GLOBETROTTER

GREEK
In Your Pocket

NEW
HOLLAND

GLOBETROTTER™

First edition published in 2005
by New Holland Publishers Ltd
London • Cape Town • Sydney
• Auckland
10 9 8 7 6 5 4 3 2

website:
www.newhollandpublishers.com

Garfield House, 86 Edgware Road
London W2 2EA
United Kingdom

80 McKenzie Street
Cape Town 8001
South Africa

14 Aquatic Drive
Frenchs Forest, NSW 2086
Australia

218 Lake Road
Northcote, Auckland
New Zealand

ISBN 1 84537 152 6

Publishing Manager (UK):
Simon Pooley
Publishing Manager (SA):
Thea Grobbelaar
Designer: Lellyn Creamer
Cover Design: Nicole Bannister
Illustrator: Marisa Galloway
Editor: Thea Grobbelaar
Translator: Doukas Coulbanis
Proofreader: Anastasia Coulbanis

Reproduction by Resolution, Cape Town
Printed and bound in Singapore by
Star Standard Industries (Pte) Ltd

Cover photograph: *Neoclassical
houses on the hillside above Yailos
harbour on Symi Island.*

CONTENTS

This PHRASE BOOK is thematically colour-coded for easy use and is organized according to the situation you're most likely to be in when you need it. The fairly comprehensive DICTIONARY section has two parts – English/Greek and Greek/English.

To make speaking Greek easy, we encourage our readers to memorize some general PRONUNCIATION rules (see page 8). After you have familiarized yourself with the basic tools of the language and the rudiments of Greek GRAMMAR (see page 14), all you need to do is turn to the appropriate section of the phrase book and find the words you need to make yourself understood. If the selection is not exactly what you are looking for, consult the dictionary for other options.

Just to get you started, here are some Greek expressions you might have heard, read or used at some time: όπα! (*opa!*), OK (which is actually an abbreviation for Όλα Καλά – *Ola Kala* – which means 'all is well') and Γειά μας! (*Gheea mas!* which means 'to our health!'). Furthermore, about 25% of the words used in English have their origins in, and sometimes are a mere transliteration of, Greek words, like 'phenomenon' which literally means 'something visible or obvious' and 'philosophy' which means 'friend of wisdom.'

4

Greek is largely a language where what you see is what you get. The same letter combinations will always be pronounced in the same way irrespective of the context in which they occur. In English, for example, **gh** can at times be silent ('thou**gh**') and at others be pronounced like an f ('cou**gh**'). This doesn't occur in Greek, making it a very easy language to read, despite the different alphabet. Another aspect which makes it easy to read is the fact that written Greek uses only a single (acute) accent to indicate the stressed syllable. To make things even easier, many English terms are used in Greek, especially in business, sport and leisure activities, so everyone will know what you mean when you say things like 'laptop', 'golf' and 'tennis'

A section on HOLIDAYS AND FESTIVALS (*see* page 82) provides some background knowledge so that you know what you're celebrating and why. There's no better way to learn a language than by joining in some enjoyment!

The brief section on manners, mannerisms and ETIQUETTE (*see* page 76) can help you make sense of the people around you. Make an effort to view your host country and its people tolerantly – that way you will be open to the new experience and able to enjoy it.

Learning a new language can be a wonderful but frightening experience. It is not the object of this book to teach you perfect Greek, but rather to equip you with just enough knowledge for a successful holiday or business trip. Luckily you are unlikely to be criticized on your grammatical correctness when merely asking for directions. The most important thing is to make yourself understood. To this end a brief section on grammar and a guide to pronunciation have been included in this book. There is, however, no substitute for listening to native speakers.

Before you leave, it might be a good idea to familiarize yourself with the sections on Pronunciation, Grammar and Etiquette. This can easily be done en route to your destination. You will also benefit from memorizing a few important phrases before you go.

The sections of the Phrase Book are arranged by topic for quick reference. Simply go to the contents list (see page 3) to find the topic you need. The Dictionary section (see page 88) goes both ways, helping you to understand and be understood. Abbreviations have been used in those instances where one English word could be interpreted as more than one part of speech, e.g. 'smoke' (a noun, the substance coming from a fire) and 'smoke' (a verb, what one would do with a cigarette). Here is a list of these and some other abbreviations used in this book:

vb	verb
n	noun
adj	adjective
adv	adverb
prep	preposition
pol	polite
fam	familiar (informal)
elec	electric/al
med	medical
anat	anatomy
rel	religion

The gender and number of Greek nouns have been specified as follows:

m	masculine
f	feminine
n	neutral
pl	plural
sing	singular

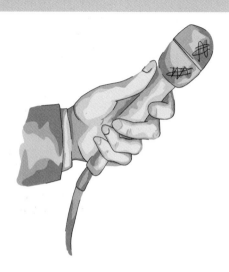

Even though the Greek alphabet might look somewhat daunting at first, you will soon get used to the letters. Greek is a phonetic language, so with a bit of practice you can soon read most of it. All the letters are always pronounced as described below, and all multisyllable Greek words have a stress mark on the vowel of the syllable that must be stressed when the word is spoken. Note, however, that capitalized words do not indicate the stress mark. So, you can learn to read Greek confidently in a very short time.

The English words given in the examples below contain sounds that approximate Greek sounds.

VOWELS
ΦΩΝΗΕΝΤΑ

◆ α – like the a in father – αλφάβητος (*alfaveetos* = alphabet)
◆ ε – like the a in hat or mat – μέρα (*mera* = day)
◆ η – like the ee in meet – ήβη (*eevee* = youth)
◆ ι – like the ee in meet, but shorter – σπίτι (*speetee* = house)
◆ ο – like the o in top – ποτό (*poto* = drink)
◆ υ – like the ee in meet – φύλο (*feelo* = gender)
◆ ω – like the o in bond, but longer – τώρα (*tora* = now)

CONSONANTS
ΣΥΜΦΩΝΑ

◆ Β β – like the v in very – βάζο (*vazo* = vase)

◆ Γ γ – something between a 'g' and an 'r', or like the French 'r' (represented as gh in this book) – γάλα (*ghala* = milk)

◆ Δ δ – like the th in there (represented as dh in this book) – δωμάτιο (*dhomateeo* = room)

◆ Ζ ζ – like the z in zebra – ζώο (*zo-o* = animal)

◆ Θ θ – like th in think – θέατρο (*theatro* = theatre)

◆ Κ κ – like the k in kitten – καθρέπτης (*kathreptees* = mirror)

◆ Λ λ – like the l in little – λεωφορείο (*leoforeeo* = bus)

◆ Μ μ – like the m in mother – μητέρα (*meetera* = mother)

◆ Ν ν – like the n night – νύχτα (*neekhta* = night)

◆ Π π – like the p in poppy – πόλη (*polee* = city/town)

◆ Ρ ρ – like the r in radio – ρόφημα (*rofeema* = hot beverage)

◆ Σ σ ς – like the s in soap – σαπούνι (*sapoonee* = soap)

◆ Τ τ – like the t in toy – τρόλλεϋ (*trole-ee* = trolley-bus)

◆ Φ φ – like the f in fork – φωτογραφία (*fotoghrafeea* = photograph)

◆ Χ χ – like ch in loch (represented as kh in this book) – χορός (*khoros* = dance)

◆ Ψ ψ – like the ps in biopsy – ψωμί (*psomee* = bread)

DIPHTHONGS
ΔΙΦΘΟΓΓΟΙ

NB: Diphthongs are used often in Greek and with the following rules in mind you will read them correctly every time! Note, however, that when the diaeresis appears on the second vowel of a vowel diphthong, then the individual letters are pronounced, as they would be had they occurred on their own. E.g. 'αι' is pronounced like the 'a' in 'hat' or 'mat' but 'αϊ' is pronounced 'a-ee'.

◆ αι – like a in hat or mat – αίσιος (*esios* = favourable/sunny)
◆ αυ – like af in after – αυτοκίνητο (*aftokeeneeto* = car)
◆ ει – like ee in meet – είμαι (*eeme* = I am)
◆ ευ – like ef in referee – ευχαριστώ (*efkhareesto* = thank you)
◆ οι – like ee in meet, but shorter – πιστοποιητικό (*peestopee-eeteeko* = certificate)
◆ ου – like oo in book – που (*poo* = where)
◆ γγ – like ng in angler – άγγελος (*angelos* = angel)
◆ γκ – like g in gun – γκαρσόνι (*garsonee* = waiter)

Ⓐⓑⓒ PRONUNCIATION

◆ ντ – like d in dad or nd in grand – ντέφι (*defee* = tambourine)

◆ μπ – like b in boy or mb in tomboy – μπύρα (*beera* = beer)

Practise a few phrases in Greek (the stressed syllables are underlined):

Καλημέρα
(kaleemera)
Good day

Γειά!
(gheea)
Hello!

Αντίο
(adeeo)
Goodbye

Μηλάτε Αγγλικά;
(meelate Anglika)
Do you speak English?

Δεν καταλαβαίνω
(dhen katalaveno)
I don't understand

Μηλάτε αργά παρακαλώ
(meelate argha para-kalo)
Please speak slowly

Πως είστε;
(pos eeste)
How are you? (pol)

Πως είσαι;
(pos eese)
How are you? (fam)

Καλά, ευχαριστώ!
(kala, efkhareesto)
Fine, thanks!

Θα ήθελα ...
(tha eethela)
I'd like ...

Πως είπατε;
(pos eepate)
Pardon?

Παρακαλώ
(parakalo)
Please

Ευχαριστώ!
(efkhareesto)
Thank you!

Λυπάμαι! (Με συγχωρείτε!)
(leepame [me seenk-horeete])
Sorry! Excuse me!

Που είναι οι τουαλέττες;
(poo eene ee tooaletes)
Where are the toilets?

Πότε έρχετε το τρένο;
(pote erkhete to treno)
When does the train arrive?

Που είναι;
(poo eene)
Where is it?

Μπορώ να...;
(mboro na)
May I ...?

εχθές
(ekhthes)
yesterday

σήμερα
(seemera)
today

αύριο
(avrio)
tomorrow

Μπορώ να χρησιμοποιήσω το τηλέφωνο;
(mboro na khree-seemopee-eeso to teelefono)
May I use the phone?

The grammar section has deliberately been kept very brief, as this is not a language course.

PERSONAL PRONOUNS
ΠΡΟΣΩΠΙΚΕΣ ΑΝΤΩΝΥΜΙΕΣ

Subject
Υποκείμενο

εγώ	I
εσύ	you (fam)
αυτός/αυτή	he/she
εμείς	we
εσείς	you (pl pol)
αυτοί/αυτές	they

Direct Object
Άμεσο Αντικείμενο

me	εμένα
you	εσένα (fam)
him	αυτόν
her	αυτήν
it	αυτό
us	εμάς
you	εσάς (pl pol)
them	αυτούς/αυτές

Indirect Object
Έμμεσο Αντικείμενο

(to) me	σ'εμένα
(to) you	σ'εσένα (fam)
(to) him	σ'αυτόν
(to) her	σ'αυτήν
(to) it	σ'αυτό
(to) us	σε μας
(to) you	σε σας (pl pol)
(to) them	σ'αυτούς

Reflexive Pronoun
Αυτοπαθής Αντωνυμία

myself	ο εαυτός μου
yourself	ο εαυτός σου (fam)
himself	ο εαυτός του
herself	ο εαυτός της
itself	ο εαυτός του
ourselves	ο εαυτός μας
yourselves	ο εαυτός σας (pl pol)
themselves	ο εαυτός τους

Possessive Pronoun
Κτητική Αντωνυμία

mine	μου
yours	σου (fam)
his	του
hers	της
its	του
ours	μας
yours	σας (pl pol)
theirs	τους

The gender of a pronoun refers to your own gender, and not to the gender of the object you are talking about. Whether the object is masculine, feminine or neutral, you would say the book (neutral) is mine (το βιβλίο είναι δικό μου), or the bag (feminine) is mine (η τσάντα είναι δική μου). However, possession in Greek is indicated with an adjective that is used in conjunction with the possessive pronoun. This adjective changes in accordance with the gender of the object being possessed. Furthermore it changes in number so that it agrees with the number of the object being possessed. This adjective is declined below:

mine (singular masculine object): δικός
mine (singular feminine object): δική
mine (singular neutral object): δικό
mine (plural masculine object): δικοί
mine (plural feminine object): δικές
mine (plural neutral object): δικά

Examples:
The books (plural, neutral) are mine:
   Τα βιβλία είναι δικά μου.
The briefcase (singular, masculine) is mine:
   Ο χαρτοφύλακας είναι δικός μου
The luggage (plural, feminine) is mine:
   Οι βαλίτσες είναι δικές μου

When referring to parts of your body, only the possessive pronoun is used, without the adjective described earlier (το πόδι μου – my leg).

VERBS
ΡΗΜΑΤΑ
Examples of REGULAR verbs, present tense:

ΑΓΑΠΑΩ (to love)
εγώ αγαπ**άω** / αγαπ**ώ**
εσύ αγαπ**άς**
αυτός/αυτή/αυτό αγαπ**ά**
εμείς αγαπ**άμε**
εσείς αγαπ**άτε**
αυτοί/αυτές/αυτά
αγαπ**άν**

ΦΟΒΑΜΑΙ (to fear)
εγώ φοβ**άμαι**
εσύ φοβ**άσαι**
αυτός/αυτή/αυτό
φοβ**άται**
εμείς φοβ**όμασται**
εσείς φοβ**όσαστε** /
φοβ**άσται**
αυτοί/αυτές/αυτά
φοβ**ούνται**

ΦΕΥΓΩ (to leave)
εγώ φεύγ**ω**
εσύ φεύγ**εις**
αυτός/αυτή/αυτό φεύγ**ει**

εμείς φεύγ**ουμε**
εσείς φεύγ**ετε**
αυτοί/αυτές/αυτά
φεύγ**ουν**

ΕΧΩ (to have)
εγώ έχω
εσύ έχεις
αυτός/αυτή/αυτό έχει
εμείς έχουμε
εσείς έχετε
αυτοί/αυτές/αυτά έχουν

ΘΕΛΩ (to want)
εγώ θέλω
εσύ θέλεις
αυτός/αυτή/αυτό θέλει
εμείς θέλουμε
εσείς θέλετε
αυτοί/αυτές/αυτά
θέλουν

ΠΑΩ (to go)
εγώ πάω
εσύ πάς
αυτός/αυτή/αυτό πάει
εμείς πάμε
εσείς πάτε
αυτοί/αυτές/αυτά πάν(ε)

ΜΠΟΡΩ (can)
εγώ μπορώ
εσύ μπορείς
αυτός/αυτή/αυτό μπορεί
εμείς μπορούμε
εσείς μπορείτε
αυτοί/αυτές/αυτά
    μπορούν

ΕΙΜΑΙ (to be)
εγώ είμαι
εσύ είσαι
αυτός/αυτή/αυτό είναι
εμείς είμαστε
εσείς είσαστε
αυτοί/αυτές/αυτά είναι

ΚΑΝΩ (to make/do)
εγώ κάνω
εσύ κάνεις
αυτός/αυτή/αυτό κάνει
εμείς κάνουμε
εσείς κάνετε
αυτοί/αυτές/αυτά
    κάνουν

ΛΕΩ (to say)
εγώ λέω
εσύ λες
αυτός/αυτή/αυτό λέει
εμείς λέμε
εσείς λέτε
αυτοί/αυτές/αυτά λέν(ε)

PUNCTUATION
ΣΤΙΞΗ

Greek punctuation is not very complex but there
are some marks that differ from their English
counterparts. The comma and full-stop are the
same in both languages, as is the exclamation
mark and the colon. However, a question mark
in Greek looks like the semi-colon in English,
and the equivalent of a semi-colon in Greek is a
raised full-stop.

NOUNS
ΟΥΣΙΑΣΤΙΚΑ

Nouns ending in -ας, -ος or -ης are usually masculine, nouns ending in -α, or -η are usually feminine, and nouns ending in -ο or -ι are usually neutral. The plural forms of nouns are constructed by replacing the previous respective suffixes by -ες, -οι or -ες for masculine, -ες for feminine, and -α for neutral nouns respectively.

Examples:

Άνδρας, Άνδρες = man, men (m)

Ταύρος, Ταύροι = bull, bulls (m)

Τραγουδιστής, Τραγουδιστές = singer, singers (m)

Γυναίκα, Γυναίκες = woman, women (f)

Σχολή, Σχολές = school, schools (f)

Παιδί, Παιδιά = child, children (n)

Βιβλίο, Βιβλία = book, books (n)

ARTICLES
ΑΡΘΡΑ

In Greek there is only a definite article. To get a form that is equivalent to the indefinite article, it suffices to omit the article altogether.

<u>Definite Article</u> (άρθρο) – the

ο – (m. sing.); η – (f. sing.)

οι – (m. pl.); οι – (f. pl.)

το – (n. sing.); τα – (n. pl.)

Examples:

Ο άνδρας **(the man);** η γυναίκα **(the woman)**

Οι άνδρες **(the men);** οι γυναίκες **(the women)**

Το βιβλίο **(the book);** Τα βιβλία **(the books)**

ADJECTIVES – ΕΠΙΘΕΤΑ

Adjectives can either follow or precede the nouns they qualify. However, they must agree in person, number and gender with the nouns they qualify.

WORD ORDER – ΣΕΙΡΑ ΤΩΝ ΛΕΞΕΩΝ

In Greek you can say a sentence in different ways using the same order. The subject, verb and predicate do not necessarily have to appear in that order. This is made possible by the fact that the endings of words are usually enough to indicate their function within the sentence, or their respective part of speech. And so, it is left to the speaker, and what he or she wishes to emphasize, to order the sentence in the way that will convey the message best. Questions and statements are distinguished by their respective intonation, although word order can also make it clear whether an articulated sentence is a question or not. Of course, any statement beginning with one of the following 'question words' is a question:

Πως = **How?**   Που = **Where?**

Πότε = **When?**   Γιατί = **Why?**

Ποιός, Ποιά, Ποιό = **Who? (m, f, n,)**

NUMBERS
ΑΡΙΘΜΟΙ (AREETHMEE)

0 μηδέν *(meedhen)*
1 ένα *(ena)*
2 δύο *(dheeo)*
3 τρία *(treea)*
4 τέσσερα *(tessera)*
5 πέντε *(pende)*
6 έξι *(eksee)*
7 επτά *(epta)*
8 οκτό *(okto)*
9 εννέα *(ennea)*
10 δέκα *(dheka)*
11 έντεκα *(endeka)*
12 δώδεκα *(dhodheka)*
13 δεκατρία *(dhekatreea)*
14 δεκατέσσερα
    (dhekatessera)
15 δεκαπέντε
    (dhekapende)
16 δεκαέξι *(dhekaeksee)*
17 δεκαεπτά *(dhekapta)*
18 δεκαοκτό *(dhekaokto)*
19 δεκαεννέα
    (dhekaennea)
20 είκοσι *(eekosee)*
21 εικοσιένα
    (eekosee-ena)
22 εικοσιδύο
    (eekoseedheeo)
30 τριάντα *(treeanda)*
31 τριάνταένα
    (treeanda-ena)

40 σαράντα *(saranda)*
50 πενήντα *(peneenda)*
60 εξήντα *(ekseenda)*
70 εβδομήντα
    (evdhomeenda)
80 ογδόντα *(oghdhonda)*
90 εννενήντα
    (enneneenda)
100 εκατό *(ekato)*
101 εκατον ένα
    (ekaton ena)
120 εκατόν είκοσι
    (ekaton eekosee)
200 διακόσια
    (dheeakoseea)
500 πεντακόσια
    (pendakoseea)
1000 χίλια *(kheeleea)*
1 million ένα
    εκατομμύριο *(ena*
    ekatomeereeo)
1 billion ένα
    δισεκατομμύριο *(ena*
    dheesekatomeereeo)

1st πρώτο *(proto)*
2nd δεύτερο *(dheftero)*
3rd τρήτο *(treeto)*
4th τέταρτο *(tetarto)*
5th πέμπτο *(pempto)*
6th έκτο *(ekto)*
7th έβδομο *(evdhomo)*
8th όγδοο *(oghdho-o)*
9th έννατο *(ennato)*
10th δέκατο *(dhekato)*

DAYS
ΗΜΕΡΕΣ (EEM<u>E</u>RES)

Monday
Δευτέρα *(dheft<u>e</u>ra)*

Tuesday
Τρίτη *(tr<u>ee</u>tee)*

Wednesday
Τετάρτη *(tet<u>a</u>rtee)*

Thursday
Πέμπτη *(p<u>e</u>mptee)*

Friday
Παρασκευή *(paraskev<u>ee</u>)*

Saturday
Σάββατο *(s<u>a</u>vvato)*

Sunday
Κυριακή *(keereeak<u>ee</u>)*

public holidays
(δημόσιες) αργίες
*([dheem<u>o</u>see-es]
argh<u>ee</u>-es)*

weekdays
μέσα στην εβδομάδα
*(m<u>e</u>sa steen evdho-
m<u>a</u>dha)*

weekends
σαββατοκύριακα
(savvatok<u>ee</u>riaka)

MONTHS
ΜΗΝΕΣ (M<u>EE</u>NES)

January
Ιανουάριος
(Eeanoo<u>a</u>reeos)

February
Φεβρουάριος
(Fevroo<u>a</u>reeos)

March
Μάρτιος *(M<u>a</u>rteeos)*

April
Απρίλιος *(Apr<u>ee</u>leeos)*

May
Μάϊος *(M<u>a</u>eeos)*

June
Ιούνιος *(Ee<u>oo</u>neeos)*

July
Ιούλιος *(Ee<u>oo</u>leeos)*

August
Αύγουστος *(<u>A</u>vghoostos)*

September
Σεπτέμβριος
(Sept<u>e</u>mvreeos)

October
Οκτώβριος *(Oktovreeos)*

November
Νοέμβριος *(Noemvreeos)*

December
Δεκέμβριος
(Dhekemvreeos)

TIME
ΩΡΑ *(ORA)*

in the morning
το πρωί
(to proee)

in the afternoon
το απόγευμα
(to apoghevma)

in the evening
το βράδυ
(to vradhee)

What is the time?
Τι ώρα είναι
(Tee ora eene?)

◆ **twenty past two**
◆ δύο και είκοσι
   (dheeo ke eekosee)

◆ **early**
◆ νωρίς *(norees)*

◆ **late**
◆ αργά *(argha)*

◆ **it's quarter to three**
◆ είναι τρείς παρά τέταρτο *(eene trees para tetarto)*

◆ **it's one o'clock**
◆ είναι μία η ώρα *(eene meea ee ora)*

◆ **it's half past two**
◆ είναι δύο και μισή *(eene dheeo ke meesee)*

at 10 a.m. (10:00)
στις δέκα προ μεσημβρίας *(stees dheka pro meseemvreeas)*

at 9 p.m. (21:00)
στις εννέα μετά μεσημβρίας *(stees ennea meta meseemvreeas)*

now
τώρα *(tora)*

the day after tomorrow
μεθαύριο *(methavreeo)*

the day before yesterday
προχθές *(prokhthes)*

this morning
σήμερα το πρωί
(seemera to proee)

yesterday evening
χθες βράδυ
(khthes vradhee)

tomorrow morning
αύριο βράδυ
(avreeo vradhee)

this week
αυτήν την εβδομάδα
(afteen teen evdhomadha)

next week
την επόμενη εβδομάδα
(teen epomenee evdhomadha)

What is today's date?
Τί ημερομηνία έχουμε σήμερα;
(Tee eemeromeeneea ekhoome seemera)

It's 13 September
Είναι 13 Σεπτεμβρίου
(Eene dhekatrees Septemvreeoo)

GREETINGS
ΧΑΙΡΕΤΙΣΜΟΙ
(KHERETEESMEE)

Good morning
Καλημέρα *(Kaleemera)*

Good afternoon
Χαίρετε *(Kherete)*

Good evening
Καλησπέρα *(Kaleespera)*

Good night
Καληνύχτα
(Kaleeneekhta)

Hello
Γειά σας (pol) / Γειά σου (fam)
(Gheea sas / Gheea soo)

Goodbye
Γειά σας (pol) / Γειά σου (fam) / Αντίο *(Gheea sas / Gheea soo / Andeeo)*

See you soon
Θα ειδοθούμε σύντομα
(Tha eedhothoome seentoma)

See you later
Θα ειδοθούμε αργότερα
(Tha eedhothoome arghotera)

Cheerio
Γειά χαρά *(Gheea khara)*

Have a good time
Να περάσετε καλά
(Na perasete kala)

I have to go now
Πρέπει να φύγω τώρα
(Prepee na feegho tora)

It was very nice
Ήταν πολύ ωραία
(Eetan polee orea)

My name is ...
Με λένε ... *(Me lene)*

What is your name?
Πως σε λένε;
(Pos se lene)

Pleased to meet you!
Χάρηκα πολύ!
(Khareeka polee)

How are you?
Τι κάνετε/κάνεις; (pol/
fam) *(Tee kanete/kanees)*

Fine, thanks. And you?
Καλά, ευχαριστώ. Κι εσείς/εσύ; (pol/fam)
(Kala efkhareesto. Kee esees/esee)

GENERAL
ΓΕΝΙΚΑ (GHENEEKA)

Do you speak English?
Μηλάτε Αγγλικά;
(Meelate Angleeka)

I don't understand
Δεν καταλαβαίνω
(Dhen katalaveno)

Please speak slowly
Μηλάτε αργά παρακαλώ
(Meelate argha parakalo)

Please repeat that
Επαναλάβετε παρακαλώ
(Epanalavete parakalo)

Please write it down
Γράψτε το παρακαλώ
(Ghrapste to parakalo)

Excuse me please
Με συγχωρείτε παρακαλώ
(Me seenkhoreete parakalo)

Could you help me?
Μπορείτε να με βοηθήσετε;
(Boreete na me voeetheesete)

Could you do me a favour?
Μπορείτε να μου κάνετε μια χάρη;
(Boreete na moo kanete meea kharee)

Can you show me?
Μπορείτε να μου δείξετε;
(Boreete na moo dheek-sete)

how?
πως; *(pos)*

where?
που; *(poo)*

when?
πότε; *(pote)*

who?
ποιός;/ποιά;/ποιό; (m/f/n) *(peeos/peea/peeo)*

why?
γιατί; *(Gheeatee)*

which?
ποιό; *(peeo)*

I need ...
Χρειάζομαι
(Khreeazome)

yes, no
ναι, όχι *(ne, okhee)*

FORMS AND SIGNS
ΕΝΤΥΠΑ ΚΑΙ ΠΙΝΑΚΙΔΕΣ
(ENDEEPA KE PEENAKEEDHES)

Please complete in block letters
Συμπληρώστε με καθαρά γράμματα παρακαλώ
(Seembleeroste me kathara ghrammata parakalo)

Surname
Επώνυμο *(Eponeemo)*

First name(s)
Όνομα(τα) *(Onoma[ta])*

Date of birth
Ημερομηνία γεννήσεως
(Eeromeeneea gheneeseos)

Place of birth
Τόπος γεννήσεως
(Topos gheneeseos)

Occupation
Επάγγελμα *(Epangelma)*

Nationality
Εθνικότητα
(Ethneekoteeta)

Address
Διεύθυνση
(Dhee-eftheensee)

Date of arrival/ departure
Ημερομηνία άφιξης/ αναχώρησης
(Eemeromeeneea afeeksees/anakhoreesees)

Passport number
Αριθμός διαβατηρίου
(Areethmos dheeavateereeoo)

I.D. number
Αριθμός Ταυτότητας
(Areethmos taftoteetas)

Issued at
Εκδόθηκε
(Ekdhotheeke)

Engaged, Vacant
Αγκαζέ, Άδειο
(Angaze, Adheeo)

No trespassing
Απαγορεύετε η είσοδος
(Apaghorevete ee eesodhos)

Out of order
Δεν λειτουργεί
(Dhen leetoorghee)

Push, Pull
Σπρώξτε, Τραβήξτε
(Sprokste, Traveekste)

Please don't disturb
Παρακαλώ, Μην ενοχλείτε *(Parakhalo, meen enokhleete)*

Lift/Elevator
Ασανσέρ *(Asanser)*

Escalator
Κυλιόμενη Σκάλα
(Khiliomenee Skala)

Wet paint
Υγρή/Νωπή/Αστέγνωτη Μπογιά *(Eeghree/Nopee/ Asteghnotee Mbogheea)*

Open, Closed
Ανοικτά, Κλειστά
(Aneekta, Kleesta)

Opening hours
Ώρες Εργασίας
(Ores erghaseeas)

Self-service
Σελφ σέρβις
(Self servees)

Waiting Room
Αίθουσα Αναμονής
(Ethoosa anamonees)

TRANSPORT

BUS/TRAM STOP
ΣΤΑΣΗ ΛΕΩΦΟΡΕΙΟΥ/
ΤΡΑΜ (STASEE
LEOFOREEOO/TRAM)

**Where is the bus/
tram stop?**
Που είναι η στάση του
λεωφορείου/τραμ;
*(Poo eene ee stasee too
leoforeeoo/tram)*

Which bus do I take?
Ποιό λεωφορείο να
πάρω;
(Peeo leoforeeo na paro)

**How often do the
buses go?**
Πόσο συχνά περνάν
τα λεωφορεία; *(Poso
seekhna pernan ta leo-
foreea)*

When is the last bus?
Πότε περνάει το
τελευταίο λεωφορείο;
*(Pote pernaee to telefteo
leoforeeo)*

Where must I go?
Που πρέπει να πάω;
(Poo prepee na pao)

**Which ticket must I
buy?**
Ποιό εισιτήριο πρέπει να
αγωράσω;
*(Peeo eeseeteereeo pre-
pee na aghoraso)*

I want to go to ....
Θέλω να πάω ...
(Thelo na pao)

What is the fare to...?
Πόσο στοιχίζει το
εισιτήριο για ... ;
*(Poso steekheezee to
eeseeteereeo gheea)*

**UNDERGROUND/
SUBWAY/METRO**
ΥΠΟΓΕΙΟΣ
ΣΙΔΗΡΟΔΡΟΜΟΣ/ΜΕΤΡΟ
(EEPOGHEEOS
SEEDHEERODHRO-
MOS/METRO)

entrance, exit
είσοδος, έξοδος
(eesodhos, eksodhos)

inner/outer zone
εσωτερική/εξωτερική
ζώνη *(esotereekee/
eksotereekee zonee)*

Where is the under-ground/subway station?
Πού είναι ο σταθμός του υπόγειου σιδηρόδρομου;
(Poo eene o stathmos too eepogheeoo seed-heerodhromoo)

Do you have a map for the metro?
Έχετε χάρτη για το μετρό;
(Ekhete khartee gheea to metro)

I want to go to ....
Θέλω να πάω ...
(Thelo na pao)

Can you give me change?
Μπορείτε να μου δώσετε ψηλά; *(Boreete na moo dhosete pseela)*

When is the next train?
Πότε περνάει το επόμενο τρένο;
(Pote pernaee to epomeno treno)

TRAIN/RAILWAY
ΤΡΕΝΟ/ΣΙΔΗΡΟΔΡΟ–ΜΙΚΗ ΣΥΓΚΟΙΝΩΝΙΑ
(TRENO/SEEDHEE-RODHROMEE- KEE SEENGEENONEEA)

Where is the railway station?
Που είναι ο σιδηρο–δρομικός σταθμός; *(Poo eene o seedheero-dhromeekos stathmos)*

departure, arrival
αναχώρηση, άφιξη
(anakhoreesee, afeeksee)

Which platform?
Ποιά πλατφόρμα;
(Peea platforma)

Do you have a time-table?
Έχετε ένα δρομολόγιο;
(Ekhete ena dhro-mologheeo)

A ... ticket please
Ένα εισιτήριο ...
παρακαλώ *(Ena eeseet-eeree ... parakalo)*

- **single**
- ατομικό *(atomeeko)*

- **return**
- επιστροφής
  (epeestrofees)

- **child's**
- παιδικό
  (pedheeko)

- **first class**
- πρώτης τάξεως
  (protees takseos)

Do I have to pay a supplement?
Πρέπει να πληρώσω παραπάνω; *(Prepee na pleeroso parapano)*

Is my ticket valid on this train?
Το εισιτήριό μου είναι έγκυρο για το τρένο αυτό; *(To eeseeteereeo moo eene engeero gheea to treno afto)*

Where do I have to get off?
Που πρέπει να κατέβω; *(Poo prepee na katevo)*

I want to book ...
Θέλω να κλείσω ... *(Thelo na kleeso)*

- **a seat/couchette**
- μια θέση/κουκέτα
  (meea thesee/kooketa)

Is this seat free?
Αυτή η θέση είναι ελεύθερη; *(Aftee ee thesee eene eleftheree)*

That is my seat
Αυτή είναι η δική μου θέση *(Aftee eene ee dheekee moo thesee)*

May I open (close) the window?
Μπορώ να ανοίξω (κλείσω) το παράθυρο; *(Boro na aneekso [kleeso] to paratheero)*

Where is the restaurant car?
Πού είναι το βαγόνι του εστιατορίου; *(Poo eene to vaghonee too esteeatoreeoo)*

Is there a sleeper?
Υπάρχει κλήνη/κρεβάτι;
*(Eeparkhee kleenee/
krevatee)*

IC – Intercity
Κ.Τ.Ε.Λ. *(K.T.E.L.)*

stationmaster
σταθμάρχης
(stathmarkhees)

BOATS
ΚΑΡΑΒΙΑ (KARABHEEA)

cruise
κρουαζιέρα
(krooazee-era)

Can we hire a boat?
Μπορούμε να
νοικιάσουμε μια λέμβο;
*(Boroome na neekeea-
soome meea lemvo)*

**How much is a
round trip?**
Πόσο κάνει το εισιτήριο
επιστροφής;
*(Poso kanee to eeseet-
eereeo epeestrofees)*

one ticket
ένα εισιτήριο
(ena eeseeteereeo)

two tickets
δύο εισιτήρια
(dheeo eeseeteereea)

**Can we eat on
board?**
Μπορούμε να φάμε κάτι
πάνω στο σκάφος;
*(Borooma na fame katee
pano sto skafos)*

**When is the last
boat?**
Πότε φεύγει το τελευταίο
καράβι; *(Pote fevghee to
telefteo karavee)*

**When is the next
ferry?**
Πότε φεύγει το επόμενο
φερυμπώτ; *(Pote
fevghee to epomeno
fereebot)*

**How long does the
crossing take?**
Πόσην ώρα παίρνει το
φερυμπώτ; *(Poseen ora
pernee to fereebot)*

Is the sea rough?
Η θάλασσα είναι
αγριεμένη; *(Ee thalasa
eene aghree-emenee)*

TAXI
ΤΑΞΙ (TAKS<u>EE</u>)

Please order me a taxi
Παρακαλώ παραγγείλετέ μου ένα ταξί.
(Parakal<u>o</u> parang<u>ee</u>lete moo <u>e</u>na taks<u>ee</u>)

To this address, please
Σ'αυτή εδώ την διεύθυνση παρακαλώ
(S'aft<u>ee</u> edh<u>o</u> teen dhee-<u>e</u>ftheensee parakal<u>o</u>)

How much is it to the centre?
Πόσο στοιχίζει να πάμε στο κέντρο;
(P<u>o</u>so steekh<u>ee</u>zee na p<u>a</u>me sto k<u>e</u>ndro)

To the airport, please
Στο αεροδρόμιο παρακαλώ (Sto aerodhr<u>o</u>meeo parakal<u>o</u>)

To the station, please
Στο σταθμό παρακαλώ
(Sto stathm<u>o</u> parakal<u>o</u>)

Keep the change
Κρατήστε τα ρέστα
(Krat<u>ee</u>ste ta r<u>e</u>sta)

I need a receipt
Χρειάζομαι απόδειξη
(Khree<u>a</u>zome ap<u>o</u>dheeksee)

AIRPORT
ΑΕΡΟΔΡΟΜΙΟ (AERODHR<u>O</u>MEEO)

arrival, departure
άφιξη, αναχώρηση
(<u>a</u>feeksee, anakh<u>o</u>reesee)

flight number
αριθμός πτήσης
(areethm<u>o</u>s pt<u>ee</u>sees)

delay
καθυστέρηση
(katheest<u>e</u>reesee)

check-in
εγγραφή κατά την άφιξη
(engraf<u>ee</u> kat<u>a</u> teen <u>a</u>feeksee)

hand luggage
χειραποσκευές
(kheeraposkev<u>e</u>s)

boarding card
κάρτα επιβίβασης
(k*arta epeeveevasees*)

valid, invalid
έγκυρο, άκυρο
(*engeero, akeero*)

lost property office
γραφείο απολεσθέντων
αντικειμένων
(*ghrafeeo apolesthendon
anteekeemenon*)

**Where do I check in
for ...?**
Που πρέπει να
παραλάβω την κάρτα
επιβίβασης για ...;
(*Poo prepee na paralavo
teen karta epeeveeva-
sees gheea*)

baggage claim
παραλαβή αποσκευών
(*paralavee aposkevon*)

**Where is the gate for
the flight to ....?**
Ποιά είναι η θύρα για
την πτήση προς...; (*Peea
eene ee theera gheea
teen pteesee pros*)

**I have nothing to
declare**
Δεν έχω τίποτα να
δηλώσω (*Dhen ekho tee-
pota na dheeloso*)

**It's for my own per-
sonal use**
Είναι για προσωπική μου
χρήση (*Eene gheea pro-
sopeekee moo khreesee*)

**An aisle/window
seat, please**
Παρακαλώ δώστε
μου θέση κοντά στο
διάδρομο/παράθυρο
(*Parakalo dhoste moo
thesee konda sto dheea-
dhromo/paratheero*)

**The flight has been
cancelled**
Η πτήση ακυρώθηκε
(*Ee pteesee
akeerotheeke*)

**The flight has been
delayed**
Υπάρχει καθυστέρηση
στην πτήση
(*Eeparkhee kathees-
tereesee steen pteesee*)

ROAD TRAVEL/ CAR HIRE
ΟΔΟΙΠΟΡΙΑ/ΕΝΟΙΚΙΑ–
ΖΟΜΕΝΑ ΑΥΤΟΚΙΝΗΤΑ
(ODHEEPOREEA/
ENEEKEEAZOMENA
AFTOKEENEETA)

Have you got a road map?
Έχετε οδικό χάρτι;
(Ekhete odheeko khatee)

How many kilo- metres is it to ...?
Πόσα χιλιόμετρα είναι
από εδώ το ...;
(Posa kheeleeometra
eene apo edho to)

Where is the nearest garage?
Που είναι το κοντινότερο
γκαράζ; (Poo eene to
kondeenotero garaz)

Fill it up, please
Γεμίστε το παρακαλώ
(Ghemeeste to parakalo)

Please check the oil, water, battery, tyres
Παρακαλώ ελέγξτε

το λάδι, το νερό, τη
μπαταρία, τα λάστιχα
(Parakalo elengkste
to ladhee, to nero, tee
batareea, ta lasteekha)

I'd like to hire a car
Θα ήθελα να νοικιάσω
ένα αυτοκίνητο
παρακαλώ (Tha eethela
na neekeeaso ena afto-
keeneeto parakalo)

How much does it cost per day/week?
Πόσο κάνει την ημέρα/
εβδομάδα;
(Poso kanee teen eem-
era/evdhomadha)

Is mileage unlimited?
Η απόσταση είναι
απεριόριστη;
(Ee apostasee eene
apereeoreestee)

Where can I pick up (leave) the car?
Που μπορώ να
παραλάβω (αφίσω) το
αυτοκίνητο;
(Poo boro na paralavo
[afeeso] to aftokeeneeto)

garage
γκαράζ *(garaz)*

headlight
προβολέας *(provoleas)*

windscreen
παρμπρίζ *(parbreez)*

indicator
φλας *(flas)*

What is the speed limit?
Ποιό είναι το όριο ταχύτητας; *(Peeo eene to oreeo takheeteetas)*

The keys are locked in the car
Τα κλειδιά είναι κλειδομένα μέσα στο αυτοκίνητο *(Ta kleedheea eene kleedhomena mesa sto aftokeeneeto)*

The engine is over-heating
Η μηχανή παραζεσταίνεται *(Ee meekhanee parazestenete)*

Have you got ...?
Έχετε...; *(Ekhete)*

◆ **a towing rope**
◆ σκοινί ρυμούλκησης *(skeenee reemoolkeesees)*

◆ **a spanner**
◆ μηχανικό κλειδί *(meekhaneeko kleedhee)*

◆ **a screwdriver**
◆ κατσαβίδι *(katsaveedhee)*

> **ROAD SIGNS**
> ΟΔΙΚΕΣ ΠΙΝΑΚΙΔΕΣ
> (ODHEEKES PEENAKEEDHES)

No through road
Δεν είναι οδός προτεραι-ότητας *(Dhen eene odhos protereoteetas)*

one-way street
οδός μιάς κατεύθυνσης *(odhos meeas kateftheensees)*

entrance, exit
είσοδος, έξοδος *(eesodhos, eksodhos)*

pedestrians
πεζοί *(pezee)*

danger
κίνδυνος *(keendheenos)*

Keep entrance clear
Κρατήστε ελεύθερη
την είσοδο *(Krateeste
eleftheree teen eesodho)*

Residents only
Μόνο κάτοικοι
(Mono kateekee)

speed limit
όριο ταχύτητας
(oreeo takheeteetas)

stop
στοπ *(stop)*

Caution
Προσοχή *(Prosokhee)*

No entry
Απαγορεύεται η είσοδος
*(Apaghorevete ee
eesodhos)*

Insert coins
Ρίξτε κέρματα
(Reekste kermata)

toll
διόδια *(dheeodheea)*

parking garage
γκαράζ για πάρκινγκ
(garaz gheea parkeeng)

roundabout
κυκλική συμβολή οδών
*(keekleekee seemvolee
odhon)*

No Parking
Απαγορεύεται το
Πάρκινγκ *(Apaghorevete
to parkeeng)*

No right turn
Όχι δεξιά
(Okhee dhekseea)

cul de sac
αδιέξοδος
(adhee-eksodhos)

roadworks
οδικά έργα
(odheeka ergha)

detour
παράκαμψη
(parakampsee)

uneven surface
ανώμαλο έδαφος
(anomalo edhafos)

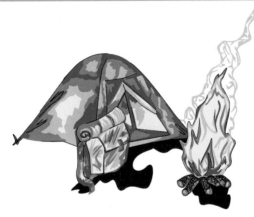

ACCOMMODATION 41
ΔΙΑΜΟΝΗ (DHEEAMON<u>EE</u>) 41

RECEPTION 43
ΡΕΣΕΨΙΟΝ (RESEPSEE<u>ON</u>) 43

SELF-CATERING 44
ΑΝΕΞΑΡΤΗΤΟ (ΔΩΜΑΤΙΟ)
(ANEKS<u>A</u>RTEETO [DHOM<u>A</u>TEEO]) 44

CAMPING 46
ΚΑΜΠΙΝΓΚ/ΚΑΤΑΣΚΗΝΩΤΙΚΗ ΖΩΗ
(K<u>A</u>MPEENG/KATASKEENOTEEK<u>EE</u> Z<u>OEE</u>) 46

ACCOMMODATION
ΔΙΑΜΟΝΗ
DHEEAMON<u>EE</u>

hotel
ξενοδοχείο
(ksenodhokh<u>ee</u>o)

bed & breakfast
δωμάτιο με πρωινό
(dhom<u>a</u>teeo me proeen<u>o</u>)

vacancies
διαθέσιμο δωμάτιο
*(dheeath<u>e</u>seemo
dhom<u>a</u>teeo)*

Have you a room ...?
Έχετε διαθέσιμο
δωμάτιο;
*(<u>E</u>khete dheeath<u>e</u>seemo
dhom<u>a</u>teeo?)*

◆ **for tonight**
◆ γι απόψε
   (ghee ap<u>o</u>pse)

◆ **with breakfast**
◆ με πρωινό
   (me proeen<u>o</u>)

◆ **with bath**
◆ με μπάνιο
   (me mb<u>a</u>neeo)

◆ **with shower**
◆ με ντουζ *(me dooz)*

◆ **a single room**
◆ μονό δωμάτιο
   (mon<u>o</u> dhom<u>a</u>teeo)

◆ **a double room**
◆ διπλό δωμάτιο
   (dhipl<u>o</u> dhom<u>a</u>teeo)

◆ **a family room**
◆ δωμάτιο για
   οικογένεια *(dhom<u>a</u>teeo
   gheea eekogh<u>e</u>neea)*

**How much is the
room per day/week?**
Πόσο κάνει το δωμάτιο
την ημέρα/εβδομάδα;
*(P<u>o</u>so k<u>a</u>nee to dhoma-
teeo teen eem<u>e</u>ra/
evdhom<u>a</u>dha?)*

**Have you anything
cheaper/better?**
Έχετε κάτι φθηνότερο/
καλύτερο; *(<u>E</u>khete k<u>a</u>tee
ftheen<u>o</u>tero/kal<u>ee</u>tero?)*

Do you have a cot?
Έχετε κρεβατάκι μωρού;
*(<u>E</u>khete krevat<u>a</u>kee
mor<u>oo</u>?)*

41

What time is breakfast/dinner?
Τι ώρα είναι το πρωινό/βραδυνό; (Tee _ora_ _ee_ne to proeeno/vradheeno?)

room service
υπηρεσία δωματίου (eepeeres_ee_a dhoma-t_ee_oo)

Please bring ...
Παρακαλώ φέρεται ... (Parakal_o_ f_e_rete...)

◆ **toilet paper**
◆ χαρτί υγείας
   (khart_ee_ eegh_ee_as)

◆ **clean towels**
◆ καθαρές πετσέτες
   (kathar_es_ pets_e_tes)

Please clean the bath
Παρακαλώ καθαρίστε το μπάνιο (parakal_o_ kathar_e_-este to mb_a_neeo)

Please put fresh sheets on the bed
Παρακαλώ αλλάξτε τα κληνοσκεπάσματα (Parakal_o_ all_a_kste ta kleenoskep_a_smata)

Please don't touch ...
Παρακαλώ μην αγγίζετε (Parakal_o_ meen ang_ee_-zete)

◆ **my briefcase**
◆ τον χαρτοφύλακά μου
   (ton khartof_ee_lak_a_ moo)

◆ **my laptop**
◆ τον φορητό υπολογιστή μου (ton foreet_o_ eepologheest_ee_ moo)

My ... doesn't work
... μου δέν δουλεύει
(... moo dhen dhool_e_vee)

◆ **toilet**
◆ Η τουαλέττα
   (Ee tooal_e_tta)

◆ **bedside lamp**
◆ Το πορτατίφ
   (To portat_ee_f)

◆ **air conditioning**
◆ Ο κλιματισμός
   (O kleemateesm_o_s)

There is no hot water
Δεν έχει ζεστό νερό
(Dhen _e_khee zest_o_ ner_o_)

RECEPTION
ΡΕΣΕΨΙΟΝ
(RESEPSEEON)

Are there any messages for me?
Υπάρχουν μηνύματα για μένα; *(Eeparkhoon meeneemata ghea mena?)*

Can I leave a message for someone?
Μπορώ να αφήσω μήνυμα για κάποιον;
(Mboro na afeeso meeneema ghea kapeeon?)

Is there a laundry service?
Έχετε υπηρεσία καθαριστηρίου;
(Ekhete eepereseea kathareesteereeoo?)

Where is the lift/ elevator?
Που είναι το ασανσέρ;
(Poo eene to asanser?)

Do you arrange tours?
Οργανώνετε τουριστικές εκδρομές;
(Orghanonete tooreesteekes ekdhromes?)

I need a wake-up call at 7 o'clock
Χρειάζομαι τηλεφώνημα για ξύπνιμα στς επτά
(Khreeazome teelefoneema ghea kseepneema stees epta)

What number must I dial for room service?
Τι αριθμό παίρνω για την υπηρεσία δωματίου;
(Tee areethmo perno ghea teen eepereseea dhomateeoo?)

Please prepare the bill
Ετοιμάσετε παρακαλώ τον λογαριασμό
(Eteemasete parakalo ton loghareeasmo)

There is a mistake in this bill
Υπάρχει λάθος στον λογαριασμό αυτό
(Eeparkhee lathos ston loghareeasmo afto)

I'm leaving tomorrow
Φεύγω αύριο
(Fevgho avreeo)

SELF-CATERING
ΑΝΕΞΑΡΤΗΤΟ (ΔΩΜΑ-
ΤΙΟ) (ANEKSARTEETO
[DHOMATEEO])

Have you any vacancies?
Έχετε διαθέσιμα δωμάτια;
(Ekhete dheeatheseema domateea)

How much is it per night/week?
Πόσο στοιχίζει το βράδι/ την εβδομάδα; (Poso steekheezee to vradhee/ teen evdhomadha?)

Do you allow children?
Επιτρέπετε παιδιά;
(Epeetrepete pedheea?)

Please, show me how ... works
Παρακαλώ, δείξτε μου πως δουλεύει ...
(Parakalo, dheekste moo pos dhoolevee...)

◆ **the cooker/stove/ oven**
◆ η κουζίνα
(ee koozeena)

◆ **the washing machine**
◆ το πλυντήριο
(to pleendeereeo)

◆ **the dryer**
◆ το στεγνοτήριο
(to steghnoteereeo)

◆ **the heater**
◆ η σόμπα (ee somba)

◆ **the water heater**
◆ ο θερμοσίφωνας
(o thermoseefonas)

Where is/are ...?
Που είναι ...;
(Poo eene ... ?)

◆ **the switch**
◆ ο διακόπτης
(o dheeakoptees)

◆ **the fuses**
◆ οι ασφάλειες
(ee asfalee-es)

Is there ...?
Υπάρχει...;
(Eeparkhee...?)

◆ **a cot**
◆ κρεβατάκι μωρού
(krevatakee moroo)

- **a high chair**
- υψιλή καρέκλα
  (eepseelee karekla)

- **a safe**
- χρηματοκιβώτιο
  (khreematokeevoteeo)

We need more ...
Χρειαζόμαστε
περισσότερ–
*(Khreeazomaste
pereesoter-)*

- **cutlery**
- -α μαχαιροπήρουνα
  (-a makheropeeroona)

- **crockery**
- -α πιάτα
  (-a peeata)

- **sheets**
- -α σεντόνια
  (-a sendoneea)

- **blankets**
- -ες κουβέρτες
  (-es koovertes)

- **pillows**
- -α μαξιλάρια
  (-a makseelareea)

Is there ... in the vicinity?
Υπάρχει ... στην περιοχή;
(Eeparkhee ... steen pereeokhee?)

- **a shop**
- μαγαζί
  (maghazee)

- **a restaurant**
- εστιατόριο
  (esteeatoreeo)

- **a bus/tram**
- λεωφορείο/τραμ
  (leoforeeo/tram)

I have locked myself out
Κλειδώθηκα απ' έξω
(Keedhotheeka ap' ekso)

the keys
τα κλειδιά
(ta kleedheea)

The window won't open/close
Το παράθυρο δεν ανοίγει/κλείνει
(to paratheero dhen aneeghee/kleenee)

ACCOMMODATION

CAMPING
ΚΑΜΠΙΝΓΚ/
ΚΑΤΑΣΚΗΝΩΤΙΚΗ ΖΩΗ
(KAMPEENG/
KATASKEENOTEEKEE
ZOEE)

caravan
τροχόσπιτο
(trokhospeeto)

Have you got a list of camp sites?
Έχετε κατάλογο με τους χώρους κατασκήνωσης/κάμπιγκ;
(Ekhete katalogho me toos khoroos kataskeenosees/kampeeng?)

Are there any sites available?
Υπάρχουν διαθέσιμοι χώροι κατασκήνωσης;
(Eeparkhoon dheeatheseemee khoree kataskeenosees?)

Can we park the caravan here?
Μπορούμε να παρκάρουμε το τροχόσπιτό εδώ;
(Mboroome na parkaroome to trokhospeeto edho?)

Can we camp here overnight?
Μπορούμε να κατασκηνώσουμε εδώ το βράδυ;
(Mboroome na kataskeenosoome edho to vradhee?)

This site is muddy
Ο χώρος αυτός είναι πολύ λασπώδης
(O khoros aftos eene polee laspodhees)

Is there a sheltered site?
Υπάρχει προστατευόμενος χώρος;
(Eeparkhee prostatevomenos khoros?)

Is there ... in the vicinity?
Έχει ... στην περιοχή;
(Ekhee ... steen pereeokhee?)

◆ **a shop**
◆ μαγαζί
  (maghazee)

◆ **a restaurant**
◆ εστιατόριο
  (esteeatoreeo)

Do you have electricity?
Έχετε ηλεκτρισμό;
(Ekhete eelektreesmo?)

We'd like to stay for three nights/a week
Θα θέλαμε να μείνουμε για τρεις βραδυές/μία εβδομάδα *(Tha thelame na meenoome ghia trees vradhee-es/meea evdhomadha)*

Is there drinking water?
Υπάρχει πόσιμο νερό;
(Eeparkhee poseemo nero?

Can I light a fire here?
Μπορώ να ανάψω φωτιά εδώ; *(Mboro na anapso foteea edho?)*

I'd like to buy fire wood
Θα ήθελα να αγοράσω ξύλο για φωτιά
(Tha eethela na aghoraso kseelo ghea foteea)

Is the wood dry?
Το ξύλο είναι στεγνό;
(To kseelo eene steghno?)

Do you have ... for rent?
Διαθέτετε ... για νοίκιασμα;
(Dheeathetete ... gia neekeeasma?)

♦ **a tent**
♦ σκηνή
  (skeenee)

♦ **a gas cylinder**
♦ φιάλη γκαζιού
  (feealee ngazeeoo)

♦ **a groundsheet**
♦ κατοσέντονο για το έδαφος
  (katosendono ghea to edhafos)

Where is/are the nearest ...?
Πού είναι οι κοντινότερες...; *(Poo eene ee kondeenoter-)*

♦ **toilets**
♦ -ες τουαλέττες;
  (-es tooalettes)

♦ **sink (for dishes)**
♦ -οι νεροχύτες (για τα πιάτα)
  (-ee nerokheetes [ghea ta peeata])

CUTLERY
ΜΑΧΑΙΡΟΠΙΡΟΥΝΑ
(MAKHERO-
PEEROONA)

knife
μαχαίρι *(makheree)*

fork, cake fork
πηρούνι, πηρουνάκι
*(peeroonee,
peeroonakee)*

spoon, teaspoon
κουτάλι, κουταλάκι
(kootalee, kootalakee)

crockery
πιατικά *(peeateeka)*

plate
πιάτο *(peeato)*

cup and saucer, mug
φλυτζάνι και πιατάκι
(fleetzanee ke peeatakee)

BREAKFAST
ΠΡΩΙΝΟ (PROEENO)

coffee
καφές *(kafes)*

◆ **with milk, cream**
◆ με γάλα, κρέμα
(me ghala, krema)

◆ **black**
◆ μαύρο *(mavro)*

◆ **without sugar**
◆ χωρίς ζάχαρι
(korees zakharee)

tea
τσαϊ *(tsaee)*

◆ **with milk, lemon**
◆ με γάλα, λεμόνι
(me ghala, lemonee)

bread
ψωμί *(psomee)*

rolls
ψωμάκια *(psomakeea)*

egg(s)
αυγό/αυγά
(avgho/avgha)

◆ **boiled – soft, hard**
◆ βραστό – μελάτο,
σφιχτό *(vrasto –
melato, sfikhto)*

◆ **fried** *(teeghaneeto)*
◆ τιγανιτό

◆ **scrambled**
◆ στραπατσάδα
◆ *(strapatsadha)*

49

◆ **poached**
◆ ποσέ (pose)

◆ **bacon and eggs**
◆ μπέικον με αυγά (mbe-eekon me avgha)

cereal
δημητριακά/κορνφλέϊκς (dheemeetreeaka/kornfle-eeks)

hot milk, cold milk
ζεστό γάλα, κρύο γάλα (zesto ghala, kreeo ghala)

fruit
φρούτα (froota)

orange juice
χυμό πορτοκάλι (kheemo portokalee)

jam
μαρμελάδα (marmeladha)

marmalade
μαρμελάδα εσπεριδο–ειδών (marmeladha espereedhoeedhon)

pepper
πιπέρι (peeperee)

salt
αλάτι (alatee)

LUNCH/DINNER
ΜΕΣΗΜΕΡΙΑΝΟ/
ΒΡΑΔΥΝΟ
(MESEEMEREEANO/
VRADHEENO)

Could we have a table ...?
Μπορείτε να μας δώσετε τραπέζι ... ; (Mboreete na mas dhosete tra-pezee)

◆ **by the window**
◆ κοντά σε παράθυρο (konda se paratheero)

◆ **outside**
◆ έξω (ekso)

◆ **inside**
◆ μέσα (mesa)

May I have ... ?
Μπορώ να έχω ...; (Mboro na echo)

◆ **the wine list**
◆ τον κατάλογο των κρασιών (ton kata-logho ton kraseeon)

◆ **the menu of the day**
◆ το μενού της ημέρας (to menoo tees eemeras)

◆ **starters**
◆ τα ορεκτικά
(ta orekteeka)

◆ **main course**
◆ το κύριο πιάτο
(to keereeo peeato)

◆ **dessert**
◆ το επιδόρπιο
(to epeedhorpeeo)

What is this?
Τί είναι αυτό;
(Tee eene afto)

That is not what I ordered
Δεν παράγγειλα αυτό
(Dhen parangeela afto)

It's tough, cold, off
Είναι μεστό, κρύο, χαλασμένο *(Eene mesto, kreeo, khalasmeno)*

What do you recommend?
Τι προτείνετε;
(Tee proteenete)

There is a mistake
Έχει γίνει λάθος
(Ekhee gheenee lathos)

Can I have the bill please?
Μου φέρνετε το λογαριασμό παρακαλό;
(Moo fernete to loghareeasmo parakalo)

We'd like to pay separately
Θα θέλαμε να πληρώσουμε χωριστά
(Tha thelame na pleerosoome khoreesta)

Thank you, that's for you
Ευχαριστώ, αυτό είναι για σας
(Efkhareesto, afto eene gheea sas)

Keep the change
Κρατήστε τα ρέστα
(Krateeste ta resta)

DRINKS
ΠΟΤΑ (POTA)

a beer/lager – large, small
μιά μπύρα/λάγκερ – μεγάλη, μικρή
(meea mbeera/langer – meghalee, meekree)

glass (1/4 litre) of cider
ένα ποτήρι χυμό μήλου/ μηλίτη (*ena poteeree kheemo meeloo/ meeleetee*)

a dry white wine
ένα ξηρό λευκό κρασί (*ena kseero lefko krasee*)

a sweet white wine
ένα γλυκό λευκό κρασί (*ena ghleeko lefko krasee*)

a light red wine
ένα ελαφρύ κόκκινο κρασί (*ena elafree kokeeno krasee*)

house wine
χύμα κρασί (*kheema krasee*)

a glass of wine with soda water
ένα ποτίρι κρασί με σόδα (*ena poteeree krasee me sodha*)

champagne
σαμπάνια (*sampaneea*)

a brandy
ένα κονιάκ (*ena koneeak*)

a whisky with ice
ένα ουίσκι με πάγο (*ena ooeeskee me pagho*)

liqueur
λικέρ (*leeker*)

a glass
ένα ποτήρι (*ena poteeree*)

a bottle
ένα μπουκάλι (*ena bookalee*)

a mineral water – still, sparkling
ένα μεταλλικό νερό – μη ανθρακούχο, ανθρακούχο (*ena metaleeko nero – mee anthrakookho, anthrakookho*)

tap water
νερό της βρύσης (*nero tees vreesees*)

fruit juice
φρουτοχυμό (*frootokheemo*)

cola and lemonade
κόλα και λεμονάδα (*kola ke lemonadha*)

another ... please
άλλο ένα ... παρακαλώ
(*allo ena ... parakalo*)

too cold
πολύ κρύο
(*polee kreeo*)

not cold enough
όχι αρκετά κρύο
(*okhee arketa kreeo*)

FOOD
ΦΑΓΗΤΟ/ΦΑΪ
(FAGHEETO/FAEE)

Soup
ΣΟΥΠΑ
(*soopa*)

pea, bean, lentil soup
σούπα μπιζελιού,
φασολάδα, φακές σούπα
(*soopa beezeleeoo,
fasoladha, fakes soopa*)

Fish
ΨΑΡΙ
(*psaree*)

sole
γλώσσα
(*ghlosa*)

red mullet
μπαρμπούνι
(*barboonee*)

cod
μπακαλιάρος
(*bakaleearos*)

perch
πέρκη
(*perkee*)

salmon
σολομός
(*solomos*)

herring
ρέγγα
(*renga*)

trout
πέστροφα
(*pestrofa*)

blackfish
ροφός
(*rofos*)

tuna
τόννος/τούνα
(*tonos/toona*)

sardines
σαρδέλλες
(*sardheles*)

fried, grilled, sautéed
τηγανητό, ψητό, σοτα-
ρισμένο *(teeghaneeto,
pseeto, sotareesmeno)*

POULTRY
ΠΟΥΛΕΡΙΚΆ
(poolereeka)

chicken
κοτόπουλο
(kotopoolo)

**crumbed roasted
chicken**
ψητό κοτόπουλο πανέ
(pseeto kotopoolo pane)

duck
πάπια *(papeea)*

goose
χήνα *(kheena)*

roasted
ψητό *(pseeto)*

MEAT
ΚΡΕΑΣ
(kreas)

mutton, lamb
πρόβειο/αρνίσιο κρέας
*(proveeo/arneeseeo
kreas)*

beef
βοδινό κρέας
(vodheeno kreas)

veal
μοσχάρι *(moskharee)*

pork
χοιρινό *(kheereeno)*

sausage
λουκάνικο *(lookaneeko)*

veal sausage
μοσχαρίσιο λουκάνικο
*(moskhareeseeo
lookaneeko)*

venison
κρέας ελαφιού/
θηράματος *(kreas
elafeeoo/theeramatos)*

meat balls/cakes
κεφτέδες/μπιφτέκια
(keftedhes/beeftekeea)

**well done, medium,
rare**
ψημένο καλά, μέτρια,
σενιάν *(pseemeno kala,
metreea, seneean)*

boiled, stewed
βραστό, γιαχνί
(vrasto, gheeakhnee)

54

smoked meats
καπνιστά κρέατα
(kapneesta kreata)

platter of cold meats
πιατέλα με αλλαντικά
(peeatela me alandeeka)

PASTA AND RICE
ΖΥΜΑΡΙΚΆ ΚΑΙ ΡΎΖΙ
(zeemareeka ke reezee)

**pasta made with
cottage cheese**
ζυμαρικά φτιαγμένα με
τυρί κόταζ
*(zeemareeka fteeaghme-
na me teeree kotaz)*

**pasta with tomato
sauce**
ζυμαρικά με σάλτσα
ντομάτα *(zeemareeka
me saltsa domata)*

rice
ρύζι *(reezee)*

**VEGETABLES, SALAD AND
FRUIT**
ΛΑΧΑΝΙΚΆ, ΣΑΛΆΤΕΣ ΚΑΙ
ΦΡΟΎΤΑ *(lakhaneeka,
salates ke froota)*

eggplant
μελιτζάνα *(meleendzana)*

onion
κρεμμύδι
(kremeedhee)

cabbage
λάχανο *(lakhano)*

cauliflower
κουνουπίδι
(koonoopeedhee)

carrots
καρότα *(karota)*

green beans
φασολάκια
(fasolakeea)

leeks
πράσσα *(prasa)*

asparagus
σπαράγγια
(sparangeea)

peppers
πιπεριές
(peeperee-es)

pumpkin
κολοκύθα *(kolokeetha)*

lettuce
μαρούλι *(maroolee)*

beetroot
παντζάρια
(pandzareea)

cucumber
αγγούρι *(angooree)*

**potatoes – boiled,
fried, mashed**
πατάτες – βραστές,
τηγανητές, πουρέ
*(patates – vrastes,
teeghaneetes, pooree)*

root celery
σέλινο *(seleeno)*

lemon
λεμόνι *(lemonee)*

grapefruit
γκρέϊπφρουτ
(gre-eepfroot)

apples
μήλο *(meelo)*

pears
αχλάδι *(akhladhee)*

bananas
μπανάνες *(bananas)*

pineapple
ανανάς *(ananas)*

cherries
κεράσια *(keraseea)*

strawberries
φράουλες *(fraooles)*

apricots
βερίκοκα *(vereekoka)*

peaches
ροδάκινα *(rodhakeena)*

raspberries
φραμπουάζ *(frambooaz)*

blackberries
βατόμουρα
(vatomoora)

plums
δαμάσκηνα
(dhamaskeena)

prunes
ξερά δαμάσκηνα
(ksera dhamaskeena)

grapes
σταφύλια *(stafeeleea)*

dried fruit
ξηροί καρποί
(kseeree karpee)

cranberries
φίγγια *(feengeea)*

DESSERTS AND CAKES
ΕΠΙΔΟΡΠΙΑ ΚΑΙ ΤΟΥΡΤΕΣ
(EPEEDHORPIA KE TOORTES)

fruit salad
φρουτοσαλάτα
(frootosalata)

jelly
ζελές *(zeles)*

crème caramel
κρέμα καραμελέ
(krema karamele)

meringue
μαρέγγα *(marenga)*

pastry with apples and raisins
μηλόπιτα με σταφίδες
(meelopeeta me stafeedhes)

light fruitcake
ελαφρό κέϊκ με φρούτα
γλασσέ
(ke-eek me froota ghlase)

baklava
μπακλαβάς *(baklavas)*

fruit flan
τάρτα με φρούτα
(tarta me froota)

kataifi
κανταΐφι *(kata-eefee)*

custard pie
γαλακτομπούρεκο
(ghalaktobooreko)

Greek-style milk-tart
μπουγάτσα *(booghatsa)*

Greek yoghurt with honey and walnuts
γιαούρτι με μέλι και
καρύδια *(Gheeaoortee me melee ke kareedheea)*

Greek 'teaspoon' sweets
γλυκά του κουταλιού
(ghleeka too kootaleeoo)

chocolate cream cake
πάστα σοκολάτα
(pasta sokolata)

vanilla cream cake
πάστα βανίλιας
(pasta vaneeleeas)

biscuits
μπισκότα *(beeskota)*

MONEY
ΧΡΗΜΑΤΑ
(KHR<u>EE</u>MATA)

bureau de change
συνάλλαγμα
(seen<u>a</u>llaghma)

cash dispenser/ATM
ATM *(E-ee Tee Em)*

Where can I change money?
Που μπορώ να αλλάξω χρήματα; *(Poo mbor<u>o</u> na all<u>a</u>kso khr<u>ee</u>mata)*

Where is an ATM, a bank?
Που θα βρω ενα ATM, μια τράπεζα; *(Poo tha vro <u>e</u>na ATM, m<u>e</u>a tr<u>a</u>peza)*

When does the bank open/close?
Πότε ανοίγει/κλείνει η τράπεζα; *(P<u>o</u>te an<u>ee</u>-ghee/kl<u>ee</u>nee ee tr<u>a</u>peza)*

How much commission do you charge?
Τι ποσοστό προμήθειας χρεώνεται; *(Tee posost<u>o</u> prom<u>ee</u>theeas khre<u>o</u>nete)*

I want to ...
Θα ήθελα ...
(Tha <u>ee</u>thela)

♦ **cash a traveller's cheque**
♦ να εξαργυρώσω μια ταξιδιωτική επιταγή
(na eksargheer<u>o</u>so m<u>e</u>a takseedhee-oteek<u>ee</u> epeetagh<u>ee</u>)

♦ **change £50**
♦ να αλλαξω πενήντα Αγγλικές Λίρες
(na all<u>a</u>kso pen<u>ee</u>nda Angleek<u>e</u>s L<u>ee</u>res)

♦ **make a transfer**
♦ να κάνω μεταφορά (χρημάτων)
(na k<u>a</u>no metafor<u>a</u> [khreem<u>a</u>ton])

POST OFFICE
ΤΑΧΥΔΡΟΜΕΙΟ
(TAKHEEDHROM<u>EE</u>O)

How much is ...?
Πόσο κάνει ... ;
(Poso k<u>a</u>nee)

♦ **a letter**
♦ ένα γράμμα
(<u>e</u>na ghr<u>a</u>mma)

◆ **a postcard to ...**
◆ μια καρτ–ποστάλ για
την ... *(meea kart-
postal ghia teen)*

◆ **a small parcel**
◆ ένα μικρό πακέτο
(ena meekro paketo

Where can I buy stamps?
Που μπορώ να πάρω
γραμματόσημα;
*(Poo mboro na paro
ghrammatoseema)*

SHOPPING
ΨΩΝΙΑ/ΑΓΟΡΕΣ
(PSONEEA/AGHORES)

What does it cost?
Πόσο κάνει; *(Poso kanee)*

Do you take travel-ler's cheques?
Δέχεστε ταξιδιωτικές
επιταγές;
*(Dhekheste takseedhee-
oteekes epeetaghes)*

Do you accept credit cards?
Δέχεστε πιστοτικές
κάρτες; *(Dhekheste
peestoteekes kartes)*

Does that include VAT?
Περιλαμβάνει ΦΠΑ; *(Per-
eelamvanee Fee Pee A)*

Do you need a deposit?
Χρειάζεστε
προκαταβολή; *(Khreea-
zeste prokatavolee)*

This isn't what I want
Δεν είναι αυτό που θέλω
*(Dhen eene afto poo
thelo)*

This isn't correct (bill)
(Ο λογαριασμός) δεν
είναι σωστός / Υπάρχει
λάθος (στο λογαριασμό)
*([O loghareeasmos] dhen
eene sostos / Eeparkhee
lathos [sto logharee-
asmo])*

I need a receipt
Χρειάζομαι απόδειξη
*(Khreeazome apo-
dheeksee)*

I want my money back
Θέλω τα λεφτά μου
πίσω *(Thelo ta lefta moo
peeso)*

This is ...
Αυτό είναι ... *(Afto eene)*

◆ **broken**
◆ σπασμένο *(spasmeno)*

◆ **damaged**
◆ ζημιωμένο *(zeemeeomeno)*

Can you repair it?
Μπορείτε να το φτιάξετε; *(Mboreete na to fteeaksete)*

BUYING FOOD
ΑΓΟΡΑ ΦΑΓΗΤΟΥ
(AGHORA FAGHEETOO)

Where can I buy ...?
Που θα βρω ... ;
(Poo tha vro)

◆ **bread**
◆ ψωμί *(psomee)*

◆ **cake**
◆ κέηκ *(ke-eek)*

◆ **cheese**
◆ τυρί *(teeree)*

◆ **butter**
◆ βούτυρο *(vooteero)*

◆ **milk**
◆ γάλα *(ghala)*

◆ **water**
◆ νερό *(nero)*

◆ **wine**
◆ κρασί *(krasee)*

◆ **sparkling wine**
◆ αφρόδες κρασί *(afrodhes krasee)*

◆ **beer**
◆ μπύρα *(beera)*

◆ **fruit juice**
◆ φρουτοχυμό *(frootokheemo)*

◆ **meat**
◆ κρέας *(kreas)*

◆ **ham**
◆ ζαμπόν *(zambon)*

◆ **polony/cold meats**
◆ αλλαντικά *(allandeeka)*

◆ **vegetables**
◆ λαχανικά *(lakhaneeka)*

◆ **fruit**
◆ φρούτα *(froota)*

- **eggs**
- αυγά *(avgha)*

I'll take ...
Θα πάρω ... *(Tha paro)*

- **one kilo**
- ένα κιλό *(ena keelo)*

- **three slices**
- τρείς φέτες
  (trees fetes)

- **a portion of**
- μια μερίδα
  (meea mereedha)

- **a packet of**
- ένα πακέτο
  (ena paketo)

- **a dozen**
- μια ντουζίνα
  (meea ndoozeena)

BUYING CLOTHES
ΑΓΟΡΑ ΡΟΥΧΩΝ
(AGHORA ROOKHON)

Can I try this on?
Μπορώ να το δοκιμάσω;
(Mboro na to dhokee-maso)

It is ...
Είναι ... *(Eene)*

- **too big**
- πολύ μεγάλο
  (polee meghalo)

- **too small**
- πολύ μικρό
  (polee mikro)

- **too tight**
- πολύ στενό
  (polee steno)

- **too wide**
- πολύ φαρδύ
  (polee fardhee)

- **too expensive**
- πολύ ακριβό
  (polee akreevo)

I'll take ...
Θα πάρω ...
(Tha paro)

- **this one**
- αυτό
  (afto)

- **size 40**
- μέγεθος σαράντα
  (meghethos saranda)

- **two**
- δύο
  (dheeo)

CLOTHING SIZES ΜΕΓΕΘΗ ΡΟΥΧΩΝ (MEGHEТHEE ROOKHON)		

Women's Wear

UK	Cont. Europe	USA
10	38	8
12	40	10
14	42	12
16	44	14
18	46	16

Menswear

UK	Cont. Europe	USA
36	46	36
38	48	38
40	50	40
42	52	42
44	54	44
46	56	46

Men's Shirts

UK	Cont. Europe	USA
14	36	14
14.5	37	14.5
15	38	15
15.5	39	15.5
16	41	16
17	43	17

Shoes

UK	Cont. Europe	USA
5	39	6
6	40	7
7	41	8
8	42	9
9	43	10
10	44	11
11	45	12

SIGHTSEEING
ΕΠΙΣΚΕΨΗ ΣΤΑ
ΑΞΙΟΘΕΑΤΑ
(EPEESKEPSEE STA
AKSEEOTHEATA)

tourist office
τουριστικό γραφείο
(tooreesteeko ghrafeeo)

Do you have leaflets?
Έχετε φυλλάδια;
(Ekhete feeladheea)

I/We want to visit ...
Θέλ–ω/–ουμε να
επισκευτ–ώ/–ούμε...
(Thel-o/-oome na
epeeskeft-o/-oome...)

**When is it open/
closed?**
Πότε ανοίγει/κλείνει;
(Pote aneeghee/kleenee)

What does it cost?
Πόσο στοιχίζει;
(Poso steekheezee)

Are there any reductions for ...?
Δίνετε έκπωση για...;
(Dheenete ekptosee
gheea...?)

◆ **children**
◆ παιδιά (pedheea)

◆ **senior citizens**
◆ υπερήλικες
(eepereeleekes)

◆ **students**
◆ μαθητές/φοιτητές
(matheetes/feeteetes)

◆ **Are there any tours?**
Γίνονται τουριστικές
εκδρομές;
(Gheenonde tooreesteekes ekdhromes?)

**When does the bus
depart/return?**
Πότε φεύγει/επιστρέφει
το λεωφορείο; (Pote
fevghee/epeestrefee to
leoforeeo?)

**From where does
the bus leave?**
Από που φεύγει το
λεωφορείο; (Apo poo
fevghee to leoforeeo?)

**Where is the
museum?**
Που είναι το μουσείο;
(Poo eene to mooseeo?)

ENTERTAINMENT
ΔΙΑΣΚΕΔΑΣΗ
(DHIASKEDHASEE)

Is there a list of cultural events?
Υπάρχει κατάλογος
με πολιτιστικές
εκδηλώσεις;
*(Eeparkhee kataloghos
me poleeteesteekes
ekdheelosees?)*

Are there any festivals?
Γίνεται κάπου γιορτή/
φεστιβάλ;
*(Gheenete kapoo
gheeortee/festeeval?)*

I'd like to go to ...
Θα ήθελα να πάω ...
(Tha eethela na pao)

◆ **the theatre**
◆ στο θέατρο
  (sto theatro)

◆ **the opera**
◆ στην όπερα
  (steen opera)

◆ **the ballet**
◆ στο μπαλέτο
  (sto balleto)

◆ **the cinema/movies**
◆ στο σινεμά
  (sto seenema)

◆ **a concert**
◆ σε μια συναυλία
  (se meea seenavleea)

Do I have to book?
Πρέπει να κλείσω θέση;
*(Prepee na kleeso
thesee?)*

How much are the tickets?
Πόσο κάνουν τα
εισητήρια; *(Poso kanoon
ta eeseeteereea?)*

Two tickets for ...
Δύο εισητήρια για...
*(Dheeo eeseeteereea
gheea...)*

◆ **tonight**
◆ απόψε *(apopse)*

◆ **tomorrow night**
◆ αύριο βράδυ
  (avreeo vradhee)

◆ **the late show**
◆ για την τελευταία πα-
  ράσταση *(gheea teen
  teleftea parastasee)*

When does the performance start/end?
Τί ώρα αρχίζει/τελειώνει
η παράσταση;
(Tee ora arkheezee/tel-eeonee ee parastasee?)

Where is ...?
Που είναι ...; *(Poo eene)*

◆ **a good bar**
◆ ένα καλό μπαρ
 (ena kalo bar)

◆ **good live music**
◆ καλή ζωντανή μουσική
 (kalee zontanee mooseekee)

Is it expensive?
Είναι ακριβά;
(Eene akreeva?)

Is it noisy, crowded?
Έχει φασαρία, πολύ
κόσμο; *(Ekhee fasareea, polee kosmo?)*

SPORT
ΣΠΟΡ/ΑΘΛΗΣΗ
(SPOR/ATHLEESEE)

Where can we ...?
Που μπορούμε να...;
(Poo mboroome na)

◆ **go skiing**
◆ πάμε για σκι
 (pame gheea skee)

◆ **play tennis/golf**
◆ παίξουμε τένις/γκολφ
 (peksoome tennis/golf)

◆ **go swimming**
◆ πάμε για κολύμπι
 (pame gheea koleembee)

◆ **go fishing**
◆ πάμε για ψάρεμα
 (pame gheea psarema)

◆ **go riding**
◆ κάνουμε ιππασία
 (kanoome eepaseea)

◆ **go cycling**
◆ κάνουμε ποδηλασία
 (kanoome podheelaseea)

◆ **hire bicycles**
◆ νοικιάσουμε ποδήλατα
 (neekeeasoome podheelata)

◆ **hire golf clubs**
◆ νοικιάσουμε μπασ–
 τούνια του γκολφ
 (neekeeasoome mbastooneea too golf)

◆ **hire skis**
◆ νοικιάσουμε πέδιλα
του σκι
*(neekeeasoome
pedheela too skee)*

◆ **hire a boat**
◆ νοικιάσουμε βάρκα
(neekeeasoome varka)

How much is it ...?
Πόσο κοστίζει....;
(Poso kosteezee)

◆ **per hour**
◆ την ώρα *(teen ora)*

◆ **per day**
◆ την ημέρα
(teen eemera)

◆ **per session/game**
◆ το παιχνίδι
(to pekhneedhee)

Is it ...?
Είναι...; *(Eene...?)*

◆ **deep**
◆ βαθιά *(vatheea)*

◆ **clean**
◆ καθαρά *(kathara)*

◆ **cold**
◆ κρύα *(kreea)*

**How do we get
there?**
Πως πάμε εκεί
(Pos pame ekee)

No swimming/diving
Απαγορεύεται το
κολύμπι/η κατάδυση
*(Apaghorevete to kolee-
mbee/ee katadheesee)*

Are there currents?
Έχει ρεύματα;
(Ekhee revmata?)

**Do I need a fishing
permit?**
Χρειάζομαι άδεια
ψαρέματος;
*(Khreeazome adheea
psarematos)*

**Where can I get
one?**
Που μπορώ να
προμηθευτώ; *(Poo
mboro na promeethefto)*

**Is there a guide for
walks?**
Υπάρχει οδηγός για
περιπάτους;
*(Eeparkhee odheeghos
gheea pereepatoos?)*

Do I need walking boots?
Χρειάζονται μπότες για περπάτιμα;
(Khreeazonde mbotes gheea perpateema?)

How much is a ski pass?
Πόσο στοιχίζει η άδεια του σκι;
(Poso steekheezee ee adheea too skee?)

Is it safe to ski today?
Είναι ασφαλές το σκι σήμερα; *(Eene asfales to skee seemera?)*

Run closed
Διάδρομος του σκι κλειστός *(Dheeadhromos too skee kleestos)*

avalanches
χιονοστιβάδες
(kheeonosteevadhes)

I'm a beginner
Είμαι αρχάριος/αρχάρια (m/f) *(Eeme arkhareeos/ arkhareea)*

Danger
Κίνδυνος *(Keendheenos)*

Which is an easy run?
Ποιός διάδρομος είναι εύκολος; *(Peeos dheeadhromos eene efkolos?)*

My skis are too long/ short
Τα σκι μου είναι πολύ μακριά/κοντά
(Ta skee moo eene polee makreea/konda)

We want to go ...
Θέλουμε να πάμε να κάνουμε ...
(Theloome na pame...)

◆ **hiking**
◆ οδοιπορία
  (odheeporeea)

◆ **sailing**
◆ ιστιοπλοΐα
  (eesteeoploeea)

◆ **ice-skating**
◆ πατινάζ *(pateenaz)*

◆ **water-skiing**
◆ θαλάσσιο σκι
  (thalaseeo skee)

PHARMACY/ CHEMIST
ΦΑΡΜΑΚΕΙΟ/ΦΑΡΜΑΚΟ-
ΠΟΙΟΣ (FARMAKEEO/
FARMAKOPEEOS)

health shop
κατάστημα προϊόντων
υγείας *(katasteema
proeeondon eegheeas)*

Have you got something for ...?
Έχετε κάτι για ...;
(Ekhete katee gheea)

◆ **diarrhoea**
◆ διάρροια *(dheeareea)*

◆ **cold, flu**
◆ κρυολόγημα, γρήπη
*(kreeologheema,
ghreepee)*

◆ **headache**
◆ πονοκέφαλος
(ponokefalos)

◆ **a sore throat**
◆ πονόλαιμος
(ponolemos)

◆ **stomachache**
◆ στομαχόπονος
(stomakhoponos)

◆ **car sickness**
◆ ναυτία επιβάτη αυτο-
κινήτου *(nafteea epee-
vatee aftokeeneetoo)*

I need ...
Χρειάζομαι ...
(Khreeazome)

◆ **indigestion tablets**
◆ χάπια για δυσπεψία
*(khapeea gheea
dheespepseea)*

◆ **laxative**
◆ καθαρτικό
(katharteeko)

◆ **sleeping tablets**
◆ υπνωτικά χάπια
(eepnoteeka khapeea)

◆ **a painkiller**
◆ παυσίπονο
(pafseepono)

Is it safe for children?
Είναι κατάλληλο/
ασφαλές για παιδιά;
*(Eene katalleelo/asfales
gheea pedheea)*

I'm a diabetic
Είμαι διαβητικός
(Eeme dheeaveeteekos)

I have high blood pressure
Έχω υψιλή πίεση/ υπέρ-
ταση *(Ekho eepseelee
pee-esee/eepertasee)*

I'm allergic to ...
Είμαι αλλεργικός στο ...
(Eeme allergheekos sto)

DOCTOR
ΓΙΑΤΡΟΣ (GHEEATROS)

I am ill
Είμαι άρρωστος
(Eeme arrostos)

I need a doctor
Χρειάζομαι γιατρό
(Khreeazome gheeatro)

He/she has a high temperature
Έχει υψιλό πυρετό
(Ekho eepseelo peereto)

It hurts
Πονάει *(Ponaee)*

I'm going to be sick!
Θα κάνω εμετό!
(Tha kano emeto)

dentist
οδοντίατρος
(odhondeeatros)

I have toothache
Έχω πονόδοντο
(Ekho ponodhondo)

optometrist
οπτικός *(opteekos)*

HOSPITAL
ΝΟΣΟΚΟΜΕΙΟ
(NOSOKOMEEO)

Will I have to go to hospital?
Θα χρειαστεί να πάω
στο νοσοκομείο;
*(Tha khreeastee na pao
sto nosokomeeo)*

Where is the hospital?
Που είναι το νοσοκομείο;
*(Poo eene to
nosokomeeo)*

When are visiting hours?
Ποιές είναι οι ώρες
επισκέψεως;
*(Pee-es eene ee ores
epeeskepseos)*

Where is casualty?
Που είναι ο θάλαμος
ατυχημάτων;
*(Poo eene o thalamos
ateekheematon)*

POLICE
ΑΣΤΥΝΟΜΙΑ
(ASTEENOMEEA)

Call the police
Φωνάξτε την αστυνομία
(Fonakste teen asteenomeea)

I have been robbed
Με έχουν ληστέψει
(Me ekhoon leestepsee)

My car has been broken into
Έχουν διαρρήξει το αυτοκίνητό μου
(Ekhoon dheeareeksee to aftokeeneeto moo)

I want to report a theft
Θα ήθελα να καταγγείλω μια κλοπή
(Tha eethela na katangeelo meea klopee)

I have been attacked
Μου έχουν επιτεθεί
(Moo ekhoon epitethee)

I have been raped
Με έχουν βιάσει
(Me ekhoon veeasee)

Where is the police station?
Που είναι το αστυνομικό τμήμα;
(Poo eene to asteenomeeko tmeema)

EMERGENCIES
ΕΠΙΓΟΝΤΑ
(EPEEGHONDA)

Call an ambulance
Φωνάξτε ασθενοφόρο
(Fonakste asthenoforo)

There's been an accident
Έγινε ένα ατύχημα
(Egheene ateekheema)

Someone is injured
Κάποιος έχει τραυματιστεί
(Kapeeos ekhee travmateestee)

Hurry up!
Γρήγορα! *(Ghreeghora)*

Could you please help me?
Μπορείτε να με βοηθήσετε;
(Mboreete na me voeetheesete)

Help!
Βοήθεια! *(Voeetheea)*

This is an emergency!
Είναι επίγον!
(Eene epeeghon)

My son/daughter is missing
Ο γιός μου / Η κόρη μου λείπει *(O gheeos moo / Ee koree moo leepee)*

I need a report for my insurance
Χρειάζομαι αναφορά για την ασφάλειά μου
(Khreeazome anaphora gheea teen asfaleea moo)

I want to phone my embassy
Θέλω να καλέσω τη πρεσβεία μου
(Thelo na kaleso teen presveea moo)

I am lost
Έχω χαθεί
(Ekho khathee)

He/she is ill
Είναι άρρωστος/ άρρωστη
(Eene arrostos/arrostee)

Look out!
Προσέξτε! *(Prosekste)*

FIRE DEPARTMENT
ΠΥΡΟΣΒΕΣΤΙΚΗ
(PEEROSVESTEEKEE)

Fire!
Φωτιά! *(Foteea)*

Call the fire department
Φωνάξτε τη πυροσβεστική *(Fonakste tee peerosvesteekee)*

It's an electrical fire
Πρόκειται για ηλεκτρική φωτιά *(Prokeete gheea eelektreekee foteea)*

The address is ...
Η διεύθυνση είναι ... *(Ee dhee-eftheensee eene)*

I need ...
Χρειάζομαι ...
(Khreeazome)

◆ **a fire extinguisher**
◆ πυροσβεστήρα
  (peerosvesteera)

◆ **medical assistance**
◆ ιατρική βοήθεια
  (eeatreekee voeetheea)

74

THE HUMAN BODY
ΤΟ ΑΝΘΡΩΠΙΝΟ ΣΩΜΑ (ΤΟ ΑΝΤΗΡΟΡΕΕΝΟ SΩMA)

brain μυαλό m<u>ee</u>alo
head κεφάλι kef<u>a</u>lee
hair μαλλιά mall<u>ee</u>a
ear αυτί aft<u>ee</u>

cheek μάγουλο m<u>a</u>ghoolo
neck λαιμός lem<u>o</u>s
shoulder ώμος <u>o</u>mos
chest στήθος st<u>ee</u>thos
arm μπράτσο mbr<u>a</u>tso
elbow αγκώνας ang<u>o</u>nas
abdomen κοιλιά keel<u>ee</u>a
hand χέρι kh<u>e</u>ree
thumb αντίχειρας and<u>ee</u>kheeras
finger δάχτυλο dh<u>a</u>khteelo
nail νύχι n<u>ee</u>khee

bone κόκαλο k<u>o</u>kalo
knee γόνατο gh<u>o</u>nato

shin καλάμι kal<u>a</u>mee

ankle αστράγαλος astr<u>a</u>ghalos
foot πόδι p<u>o</u>dhee

toe δάχτυλο ποδιού dh<u>a</u>khteelo podh<u>ee</u><u>oo</u>

forehead μέτοπο m<u>e</u>toro
eyebrow φρύδι fr<u>ee</u>dhee
eyelash βλεφαρίδα vlefar<u>ee</u>dha
eye μάτι m<u>a</u>tee
face πρόσωπο pr<u>o</u>sopo
nose μύτη m<u>ee</u>tee
lip χείλη kh<u>ee</u>lee
mouth στώμα st<u>o</u>ma
chin σαγόνι sagh<u>o</u>nee

lung πνεύμονας pn<u>e</u>vmonas
heart καρδιά kardh<u>ee</u>a
stomach στομάχι stom<u>a</u>khee
liver συκώτι seek<u>o</u>tee
intestines έντερα <u>e</u>ntera

leg πόδι p<u>o</u>dhee

skin δέρμα dh<u>e</u>rma
heel φτέρνα ft<u>e</u>rna

FORMS OF ADDRESS

ΤΡΟΠΟΙ ΠΡΟΣΦΩΝΗΣΗΣ

(TROPEE PROSFONEESEES)

There are two ways of translating the English word 'you'. The formal way is εσείς *(esees)*. This form of address is a sign of courtesy and respect, and would normally be used when addressing elderly people, teachers, bosses, shopkeepers and people you don't know very well, especially if they are older than you.

The less formal translation of 'you' is εσύ *(esee)*, which is the form generally used when addressing family, friends and people you know well.

GREETING PEOPLE

ΧΑΙΡΕΤΙΣΜΟΣ (KHERETEESMOS)

When it comes to greeting each other, the Greek people are rather formal, and the usual form of greeting is to shake hands followed, optionally, by reciprocal kissing on both cheeks if the parties know each other. This applies to both young and old people and is irrespective of gender.

Hugging is also a very Greek custom, and men who know each other well will usually hug each other.

Kissing varies from country to country. In Greece a greeting will usually consist of two kisses, one on each cheek.

Eye contact is important, and Greeks expect you to make eye contact when you speak to them. Not establishing eye contact may be taken as a sign of respect toward an elder party, or a figure of authority, but this behaviour is fading away in modern times.

MANNERS
ΚΑΛΟΙ ΤΡΟΠΟΙ (KALEE TROPEE)

The well-known fiery Mediterranean temperament means that Greek people are usually quite outspoken and direct. This same temperament also leads to rather high levels of noise. The people speak loudly, and the drivers generally hoot a lot, so don't expect an especially quiet time when visiting Greece and Cyprus!

On the other hand, there is the very Greek custom of the ώρες κοινής ησυχίας (*ores keenees eeseekheeas*), like the Spanish siesta, and in most Greek-speaking countries everything comes to a standstill during the hottest part of the day, when people usually have a rest.

The Greek people can be very helpful towards strangers. The more you try to talk to them, no matter how excruciating your Greek pronunciation is, the more they will want to help you. They may even offer to accompany you to whichever place it is you are trying to find. So it would be well worth your while to learn the basics of the language before you embark on a visit to Greece or Cyprus, whether you are going on holiday or on a business trip. If you make the effort it will be appreciated.

COMMUNICATION
ΕΠΙΚΟΙΝΩΝΙΑ (EPEEKEENONEEA)

There are many Greek words that cannot be simply and literally translated into English, for example words such as κέφι (a very cheer-ful mood experienced in good company) or φιλότιμο (literally 'a friend of honour'), which have many more connotations attached to them than their literal meanings tell us.

The Greek phrase έχει πολύ κέφι (<u>e</u>khee pol<u>ee</u> k<u>e</u>fee), for instance, literally means 'there is much cheer', but it carries with it a wealth of social images such as a group of people, both acquaintances and not, who are at the same place having an extremely jovial party with good music, lots of dancing and a sense that one is having the best time of one's life. In Greece and Cyprus, the people enjoy a good party with a big variety of μεζέδες (mez<u>e</u>dhes) on the table, which you can enjoy with your favourite drink, while enjoying ample good music and dancing in the company of family and good friends.

FOOD AND MEALS
ΦΑΓΗΤΟ ΚΑΙ ΓΕΥΜΑΤΑ
(FAGHEET<u>O</u> KE GH<u>E</u>VMATA)

Greek cuisine varies from region to region. Dishes found on mainland Greece may be very different to dishes found on the islands, even though they have the same or similar names, and the same may apply to drinks. For example, ρακί (rak<u>ee</u>) in Lesbos is actually what we know as Ouzo, whereas in Crete it is a very strong drink distilled from the pulp of grapes that have already been squeezed for the purpose of making wine. Similarly, ντολμάδες (dolmadhes) served on the island of Crete can consist of stuffed courgette flowers, whereas in the rest of Greece it typically implies parcels of mince and rice wrapped in vine leaves.

Unlike the West, where people normally sit down to have a meal consisting of a starter, a main course and a dessert, in Greece, and at most social gatherings, many varieties of food are served at once and are put in the middle of the table for everyone to enjoy. Hence a Greek meal can often mean continuous snacking from a large selection of μεζέδες (mezedhes – from which we get the term 'meze platters') enjoyed in good company, with music and dance an absolutely essential accompaniment. Greeks normally need very little reason to break out into a party and you will have ample opportunity to experience this first-hand if you follow the locals into the tavernas they prefer to frequent rather than going to the tourist-accommodating restaurants.

OFFICIAL HOLIDAYS 83
ΕΠΙΣΗΜΕΣ ΓΙΟΡΤΕΣ
(EP<u>EE</u>SEEMES GHEEORT<u>E</u>S) 83

REGIONAL HOLIDAYS 85
ΤΟΠΙΚΕΣ ΓΙΟΡΤΕΣ
(TOPEEK<u>E</u>S GHEEORT<u>E</u>S) 85

New Year's Day
Πρωτοχρονιά
Protokhroneea
(1 January)
Exuberant parties and dances are held on 31 December – παραμονή πρωτοχρονιάς (*paramonee protokhroneeas*) – so most people spend New Year's Day recovering.

Epiphany
Τα Άγια Θεοφάνεια
Ta Agheea Theofaneea
(6 January)
A religious holiday commemorating the manifestation of Holy Trinity during the baptism of Jesus Christ in the Jordan River.

Holy Week – Easter
Μεγάλη Εβδομάδα – Πάσχα
Meghalee Evdhomadha – Paskha
(March/April)
In Greece and the Orthodox Christian world, Easter is preceded by the Holy Week, which starts on Palm Sunday (Κυριακή των Βαΐων) and ends at midnight on Holy Saturday (Μεγάλο Σάββατο) with the proclamation 'Χριστός Ανέστη!' (Christ is Risen!). Church services are held once or twice a day during Holy Week and the general mood is sombre and austere, culminating in a very mournful atmosphere permeating the land on Holy Friday (Μεγάλη

Παρασκευή). **During Holy Week, most Greeks observe the strictest Lent in commemoration of the Passion of Christ and His sacrifice. Some important events during Holy Week are the Sacrament of Unction on Holy Wednesday, the Passion and Crucifixion of Christ on Holy Thursday, the Burial and Litany of Christ's Body on Holy Friday, and of course, the Resurrection on Easter Sunday. Easter Sunday is celebrated loudly all over Greece and Cyprus and everyone is in the outdoors, spit-roasting lamb, cracking Greek Easter-Eggs and endlessly proclaiming to one another: 'Christ is Risen'.**

May Day, Labour Day
Πρωτομαγιά
Protomagheea
(1 May)
An official holiday for the workers.

Greek Independence Day
25 η Μαρτίου,
Ευαγγελισμός της
Θεοτόκου
*Eekostee Pemptee Marteeoo,
Evangeleesmos tees Theotokoo*
(25 March)
All around Greece people celebrate the country's independence from Turkish Occupation since 25 March 1821. The same date (25 March) is also the day on which the Immaculate Conception of Christ is celebrated in the Christian churches.

Christmas

Χριστούγεννα
Khreestooghenna
(25 December)

From the first Sunday of Advent private and public festivities mark this special season, leading up to the highlight of Christmas Eve (Παραμονή Χριστουγέννων).

REGIONAL HOLIDAYS
ΤΟΠΙΚΕΣ ΓΙΟΡΤΕΣ
TOPEEKES
GHEEORTES

All over Greece and Cyprus are churches and chapels dedicated to the memories of the myriad saints of the Greek Orthodox Church. In each region some saints have special significance as patron saints of towns or villages. It is not uncommon then for one region to hold special festivities on their patron saint's feast day, whereas the rest of the country continues its normal daily routine. Such regional festivities are not necessarily limited to religious observances. There are also non-religious celebrations in various parts of Greece commemorating events of Greece and Cyprus' tumultuous history. In Greece for example, even though liberation from Turkish occupation started in 1821, many regions of modern Greece remained occupied for longer. Hence in many parts of Greece, liberation is celebrated on different dates.

ENGLISH → GREEK

A

abbey μοναστήρι
monasteeree

abortion έκτρωση
ektrosee

about (approximately)
περίπου *pereepoo*

above παραπάνω
parapano

abroad εξωτερικό
eksotereeko

abscess απόστημα
aposteema

absolutely απόλυτα
apoleeta

accelerator γκάζι *gazee*

accent προφορά *profora*

accept δέχομαι *dhekhome*

accident ατύχημα
ateekheema

accommodation διαμονή
dheeamonee

account λογαριασμός
loghareeasmos

accurate ακριβής
akreevees

ache πόνος *ponos*

adapter μετασχηματιστής
metaskheemateestees

adhesive tape
αυτοκόλλητη ταινία
aftokoleetee teneea

admission fee είσοδος
eesodhos

adult ενήλικας *eneeleekas*

advance, in advance
προκαταβολή, προκατα-
βολικά *prokatavolee,*
prokatavoleeka

advertisement δια-
φήμηση *dheeafeemeesee*

advice συμβουλή
seemvoolee

advise συνιστώ *seeneesto*

aeroplane αεροπλάνο
aeroplano

afraid, be afraid of
φοβάμαι *fovame*

after ύστερα *eestera*

afternoon απόγευμα
apoghevma

afterwards κατόπιν
katopeen

again πάλι, ξανά *palee, xana*

against εναντίον
enandeeon

age ηλικία *eeleekeea*

agree συμφωνώ *seemfono*

agreement συμφωνία
seemfoneea

air αέρας *aeras*

air conditioning κλιματισμός *kleemateesmos*

air ticket αεροπορικό
εισιτήριο *aeroporeeko*
eeseeteereeo

airmail αεροπορικώς
aeroporeekos

airport αεροδρόμιο
aerodhromeeo

aisle διάδρομος
dheeadhromos

aisle seat κάθισμα κοντά
στο διάδρομο *katheesma*
konda sto dheeadhromo

all right εντάξι *endaksee*

allow επιτρέπω *epeetrepo*

almond αμύγδαλο
ameeghdhalo

almost σχεδόν *skhedhon*

alone μόνος *monos*

already ήδη *eedhee*

also επίσης *epeesees*

although μολονότι/αν και
molonotee/an ke

altogether συνολικά
seenoleeka

always πάντοτε *pandote*

a.m. (before noon)
π.μ. (προ μεσημβρείας)
pro meseemvreeas)

am, I am είμαι *eeme*

amazing καταπληκτικό
katapleekteeko

amber κεχριμπάρι
kekhreembaree

ambulance ασθενοφόρο
asthenoforo

among ανάμεσα/μεταξύ
  anamesa/metaksee
amount ποσό *poso*
anaesthetic αναισθητικό
  anestheeteeko
ancient αρχαίο *arkheo*
and και *ke*
angry θυμωμένος
  theemomenos
animal ζώο *zo-o*
ankle αστράγαλος
  astraghalos
anniversary επέτειος
  epeteeos
annoy ενοχλώ *enokhlo*
annual ετήσιος *eteeseeos*
another άλλος *allos*
answer (n, response)
  απάντηση *apandeesee*
answer (n, solution) λύση
  leesee
ant μυρμήγκι *meermeengee*
antacid αντιοξύ
  andeeoksee
anybody οποιοσδήποτε
  opeeosdheepote
anything οτιδήποτε
  oteedheepote
apartment διαμέρισμα
  dheeamereesma
apology συγγνώμη
  seenghnomee
appendicitis
  σκωληκοειδίτιδα
  skoleekoeedheeteedha
appointment ραντεβού
  randevoo
approximately περίπου
  pereepoo
apron ποδιά *podheea*
are είναι *eene*
area έκταση *ektasee*
armchair πολυθρόνα
  poleethrona
arrange κανονίζω
  kanoneezo
arrest συλλαμβάνω
  seelamvano
arrival άφιξη *afeeksee*
arrive φθάνω *fthano*

art τέχνη *tekhnee*
artist καλλιτέχνης
  kaleetekhnees
ask ζητώ *zeeto*
astonishing εκπληκτικός
  ekpleekteekos
at στον, στην, στο
  ston (m), steen (f), sto (n)
attack (n) επίθεση
  epeethesee
attack (vb) επιτίθεμαι
  epeeteetheme
attic σοφίτα *sofeeta*
audience ακροατήριο
  akroateereeo
aunt θεία *theea*
autumn φθινόπωρο
  ftheenoporo
available διαθέσιμο
  dheeatheseemo
avalanche χιονοστιβάδα
  kheeonosteevadha
avenue λεωφόρος *leoforos*
average μέσος όρος
  mesos oros
avoid αποφεύγω
  apofevgho
awake ξυπνώ *kseepno*
away λείπει *leepee*
awful απαίσιο *apeseeo*

B
baby food φαγητό μωρού
  fagheeto moroo
back πίσω, πλάτη *peeso,*
  platee
backache οσφυαλγία
  osfeealgheea
backpack (εκδρομικό)
  σακίδιο *(ekdhromeeko)*
  sakeedheeo
bacon μπέικον *mbe-eekon*
bad κακός, άσχημος *kakos,*
  askheemos
bag τσάντα *tsanta*
baggage αποσκευές
  aposkeves
baggage reclaim
  αναζήτηση αποσκευών
  anazeeteesee aposkevon

bait δόλωμα *dholoma*
bakery φούρνος, ζαχαροπλαστείο *foornos, zakharoplasteeo*
balcony μπαλκόνι *balkonee*
ballpoint pen στυλός διαρκείας *steelos dheearkeeas*
Baltic Sea Βαλτική Θάλασσα *Valteekee Thalassa*
bandage επίδεσμος *epeedhesmos*
bar of chocolate πλάκα σοκολάτας *plaka sokolatas*
barber's shop κουρείο *kooreeo*
bark (n, of dog) γαύγισμα *ghavgheesma*
bark (n, of tree) φλοιός *fleeos*
barn αποθήκη, στάβλος *apotheekee, stavlos*
barrel βαρέλι *varelee*
basement υπόγειο *eepogheeo*
basket καλάθι *kalathee*
bath μπάνιο *mbaneeo*
bathroom μπανιέρα *mbanee-era*
bay κόλπος *kolpos*
bay leaf βαγιόφυλο *vagheeofeelo*
be είμαι *eeme*
beach πλαζ *plaz*
bean φασόλι *fasolee*
beard γένια *gheneea*
beautiful όμορφος *omorfos*
beauty salon ινστιτούτο καλλονής *eensteetooto kallonees*
because επειδή *epeedhee*
because of εξ'αιτίας *eks'eteeas*
bed κρεββάτι *krevatee*
bed & breakfast διαμονή και πρωινό *dheeamonee ke proeeno*

bed linen κλινοσκεπάσματα *kleenoskepasmata*
bedspread στρωσίδι *stroseedhee*
bee μέλισσα *meleesa*
beef βοδινό *vodheeno*
beer μπύρα *beera*
before πριν, μπροστά *preen, mbrosta*
beginner αρχάριος *arkhareeos*
behind πίσω *peeso*
Belgian Βέλγος *Velghos*
Belgium Βέλγιο *Velgheeo*
believe πιστεύω *peestevo*
bell κουδούνι, καμπάνα *koodhoonee, kambana*
below από κάτω *apo kato*
belt ζώνη *zonee*
bend σκύβω *skeevo*
beside πλάϊ, δίπλα *plaee, dheepla*
bet στοίχημα *steekheema*
better καλύτερος *kaleeteros*
beyond πέρα από *pera apo*
bicycle ποδήλατο *podheelato*
big μεγάλος *meghalos*
bill λογαριασμός *loghareeasmos*
bin δοχείο *dhokheeo*
binoculars κιάλια *keealeea*
bird πουλί *poolee*
birth γέννηση *gheneesee*
birth certificate πιστοποιητικό γεννήσεως *peestopee-eeteeko gheneeseos*
birthday γεννέθλια *ghenethleea*
birthday card κάρτα γεννεθλίων *karta ghenethleeon*
birthday present δώρο γεννεθλίων *dhoro ghenethleeon*
biscuit μπισκότο *beeskoto*

bit κομμάτι *komatee*
bite (vb) δαγκώνω *dhangono*
black μαύρος *mavros*
blackcurrant μαύρη σταφίδα *mavree stafeedha*
blanket κουβέρτα *kooverta*
bleach (n) λευκαντικό
lefkandeeko
bleed ματώνω *matono*
blind (adj) τυφλός *teeflos*
blind (n) ρολό *rolo*
blister φουσκάλα *fooskala*
block of flats πολυ-
κατοικία *poleekateekeea*
blocked φραγμένο
fraghmeno
blood αίμα *ema*
blood pressure πίεση
pee-esee
blouse μπλούζα *blooza*
blow-dry στεγνώνω
μαλλιά *steghnono maleea*
blue γαλάζιο *ghalazeeo*
blunt αμβλύς *amvlees*
blusher κοκκινάδι
kokeenadhee
boar αγριόχοιρος
aghreeokheeros
boarding card δελτίο
επιβίβασης *dehlteeo
epeeveevasees*
boarding house πανσιόν
panseeon
boat πλοίο *pleeo*
boat trip ταξίδι με πλοίο
takseedhee me pleeo
body σώμα *soma*
boil (vb) βράζω *vrazo*
boil (n) καλόγερος *kalogheros*
bone κόκαλο *kokalo*
bonnet (car) καπό *kapo*
book βιβλίο *veevleeo*
bookshop βιβλιοπωλείο
veevleeopoleeo
boots μπότες *botes*
border σύνορα *seenora*
boring πληκτικός
pleekteekos

born γεννημένος
gheneemenos
borrow δανίζομαι, δανίζω
dhaneezome, dhaneezo
both και οι δύο *ke ee dheeo*
bottle μπουκάλι *bookalee*
bottle opener ανοιχτήρι
aneekhteeree
bottom (at the) από
κάτω *apo kato*
bow tie παπιόν *papeeon*
bowl λεκάνη *lekanee*
box κουτί *kootee*
boy αγόρι *aghoree*
boyfriend φίλος *feelos*
bra σουτιέν *sootee-en*
bracelet βραχιόλι
vrakheeolee
brake (n) φρένο *freno*
brake fluid υγρό φρένων
eeghro frenon
brake light φανάρι
φρένων *fanaree frenon*
branch (office)
παράρτημα *pararteema*
brand μάρκα *marka*
brandy κονιάκ *koneeak*
bread ψωμί *psomee*
break σπάω *spao*
breakable εύθραυστος
efthrafstos
breakdown (of car)
βλάβη αυτοκινήτου *vlavee
aftokeeneetoo*
breakdown van συνερ-
γείο διάσωσης *seener-
gheeo dheeasosees*
breakfast πρωινό *proeeno*
break-in διάρρηξη
dheeareeksee
breast στήθος *steethos*
breathe αναπνέω *anapneo*
breeze ρεύμα *revma*
brewery ζυθοποιείο
zeethopee-eeo
brick τούβλο *toovlo*
bride νύφη *neefee*
bridegroom γαμπρός
ghambros

89

ENGLISH → GREEK

bridge γεφύρι *ghefeeree*
briefcase χαρτοφύλακας *khartofeelakas*
bright λαμπρό *lambro*
bring φέρω *fero*
bring in αποφέρω *apofero*
brochure φυλλάδιο *feeladheeo*
broken σπασμένο *spasmeno*
bronchitis βρογχίτιδα *vronkheeteedha*
brooch καρφίτσα *karfeetsa*
broom σκούπα *skoopa*
brother αδελφός *adhelfos*
brother-in-law γαμπρός/κουνιάδος *ghambros/kooneeadhos*
brown καφετί *kafetee*
bruise (n) μελανιά *melaneea*
brush βούρτσα *voortsa*
Brussels Βρυξέλλες *Vreekseles*
bucket κουβάς *koovas*
buffet car βαγόνι του μπουφέ *vaghonee too boofe*
buggy αμαξάκι *amaksakee*
build χτίζω *khteezo*
building οικοδομή *eekodhomee*
bulb (light) λάμπα *lamba*
bulb (plant) βολβός *volvos*
bumper προφυλακτήρας *profeelakteeras*
bun ψωμάκι *psomakee*
bunch τσαμπί *tsambee*
bureau de change γραφείο συναλλάγματος *ghrafeeo seenalaghmatos*
burglar κλέφτης *kleftees*
burglary διάρρηξη *dheeareeksee*
burn καίω *keo*
burst σκάω *skao*
bus λεωφορείο *leoforeeo*
bus stop στάση λεωφορείου *stasee leoforeeoo*
bush θάμνος *thamnos*

business επιχείρηση *epeekheereesee*
business trip ταξίδι για δουλειά *takseedhee gheea dhooleea*
busy απασχολημένος/πολυάσχολος *apaskholeemenos/poleeaskholos*
but αλλά/μα *ala ma*
butcher χασάπης *khasapees*
butter βούτυρο *vooteero*
butterfly πεταλούδα *petaloodha*
button κουμπί *koobee*
buy αγοράζω *aghorazo*
by κοντά/από *konda/apo*
bypass (road) πάροδος *parodhos*

C

cab ταξί *taksee*
cabbage λάχανο *lakhano*
cabin καμπίνα *kambeena*
cable car τελεφερίκ *telefereek*
cake τούρτα/κέικ *toorta/ke-eek*
cake shop ζαχαροπλαστείο *zakharoplasteeo*
calculator κομπιουτεράκι *kombeeooterakee*
calf μοσχάρι *moskharee*
call (to call someone) φωνάζω *fonazo*
call (to phone someone) πέρνω τηλέφωνο *perno teelefono*
calm ήρεμος *eeremos*
camp (vb) κατασκηνώνω *kataskeenono*
camp site κατασκήνωση *kataskeenosee*
can (n) τενεκές *tenekes*
can (vb) μπορώ *mboro*
can't δεν μπορώ *dhen boro*
can opener ανοιχτήρι *aneekhteeree*

90

Canada Καναδάς
Kanadhas
canal κανάλι *kanalee*
cancel ακυρώνω *akeerono*
cancellation ακύρωση
akeerosee
cancer καρκίνος *karkeenos*
candle κερί *keree*
candy γλυκά/καραμέλες
ghleeka / karamelees
canoe κανό *kano*
cap σκούφος *skoofos*
capital (city) πρωτεύουσα
protevoosa
capital (money)
κεφάλαιο *kefaleo*
car αυτοκίνητο
aftokeeneeto
car ferry φερυμπώτ
αυτοκηνίτων *fereembot
aftokeeneeton*
car hire ενοικιαζόμενα
αυτοκίνητα *eneekeea-
zomena aftokeeneeta*
car insurance ασφάλεια
αυτοκηνήτων *asfaleea
aftokeeneeton*
car keys κλειδιά
αυτοκινήτου *kleedheea
aftokeeneetoo*
car parts εξαρτήματα
αυτοκινήτου *eksarteema
aftokeeneetoo*
car wash πλήσιμο
αυτοκινήτου *pleeseemo
aftokeeneetoo*
caravan τροχόσπιτο
trokhospeeto
caravan site χώρος
στάθμευσης για
τροχόσπιτα *khoros
stathmefshees gheea
trokhospeeta*
carburettor καρμπυρατέρ
karbeerater
card κάρτα *karta*
cardboard χαρτόνι
khartonee
cardigan ζακέτα *zaketa*

careful προσεκτικός
prosekteekos
caretaker επιστάτης
epeestatees
carpenter μαραγκός
marangos
carpet χαλί *khalee*
carriage καρότσα *karotsa*
carrier bag τσάντα *tsanta*
carrot καρότο *karoto*
carry βαστώ *vasto*
carry-cot φορητή κουκέτα
foreetee kooketa
carton χαρτόκουτο
khartokooto
case περίπτωση
pereeptosee
cash μετρητά *metreeta*
cash desk ταμείο *tameeo*
cash dispenser
αυτόματος διανομέας
χρημάτων *aftomatos
dheanomeas khreematon*
cash register ταμειακή
μηχανή *tameeakee
meekhanee*
cashier ταμίας *tameeas*
cassette κασέτα *kaseta*
castle κάστρο *kastro*
casualty department
θάλαμος ατυχημάτων
thalamos ateekheematon
cat γάτα *ghata*
catch (vb) πιάνω *peeano*
catch (arrest) συλλαμβάνω *seelamvano*
cathedral καθεδρικός
ναός *kathedhreekos naos*
Catholic Καθολικός
Katholeekos
cauliflower κουνουπίδι
koonoopeedhee
cave σπηλιά *speeleea*
CD player Ση-Ντη Πλέγιερ
See-Dee Pleghee-er
ceiling ταβάνι *tavanee*
celery σέλινο *seleeno*
cellar κελάρι/κάβα
kelaree/kava

cemetery νεκροταφείο/
κοιμητήριο *nekrotafeeo/
keemeeteereeo*
Centigrade εκατοντά-
βαθμο *ekatondavathmo*
centimetre πόντος/εκα-
τοστό *pondos/ekatosto*
central heating κεντρική
θέρμανση *kendreekee
thermansee*
central locking
κεντρικό κλείδωμα
kendreeko kleedhoma
centre κέντρο *kendro*
century αιώνας *eonas*
certain βέβαιος *veveos*
certainly ασφαλώς *asfalos*
certificate πιστοποιητικό
peestopee-eeteeko
chair καρέκλα *karekla*
chair lift ασανσέρ
αναπηρικής πολυθρώνας
*asanser anapeereekees
poleethronas*
chambermaid καμαριέρα
kamaree-era
champagne σαμπάνια
sampaneea
change (money) ρέστα/
ψιλά *resta/pseela*
change (clothes)
αλλάζω *alazo*
changing room
δοκιμαστήριο *dhokee-
masteereeo*
channel κανάλι/πορθμός
kanalee/porthmos
chapel παρεκκλήσι
parekleesee
charcoal κάρβουνο
karvoono
charge χρεώνω/
κατηγορώ/επιτίθεμαι
*khreono/kateegoro/
epeeteetheme*
charge card πιστωτική
κάρτα *peestoteekee karta*
charter flight πτήση
τσάρτερ *pteesee tsarter*

cheap φτηνό *fteeno*
cheap rate φτηνή τιμή
fteenee teemee
cheaper φτηνότερος
fteenoteros
check ελέγχω *elengkho*
check in (at hotel)
υπογραφή στο ξενοδοχείο
κατά την άφιξη *eepoghra-
fee sto ksenodhokheeo
kata teen afeeksee*
check in (at airport)
τσεκάρισμα αποσκευών
και εισιτηρίου προ της
αναχώρησης *tseka-
reesma aposkevon ke
eeseeteereeon pro tees
anakhoreesees*
cheek μάγουλο *maghoolo*
Cheers! Στην υγειά μας!
Steen eegheea mas!
cheese τυρί *teeree*
chef σεφ/αρχιμάγειρας
sef/arkheemagheeras
chemist φαρμακείο/
φαρμακοποιός *farma-
keeo/farmakopeeos*
cheque επιταγή
epeetaghee
cheque book βιβλίο
επιταγών *veevleeo
epeetaghon*
cheque card κάρτα
λογαριασμού επιταγών
*karta loghareeasmoo
epeetaghon*
cherry κερασάκι *kerasakee*
chess σκάκι *skakee*
chest στήθος *steethos*
chest of drawers
συρτάρια *seertareea*
chestnut κάστανο *kastano*
chewing gum τσίχλα
tseekhla
chicken κοτόπουλο
kotopoolo
chicken pox ανεμοβλογιά
anemovlogheea
child παιδί *pedhee*

child car seat κάθισμα παιδιού *katheesma pedheoo*
chimney καπνοδόχος *kapnodhokhos*
chin πηγούνι *peeghoonee*
China Κίνα *Keena*
china πορσελάνη *porselanee*
chips τσίπς/πατατάκια *tseeps/patatakeea*
chocolate σοκολάτα *sokolata*
chocolates σοκολατάκια *sokolatakeea*
choir χορωδία *khorodheea*
choose διαλέγω *dhealegho*
chop κομματιάζω *komateeazo*
Christian name βαφτιστικό όνομα *vafteesteeko onoma*
Christmas Χριστούγεννα *Khreestooghena*
Christmas Eve Παραμονή Χριστουγέννων *Paramonee Khreestoghenon*
church εκκλησία *ekleeseea*
cider μηλίτης *meeleetees*
cigar πούρο *pooro*
cigarette τσιγάρο *tseegharo*
cigarette lighter αναπτήρας *anapteeras*
cinema σινεμά *seenema*
circle κύκλος *keeklos*
cistern δεξαμενή *dheksamenee*
citizen πολίτης *poleetees*
city πόλη *polee*
city centre κέντρο της πόλης *kendro tees polees*
class τάξη *taksee*
clean (vb) καθαρίζω *kathareezo*
clean (adj) καθαρός *katharos*
cleaning solution καθαριστικό διάλυμα *kathareesteeko dheealeema*

cleansing lotion λοσιόν καθαρισμού *loseeon kathareesmoo*
clear (adj) σαφής *safees*
clever έξυπνος *ekseepnos*
client πελάτης *pelatees*
cliff γκρεμός *gremos*
climate κλίμα *kleema*
climb σκαρφαλώνω *skarfalono*
cling film σελοφάν *selofan*
clinic κλινική *kleeneekee*
cloakroom τουαλέτα *tooaleta*
clock ρολόι *roloee*
closed κλειστό *kleesto*
cloth πανί/ύφασμα *panee/eefasma*
clothes ρούχα *rookha*
clothes line σκοινί ρούχων *skeenee rookhon*
clothes peg μανταλάκι *mandalakee*
clothing ρουχισμός *rookheesmos*
cloud σύνεφο *seenefo*
clutch (car) αμπραγιάτζ *abragheeaz*
coach πούλμαν *poolman*
coal κάρβουνο *karvoono*
coast παραλία/ακτή *paraleea/aktee*
coastguard ακτοφύλακας *aktofeelakas*
coat παλτό *palto*
coat hanger κρεμαστάρι *kremastaree*
cockroach κατσαρίδα *katsareedha*
cocoa κακάο *kakao*
coconut καρύδα *kareedha*
cod μπακαλιάρος *bakaleearos*
code κώδικας *kodheekas*
coffee καφές *kafes*
coil (rope) κουλούρα σχοινιού *kooloora skeeneeoo*
coin κέρμα *kerma*

Coke Κόκα Κόλα *Koka Kola*

colander τρυπητό *treepeeto*

cold κρύο *kreeo*

collapse καταρρέω *katareo*

collar κολάρο *kolaro*

collarbone κλείδωση του ώμου *kleedhosee too omoo*

colleague συνάδελφος *seenadhelfos*

collect μαζεύω *mazevo*

collect call τηλεφώνημα με χρέωση του καλού- μενου *teelefoneema me khreosee too kaloomenoo*

colour χρώμα *khroma*

colour blind αχρωματοψία *akhromatopseea*

colour film έγχρωμο φιλμ *engkhromo feelm*

comb (n) χτένα *khtena*

comb (vb) χτενίζω *khteneezo*

come έρχομαι *erkhome*

come back επιστρέφω *epeestrefo*

come in μπαίνω *mbeno*

comedy κωμωδία *komodheea*

comfortable άνετος *anetos*

company παρέα *parea*

compartment τμήμα/ βαγόνι *tmeema/ vaghonee*

compass πυξίδα *peekseedha*

complain παραπονιέμαι *paraponee-eme*

complaint παράπονο *parapono*

completely εξ'ολοκλήρου *eks'olokleeroo*

composer συνθέτης *seenthetees*

compulsory υποχρεω- τικός *eepokhreoteekos*

computer υπολογιστής *eepologheestees*

concert συναυλία *seenavleea*

concession παραχώρηση *parakhoreesee*

concussion διάσειση *dheeaseesee*

condition κατάσταση *katastasee*

condom προφυλακτικό *profeelakteeko*

conference διάσκεψη *dheeaskepsee*

confirm επιβεβαιώνω *epeeveveono*

confirmation επιβεβαί- ωση *epeeveveosee*

confused μπερδεμένος *mberdhemenos*

Congratulations! Συγχαρητήρια! *Seengkhareeteereea!*

connecting flight πτήση ανταπόκρισης *pteesee andapokreesees*

connection (elec) ηλεκτρική σύνδεση *eelektreekee seendhesee*

connection (phone) τηλεφωνική σύνδεση *teelefoneekee seendhesee*

conscious συναισθανό- μενος *seenesthanomenos*

constipated δυσκοίλιος *dheeskeeleeos*

consulate προξενείο *prokseneeo*

contact επαφή *epafee*

contact lenses φακοί επαφής *fakee epafees*

continue συνεχίζω *seenekheezo*

contraceptive αντισυλληπτικό *andeeseeleepteeko*

contract συμβόλαιο *seemvoleo*

convenient βολικός
voleekos
cook (vb) μαγειρεύω
magheerevo
cook (n) μάγειρας
magheeras
cooker κουζίνα *koozeena*
cookie μπισκότο *beeskoto*
cooking utensils εργαλεία
μαγειρικής *erghaleea*
magheereekees
cool δροσερό *dhrosero*
cool bag, cool box
ψυκτικός σάκος, δοχείο
ψύξης *pseekteekos*
sakos, dhokheeo
pseeksees
copy αντίγραφο
andeeghrafo
cork φελλός *felos*
corkscrew τιρμπουσόν
teerbooson
corner γωνία *ghoneea*
correct (adj) σωστός *sostos*
corridor διάδρομος
dheeadhromos
cost κόστος *kostos*
cot κρεβατάκι μωρού
krevatakee moroo
cotton βαμβακερή κλωστή
vamvakeree klostee
cotton wool βαμβάκι
vamvakee
couch καναπές *kanapes*
couchette κουκέτα
kooketa
cough (vb) βήχω *veekho*
cough (n) βήχας *veekhas*
cough mixture σιρόπι
για βήχα *seeropee*
gheea veekha
Could I? Θα μπορούσα;
Tha mboroosa?
couldn't δεν θα μπορούσα
dhen tha mboroosa
counter ταμείο *tameeo*
country χώρα *khora*
countryside ύπαιθρος
eepethros

couple ζευγάρι *zevgharee*
courier service υπηρεσία
κούριερ *eepeereseea*
kooree-er
course διαδρομή
dheeadhromee
cousin εξάδελφος
eksadhelfos
cover charge κουβέρ
koover
cow αγελάδα *agheladha*
crab καβούρι *kavooree*
craft τέχνη *tekhnee*
cramp κράμπα *kramba*
crash (n) δυστύχημα
dheesteekheema
crash helmet κράνος
kranos
crazy τρελός *trelos*
cream κρέμα *krema*
crèche βρεφικός σταθμός
vrefeekos stathmos
credit card πιστωτική
κάρτα *peestoteekee karta*
crime έγκλημα *engleema*
crisps πατατάκια
patatakeea
crockery πιατικά
peeateeka
cross (n) σταυρός *stavros*
cross (adj) θυμωμένος
theemomenos
crossing διάβαση
dheeavasee
crossroads διασταύρωση
dheeastavrosee
crossword puzzle
σταυρόλεξο *stavrolekso*
crowd πλήθος *pleethos*
crowded γεμάτος
ghematos
crown (royal) στέμμα
stema
crown (anat) κορυφή
koreefee
cruise κρουαζιέρα
krooazee-era
crutches δεκανίκια
dhekaneekeea

cry κλαίω *kleo*
cucumber αγγούρι
  angooree
cufflinks μανικετόκουμπα
  maneeketokoomba
cup φλυτζάνι *fleetzanee*
cupboard ντουλάπα
  ndoolapa
curly κατσαρός *katsaros*
currency νόμισμα
  nomeesma
current (adj) τρέχων/
  τωρινός *trekhon/toreenos*
curtain κουρτίνα
  koorteena
cushion μαξιλάρι
  makseelaree
custard κρέμα *krema*
custom έθιμο *etheemo*
customer πελάτης
  pelatees
customs τελωνείο
  teloneeo
cut κόβω *kovo*
cutlery μαχαιροπήρουνα
  makheropeeroona
cycle (shape) κύκλος
  keeklos
cycle (vehicle) ποδήλατο
  podheelato
cycle track κυκλική
  κούρσα *keekleekee
  koorsa*
cyst κύστη *keestee*
cystitis κυστίτιδα
  keesteeteedha
Czech Republic
  Δημοκρατία της Τσεχίας
  *Dheemokrateea tees
  Tsekheeas*

D

daily καθημερινά
  katheemereena
damage ζημιά *zeemeea*
damp υγρός *eeghros*
dance (vb) χορεύω *khorevo*
danger κίνδυνος
  keendheenos

dangerous επικίνδυνος
  epeekeendheenos
dark σκοτεινός *skoteenos*
darkness σκοτάδι
  skotadhee
date (appointment)
  ραντεβού *randevoo*
date (fruit) χουρμάς
  khoormas
date (of year) ημερομηνία
  eemeromeeneea
date of birth ημερομηνία
  γεννήσεως *eemero-
  meeneea gheneeseos*
daughter κόρη *koree*
daughter-in-law νύφη
  neefee
dawn αυγή *avghee*
day ημέρα *eemera*
dead νεκρός *nekros*
deaf κουφός *koofos*
deal (it's a ...) συμφωνία
  seemfoneea
dear αγαπητός *aghapeetos*
death θάνατος *thanatos*
debts χρέη *khre-ee*
decaffeinated ντεκαφεϊνέ/
  χωρίς καφεΐνη *dekafe-
  eene/khorees kafe-eenee*
December Δεκέμβριος
  Dhekemvrios
decide αποφασίζω
  apofaseezo
decision απόφαση
  apofasee
deck chair ξαπλώστρα/
  σαιζλόνγκ *ksaplostra/
  sezlong*
deduct (subtract)
  αφαιρώ *afero*
deduct (discount)
  εκπίπτω *ekpeepto*
deep βαθύς *vathees*
definitely οριστικά
  oreesteeka
degree (measurement)
  βαθμός *vathmos*
degree (qualification)
  πτυχίο *pteekheeo*

delay καθυστέρηση
katheestereesee
deliberately σκόπιμα
skopeema
delicious νοστιμώτατος
nosteemotatos
deliver παραδίδω
paradheedho
delivery παράδοση
paradhosee
Denmark Δανία *Dhaneea*
dental floss κλωστή
για καθάρισμα ανάμεσα
στα δόντια *klostee gheea
kathareesma anamesa
sta dhonteea*
dentist οδοντίατρος
odhondeeatros
dentures οδοντοστοιχία,
μασέλα *odhondos-
teekheea, masela*
depart αναχωρώ *anakhoro*
department τμήμα
tmeema
department store
πολυκατάστημα
poleekatasteema
departure αναχώρηση
anakhoreesee
departure lounge σαλόνι
αναχώρησης *anakhoreese*
deposit καταθέτω
katatheto
describe περιγράφω
perighrafo
description περιγραφή
perighrafee
desert έρημος *ereemos*
desk γραφείο *ghrafeeo*
dessert επιδόρπιο
epeedhorpeeo
destination προορισμός
prooreesmos
details λεπτομέρειες
leptomeree-es
detergent απορρυπαντικό
aporeepandeeko
detour παράκαμψη
parakampsee

develop αναπτύσσω
anapteeso
diabetic (adj) διαβητικός
dheeaveeteekos
dial (vb) καλώ τον αριθμό
(τηλεφώνου) *kalo ton
areethmo (teelefonoo)*
dial (n) καντράν *kandran*
dialling code κωδικός
αριθμός *kodheekos
areethmos*
dialling tone σήμα *seema*
diamond διαμάντι
dheeamandee
diaper πάνα *pana*
diarrhoea διάρροια
dheeareea
diary ημερολόγιο
eemerologheeo
dice ζάρια *zareea*
dictionary λεξικό *lekseeko*
die (n) ζάρι *zaree*
die (vb) πεθαίνω *petheno*
diesel ντήζελ *ndeezel*
diet δίαιτα *dhee-eta*
difference διαφορά
dheeafora
different διαφορετικός
dheeaforeteekos
difficult δύσκολος
dheeskolos
dinghy λαστιχένια
(φουσκωτή) βάρκα
*lasteekheneea
(fooskotee) varka*
dining room τραπεζαρία
trapezareea
dinner δείπνο *dheepno*
direct (vb) κατευθύνω
kateftheeno
direct (adj) άμεσος
amesos
direction κατεύθυνση
katfetheensee
dirty (vb) λερώνω *lerono*
dirty (adj) βρώμικος
vromeekos
disabled ανάπηρος
anapeeros

disappear εξαφανίζομαι
eksafaneezome
disappointed
απογοητευμένος
apoghoeetevmenos
disaster καταστροφή
katastrofee
disconnected
αποσυνδεμένος
aposendhemenos
discount έκπωση *ekptosee*
discover ανακαλύπτω
anakaleepto
disease αρρώστεια
arosteea
dish πιάτο *peeato*
dishtowel πανί για πιάτα
panee gheea peeata
dishwasher πλυντήριο
πιάτων *pleendeereeo
peeaton*
disinfectant
απολυμαντικός
apoleemandeekos
disk δίσκος *dheeskos*
**disposable diapers/
nappies** πάνες μιάς
χρήσης *panes meeas
khreesees*
distance απόσταση
apostasee
district περιοχή
pereeokhee
disturb ενοχλώ *enokhlo*
dive καταδύομαι
katadheeome
diving board εξέδρα
καταδύσεων *eksedhra
katadheeseon*
divorced χωρισμένος
khoreesmenos
DIY shop κατάστημα
κατασκευαστικών υλικών
*katasteema kataskevas-
teekon eeleekon*
dizzy ζαλισμένος
zaleesmenos
do κάνω *kano*
doctor γιατρός *gheeatros*

document (n) έγγραφο
engrafo
dog σκύλος *skeelos*
doll κούκλα *kookla*
domestic οικιακός
eekeeakos
door πόρτα *porta*
doorbell κουδούνι πόρτας
koodhoonee portas
doorman θυρωρός
theeroros
double διπλός *dheeplos*
double bed διπλό
κρεββάτι *dheeplo
krevatee*
double room διπλό
δωμάτιο *dheeplo
dhomateeo*
doughnut ντόνατ,
λουκουμάς *donat,
lookoomas*
downhill κατηφόρα
kateefora
downstairs κάτω *kato*
dozen ντουζίνα, δωδεκάδα
doozeena, dhodhekadha
drain (n) οχετός *okhetos*
draught ρεύμα *revma*
draught beer μπύρα χύμα
beera kheema
drawer συρτάρι *seertaree*
drawing ζωγραφιά
zoghrafeea
dreadful τρομερός,
φοβερός *tromeros,
foveros*
dress φόρεμα *forema*
dressing (bandage)
επίδεσμος *epeedhesmos*
dressing (salad)
καρύκευμα, σάλτσα
kareekevma, saltsa
dressing gown ρόμπα
romba
drill (n) τρυπάνι *treepanee*
drink (vb) πίνω *peeno*
drink (n) ποτό *poto*
drinking water πόσιμο
νερό *poseemo nero*

ENGLISH → GREEK

drive οδηγώ *odheegho*
driver οδηγός *odheeghos*
driving licence άδεια
οδήγησης *adheea
odheegheesees*
drop (vb) ρίχνω *reekhno*
drug (medicine)
φάρμακο *farmako*
drug (narcotic)
ναρκωτικό *narkoteeko*
drunk (adj) μεθυσμένος
metheesmenos
dry στεγνός *steghnos*
dry cleaner's
στεγνοκαθαριστήριο
steghnokathareesteereeo
dryer (for clothes)
στεγνωτήριο
steghnoteereeo
dryer (for hair) σεσουάρ
sesooar
duck πάπια *papeea*
due οφειλόμενος
ofeelomenos
dull μουντός *moondos*
dummy πιπίλα *peepeela*
during κατά τη διάρκεια
kata tee dheearkeea
dust σκόνη *skonee*
dustbin σκουπιδοτενεκές
skoopeedhotenekes
duster ξεσκονόπανο
kseskonopano
dustpan φαράσι *farasee*
**Dutch, Dutchman,
Dutchwoman**
Ολλανδός, Ολλανδή
Olandhos, Olandhee
duty-free αφορολόγητος
aforologheetos
duvet πάπλωμα *paploma*
duvet cover κάλυμμα
παπλώματος *kaleema
paplomatos*
dye (vb) βάφω *vafo*
dye (n) βαφή *vafee*
dynamo γεννήτρια
gheneetreea

E
each κάθε *kathe*
eagle αετός *aetos*
ear αυτί *aftee*
earache ωταλγία, πόνος
στο αυτί *otalgheea,
ponos sto aftee*
earphones ακουστικά
akoosteeka
earrings σκουλαρίκια
skoolareekeea
earth γη *ghee*
earthquake σεισμός
seesmos
east ανατολή *anatolee*
Easter Πάσχα *Paskha*
Easter egg Πασχαλιάτικο
αυγό *Paskhaleeateeko
avgho*
easy εύκολο *efkolo*
eat τρώω *tro-o*
EC Ευρωπαϊκό Συμβούλιο
Evropaeeko Seemvooleeo
economy οικονομία
eekonomeea
economy class τουριστική
θέση *tooreesteekee thesee*
edge άκρη *akree*
eel χέλι *khelee*
egg αυγό *avgho*
either ... or είτε ... είτε
eete ... eete
elastic ελαστικός
elasteekos
elbow αγκώνας *angonas*
electric ηλεκτρικός
eelektreekos
electrician ηλεκτρολόγος
eelektrologhos
electricity ηλεκτρισμός
eelektreesmos
elevator ασανσέρ *asanser*
embassy πρεσβεία
presveea
emergency ανάγκη
anangee
emergency exit έξοδος
ανάγκης *eksodhos
anangees*

ENGLISH → GREEK

empty άδειος _adheeos_
end τέλος _telos_
engaged (occupied) κατειλημμένος _kateeleemenos_
engaged (to be married) αρραβωνιασμένος _aravoneeasmenos_
engine μηχανή _meekhanee_
engineer μηχανικός _meekhaneekos_
England Αγγλία _Angleea_
English (language) Αγγλικά _Angleeka_
English Channel Κανάλι της Αγγλίας _Kanalee tees Angleeas_
English, Englishman/woman Άγγλος/Αγγλίδα _Anglos, Angleedha_
enjoy απολαμβάνω _apolamvano_
enlargement μεγένθυση _meghentheese_
enough αρκετός _arketos_
enquiry ζήτηση πληροφοριών _zeeteesee pleeroforeeon_
enquiry desk πληροφορίες _pleeroforee-es_
enter μπαίνω _mbeno_
entrance είσοδος _eesodhos_
entrance fee τιμή εισόδου _teemee eesodhoo_
envelope φάκελος _fakelos_
epilepsy επιληψία _epeeleepseea_
epileptic επιληπτικός _epeeleepteekos_
equipment εξοπλισμός _eksopleesmos_
error λάθος _lathos_
escalator κυλιόμενη σκάλα _keeleeomenee skala_
escape (vb) δραπετεύω, διαφεύγω _dhrapetevo, dheeafevgho_

especially ιδιαιτέρως _eedhee-eteros_
essential απαραίτητος _apareteetos_
estate agent κτηματομεσίτης _kteematomeseetees_
Estonia Εστονία _Estoneea_
EU Ευρωπαϊκή Ένωση _Evropaeekee Enosee_
Europe Ευρώπη _Evropee_
European Ευρωπαίος _Evropeos_
even (number) άρτιος _arteeos_
even (adv) ακόμη και _akomee ke_
evening βράδυ _vradhee_
eventually τελικά _teleeka_
every κάθε _kathe_
everyone καθένας _kathenas_
everything κάθε τι, όλα _kathe tee, ola_
everywhere παντού _pandoo_
exactly ακριβώς _akreevos_
examination εξέταση _eksetasee_
example, for example παράδειγμα, για παράδειγμα _paradheeghma, gheea paradheeghma_
excellent τέλειος _teleeos_
except εκτός από _ektos apo_
excess luggage υπέρβαρες αποσκευές _eepervares aposkeves_
exchange (n) συνάλλαγμα _seenalaghma_
exciting συναρπαστικός _seenarpasteekos_
exclude αποκλείω _apokleeo_
excursion εκδρομή _ekdhromee_
excuse (vb) συγχωρώ _seengkhoro_
excuse (n) δικαιολογία _dheekeologheea_

Excuse me! Με συγχω
ρείτε! *Me seengkhoreete!*
exhaust pipe εξάτμιση
eksatmeesee
exhausted εξαντλημένος
eksandleemenos
exhibition έκθεση *ekthesee*
exit έξοδος *eksodhos*
expect προσδοκώ
prosdhoko
expenses έξοδα *eksodha*
expensive ακριβός
akreevos
experienced έμπειρος
embeeros
expire λήγω *leegho*
explain εξηγώ *ekseegho*
explosion έκρηξη
ekreeksee
export εξαγωγή
eksaghoghee
exposure αποκάλυψη
apokaleepsee
express (train) ταχύς
takhees
extension επέκταση
epektasee
extension lead καλόδιο
επέκτασης *kalodheeo
epektasees*
extra πρόσθετος *prosthetos*
extraordinary εξαιρετικός
eksereteekos
eye μάτι *matee*
eye drops σταγόνες ματιού
staghones mateeoo
eye make-up remover
λοσιόν αφαίρεσης
καλλυντικών ματιού
*loseeon aferesees
kaleendeekon mateeoo*
eye shadow σκιά ματιού
skeea mateeoo

F
fabric ύφασμα *eefasma*
façade πρόσοψη
prosopsee
face πρόσωπο *prosopo*

factory εργοστάσιο
erghostaseeo
faint (vb) λιποθυμώ
leepotheemo
fair (fête)
εμποροπανήγυρη
emboropaneegheeree
fair (hair colour) ξανθός
kshanthos
fair (just) τίμιος, δίκαιος
teemeeos, dheekeos
fairly δίκαια *dheekea*
fake (adj) απομίμηση
apomeemeesee
fake (vb) παραποιώ
parapeeo
fall πέφτω *pefto*
false ψεύτικος *psefteekos*
family οικογένεια
eekogheneea
famous διάσημος
dheeaseemos
fan θαυμαστής
thavmastees
fanbelt λουρί του
βεντιλατέρ *looree too
vendeelater*
far (adv) μακρυά *makreea*
far (adj) μακρυνός
makreenos
fare εισιτήριο
eeseeteereeo
farm φάρμα *farma*
farmer αγρότης *aghrotees*
farmhouse αγροικία
aghreekeea
fashionable μοντέρνος
mondernos
fast γρήγορος *ghreeghoros*
fasten στερεώνω *stereono*
fasten seatbelt
προσδένομαι με ζώνη
ασφαλείας *prosdhenome
me zonee asfaleeas*
fat παχύς *pakhees*
father πατέρας *pateras*
father-in-law πεθερός
petheros
fatty λιπαρός *leeparos*

ENGLISH → GREEK

fault βλάβη *vlavee*
faulty επιβλαβές *epeevlaves*
favourite προτιμώμενος *proteemomenos*
fax φαξ *faks*
February Φεβρουάριος *Fevrooareeos*
feed ταΐζω *taeezo*
feel αισθάνομαι *esthanome*
feet πόδια *podheea*
female θηλυκός *theeleekos*
fence φράχτης *frakhtees*
fender προφυλακτήρας *profeelakteeras*
ferry φερυμπώτ *fereembot*
festival φεστιβάλ *festeeval*
fetch φέρνω *ferno*
fever πυρετός *peeretos*
few, a few μερικά, λίγα *mereeka, leegha*
fiancé αρραβωνιαστικός *aravoneeasteekos*
fiancée αρραβωνιαστικιά *aravoneeasteekeea*
field αγρός, χωράφι *aghros, khorafee*
fight (vb) μαλώνω *malono*
fight (n) καυγάς *kavghas*
file (folder) φάκελος *fakelos*
file (tool) λίμα *leema*
fill, fill in, fill up γεμίζω, συμπληρώνω, γεμίζω *ghemeezo, seemblee-rono, ghemeezo*
fillet φιλέτο *feeleto*
filling (sandwich) γέμιση *ghemeesee*
filling (tooth) σφράγισμα *sfragheesma*
film (vb) κινηματογραφώ *keeneematoghrafo*
film (n) φιλμ *feelm*
film processing επεξεργασία φιλμ *epekserghaseea feelm*
filter φίλτρο *feeltro*
filthy βρώμικος *vromeekos*

find βρίσκω *vreesko*
fine (e.g. for speeding) πρόστιμο *prosteemo*
fine (adj) καλός *kalos*
finger δάχτυλο *dhakhteelo*
finish (vb) τελειώνω *teleeono*
fire φωτιά *foteea*
fire brigade πυροσβεσ-τική *peerosvesteekee*
fire exit έξοδος κινδύνου *eksodhos keendheenoo*
fire extinguisher πυροσβεστήρας *peerosvesteeras*
first, at first πρώτος, πρώτα *protos, prota*
first aid πρώτες βοήθειες *protes voeethee-es*
first-aid kit φαρμακείο πρώτων βοηθειών *farmakeeo proton voeetheeon*
first class πρώτη τάξη *protee taksee*
first floor πρώτος όροφος *protos orofos*
first name όνομα *onoma*
fish ψάρι *psaree*
fishing permit άδεια αλιείας *adheea alee-eeas*
fishing rod καλάμι ψαρέματος *kalamee psarematos*
fishmonger's στου ψαρά/ ψαροπώλη *stoo psara/ psaropolee*
fit (healthy) ικανός *eekanos*
fitting room δοκιμαστήριο *dhokeemasteereeo*
fix φτιάχνω, διορθώνω *fteeakhno, dheeorthono*
fizzy ανθρακούχο *anthrakookho*
flannel φανέλα *fanela*
flash (of lightning) αστραπή *astrapee*
flashlight ηλεκτρικός φακός *eelektreekos fakos*
flask παγούρι, φλάσκο *paghooree, flasko*

flat (adj) επίπεδος
  epeepedhos
flat battery άδεια μπαταρία *adheea batareea*
flat tyre ξεφούσκωτα λάστιχα *ksefooskota lasteekha*
flavour γεύση *ghefsee*
flaw ελάττωμα *elatoma*
flea ψύλλος *pseelos*
flight πτήση *pteesee*
flip flops πέδιλα *pedheela*
flippers βατραχοπέδιλα *vatrakhopedheela*
flood πλημμύρα *pleemeera*
floor (of room) πάτωμα *patoma*
floor (storey) όροφος *orofos*
floorcloth πατσαβούρα *patsavoora*
florist ανθοπώλης *anthopolees*
flour αλεύρι *alevree*
flower λουλούδι *looloodhee*
flu γρίπη *ghreepee*
fluent ευφραδής *effradhees*
fly (vb) πετάω *petao*
fly (n) μύγα *meegha*
fog ομίχλη *omeekhlee*
folk άνθρωποι *anthropee*
follow ακολουθώ *akolootho*
food φαγητό *fagheeto*
food poisoning τροφική δηλητηρίαση *trofeekee dheeleeteereeasee*
food shop κατάστημα τροφίμων *katasteema trofeemon*
foot πόδι *podhee*
football ποδόσφαιρο *podhosfero*
football match αγώνας ποδοσφαίρου *aghonas podhosferoo*
footpath μονοπάτι *monopatee*
for για *gheea*

forbidden απαγορευμένος *apaghorevmenos*
forehead μέτωπο *metopo*
foreign (person) ξένος *ksenos*
foreign (country) εξωτερικός *eksotereekos*
foreigner ξένος *ksenos*
forest δάσος *dhasos*
forget ξεχνάω *ksekhnao*
fork πηρούνι *peeroonee*
form (document) φόρμα, έντυπο *forma, enteepo*
form (shape) σχήμα *skheema*
formal επίσημος *epeeseemos*
fortnight δεκαπενθήμερο *dhekapentheemero*
fortress φρούριο *frooreeo*
fortunately ευτυχώς *efteekhos*
fountain συντριβάνι, βρύση *seendreevanee, vreesee*
fox αλεπού *alepoo*
fracture κάταγμα *kataghma*
frame σκελετός *skeletos*
France Γαλλία *Ghaleea*
free ελεύθερος *eleftheros*
free (cost) δωρεάν *dhorean*
freelance μισθοφόρος *meesthoforos*
freeway εθνική οδός *ethneekee odhos*
freezer κατάψυξη *katapseeksee*
French, Frenchman/woman Γάλλος, Γαλλίδα *Ghalos, Ghaleedha*
French fries τηγανιτές πατάτες *teeghaneetes patates*
frequent συχνός *seekhnos*
fresh φρέσκος *freskos*
Friday Παρασκευή *Paraskevee*

fridge ψυγείο *pseegheeo*
fried τηγανιτός
  teeghaneetos
friend φίλος *feelos*
friendly φιλικός *feeleekos*
frog βάτραχος *vatrakhos*
from (origin) από *apo*
from (time) από *apo*
front μπροστά *mbrosta*
frost παγετός *paghetos*
frozen παγωμένος
  paghomenos
fruit φρούτα *froota*
fruit juice φρουτοχυμός
  frootokheemos
fry τηγανίζω *teeghaneezo*
frying pan τηγάνι
  teeghanee
fuel καύσιμο *kafseemo*
fuel gauge δείκτης
  πετρελαίου *dheektees*
  petreleoo
full γεμάτος *ghematos*
full board φουλ πανσιόν
  fool panseeon
fun (to have) κέφι,
  διασκέδαση *kefee,*
  dheeaskedhasee
fun (to make ... of)
  πλάκα *plaka*
funeral κηδεία *keedheea*
funicular τελεφερίκ
  telefereek
funny αστείο *asteeo*
fur γούνα *ghoona*
fur coat γούνινο παλτό
  ghooneeno palto
furnished επιπλωμένο
  epeeplomeno
furniture έπιπλα
  epeepla
further μακρύτερα
  makreetera
fuse ασφάλεια *asfaleea*
fuse box πίνακας με
  ασφάλειες *peenakas me*
  asfalee-es
future μέλλον *melon*

G
gallery γκαλερί *galeree*
gallon γαλόνι *ghalonee*
game παιχνίδι
  pekhneedhee
garage γκαράζ, βενζινάδικο
  garaz, venzeenadheeko
garden κήπος *keepos*
garlic σκόρδο *skordho*
gas αέριο, υγραέριο
  aereeo, eeghraereeo
gas cooker στόφα
  υγραερίου *stofa*
  eeghraereeoo
gate καγκελόπορτα
  kangeloporta
gay γκέι, ομοφυλόφιλος
  ge-ee, omofeelofeelos
gay bar γκέι μπαρ
  ge-ee bar
gear (car) ταχύτητα
  takheeteeta
gear lever μοχλός
  ταχυτήτων *moklos*
  takheeteeton
gearbox κιβώτιο
  ταχυτήτων *keevoteeo*
  takheeteeton
general γενικός *gheneekos*
generous γενναιόδωρος
  gheneodhoros
Geneva Γενεύη *Ghenevee*
gents' toilet τουαλέτες
  ανδρών *tooaletes andhron*
genuine γνήσιο *ghneeseeo*
German (m) Γερμανός
  Ghermanos
German (f) Γερμανίδα
  Ghermaneedha
German measles ερυθρά
  ereethra
Germany Γερμανία
  Ghermaneea
get παραλαμβάνω
  paralamvano
get off κατεβαίνω
  kateveno
get on ανεβαίνω *aneveno*

get up σηκώνομαι
seekonome
gift δώρο *dhoro*
girl κορίτσι *koreetsee*
girlfriend φιλενάδα
feelenadha
give δίνω *dheeno*
give back δίνω πίσω
dheeno peeso
glacier παγετώνας
paghetonas
glad χαρούμενος
kharoomenos
glass (tumbler) ποτήρι
poteeree
glasses (spectacles)
γυαλιά *gheealeea*
gloomy σκοτεινός,
μελαγχολικός *skoteenos,
melangkholeekos*
gloves γάντια *ghandeea*
glue κόλα *kola*
go πηγαίνω *peegheno*
go (by car) πηγαίνω με
αυτοκίνητο *peegheno me
aftokeeneeto*
go (on foot) πηγαίνω με
τα πόδια *peegheno me
ta podheea*
go away φεύγω *fevgho*
go back πηγαίνω πίσω
peegheno peeso
goat κατσίκι *katseekee*
God Θεός *Theos*
goggles γυαλιά *gheealeea*
gold χρυσός *khreesos*
golf club (place) λέσχη
γκολφ *leskhee golf*
golf club (stick)
μπαστούνι του γκολφ
bastoonee too golf
golf course γήπεδο γκολφ
gheepedho golf
good καλός *kalos*
good afternoon καλό
απόγευμα *kalo
apoghevma*
good day καλή μέρα
kalee mera

good evening καλό βράδυ
kalo vradhee
Good Friday Μεγάλη
Παρασκευή *Meghalee
Paraskevee*
good luck καλή τύχη
kalee teekhee
good morning καλή μέρα
kalee mera
good night καλή νύχτα
kalee neekhta
goodbye αντίο *andeeo*
goose χήνα *kheena*
Gothic Γοτθικός
Ghottheekos
government κυβέρνηση
keeverneesee
gradually σταδιακά
stadheeaka
gram γραμμάριο
ghramareeo
grammar γραμματική
ghramateekee
grand μεγάλος,
μεγαλοπρεπής *meghalos,
meghaloprepees*
granddaughter εγγονή
engonee
grandfather παπούς
papoos
grandmother γιαγιά
gheeagheea
grandparents ο παπούς
και η γιαγιά *o papoos ke
ee gheeagheea*
grandson εγγονός
engonos
grapes σταφύλια
stafeeleea
grass γρασίδι, γκαζόν
ghraseedhee, gazon
grated τριμμένο *treemeno*
grateful ευγνώμων
evghnomon
gravy σάλτσα *saltsa*
greasy λαδερό, παχύ
ladhero, pakhee
great μεγάλος *meghalos*

Great Britain Μεγάλη
Βρετανία *Meghalee
Vretaneea*
Greece Ελλάδα *Eladha*
Greek (m) Έλληνας
Eleenas
Greek (f) Ελληνίδα
Eleeneedha
Greek (n) Ελληνικό
Eleeneeko
green πράσινος *praseenos*
greengrocer's στου
μανάβη *stoo manavee*
greeting χαιρετισμός
khereteesmos
grey γκρίζος *greezos*
grilled ψητός *pseetos*
ground χώμα, έδαφος
khoma, edhafos
ground floor ισόγειο
eesogheeo
group ομάδα *omadha*
guarantee εγγύηση
engee-eesee
guard φύλακας *feelakas*
guest καλεσμένος
kalesmenos
guesthouse πανσιόν
panseeon
guide οδηγός *odheeghos*
guide book οδηγός
odheeghos
guided tour εκδρομή
με τουριστικό οδηγό
*ekdhromee me
tooreesteeko odheegho*
guitar κιθάρα *keethara*
gun περίστροφο
pereestrofo
gym γυμναστήριο
gheemnasteereeo

H
hail χαλάζι *khalazee*
hair μαλλιά *maleea*
hairbrush βούρτσα *voortsa*
haircut κούρεμα *koorema*
hairdresser κωμμοτής
komotees

hairdresser's στου
κωμμοτή *stoo komotee*
hairdryer σεσουάρ *sesooar*
half μισός *meesos*
hall σάλα, αίθουσα *sala,
ethoosa*
ham ζαμπόν *zambon*
hamburger χάμπουργκερ
khamboorger
hammer σφυρί *sfeeree*
hand χέρι *kheree*
hand luggage
χειραποσκευές
kheeraposkeves
handbag τσάντα *tsanta*
handbrake χειρόφρενο
kheerofreno
handicapped ανάπηρος
anapeeros
handkerchief μαντίλι
mandeelee
handle χερούλι *kheroolee*
handmade χειροποίητο
kheeropee-eeto
handsome όμορφος
omorfos
hang up (phone) κλείνω
το τηλέφωνο *kleeno to
teelefono*
hanger κρεμάστρα
kremastra
hang-gliding ανεμοπορία
anemoporeea
hangover πονοκέφαλος
ponokefalos
happen συμβαίνω
seemveno
happy χαρούμενος
kharoomenos
Happy Easter! Καλό
Πάσχα! *Kalo Paskha!*
Happy New Year! Καλή
Χρονιά! *Kalee Khroneea!*
harbour λιμάνι *leemanee*
hard σκληρός *skleeros*
hard disk σκληρός δίσκος
skleeros dheeskos
hardly σχεδόν ποτέ
skhedhon pote

hardware shop κατάστημα σιδηροπωλείο, είδη κιγκαλερίας *katasteema seedheeropoleeo, eedhee keengalereeas*
harvest συγκομιδή *seengomeedhee*
hat καπέλο *kapelo*
have έχω *ekho*
have to πρέπει να *prepee na*
hay fever αλλεργική καταρροή *alergheekee kataroee*
hazelnut φουντούκι *foondookee*
he αυτός *aftos*
head κεφάλι *kefalee*
headache πονοκέφαλος *ponokefalos*
headlight/s προβολέας/ προβολείς *provoleas/ provolees*
headphones ακουστικά *akoosteeka*
health food shop κατάστημα υγιεινών τροφών *katasteema eghee-eenon trofon*
healthy υγιείς *eeghee-ees*
hear ακούω *akoo-o*
hearing aid ακουστικό βαρυκοΐας *akoosteeko vareekoeeas*
heart καρδιά *kardheea*
heart attack καρδιακή προσβολή *kardheeakee prosvolee*
heartburn καούρα *kaoora*
heat ζέστη *zestee*
heater θερμάστρα *thermastra*
heating θερμαίνομενος *thermenomenos*
heavy βαρύς *varees*
heel φτέρνα *fterna*
height ύψος *eepsos*
helicopter ελικόπτερο *eleekoptero*

helmet κράνος *kranos*
Help! Βοήθεια! *Voeetheea!*
help βοήθεια *voeetheea*
hem στρίφωμα *streefoma*
her αυτή *aftee*
herbal tea τσάι από βότανα *tsaee apo votana*
herbs βότανα *votana*
here εδώ *edho*
hernia κήλη *keelee*
hide κρύβω *kreevo*
high υψηλός *eepseelos*
high blood pressure υπέρταση *eepertasee*
high chair ψηλή καρέκλα *pseelee karekla*
him, to him αυτός, σ'αυτόν *aftos, s'afton*
hip γοφός *ghofos*
hire (vb) νοικιάζω *neekeeazo*
hire car νοικιασμένο αυτοκίνητο *neekeeazomeno aftokeeneeto*
his δικό του/αυτουνού *dheeko too/aftoonoo*
historic ιστορικός *eestoreekos*
history ιστορία *eestoreea*
hit χτυπάω *khteepao*
hitchhike οτοστόπ *otostop*
hold κρατάω *kratao*
hole τρύπα *treepa*
holidays διακοπές *dheeakopes*
holy ιερός *ee-eros*
home σπίτι *speetee*
homesickness νοσταλγός *nostalghos*
homosexual ομοφυλόφιλος *omofeelofeelos*
honest ειλικρινής *eeleekreenees*
honey μέλι *melee*
honeymoon μήνας του μέλιτος *meenas too meleetos*
hood (car) καπό *kapo*

hood (garment)
κουκούλα *kookoola*
hope ελπίζω *elpeezo*
hopefully αισιόδοξα
eseeodhoksa
horn (animal) κέρατο
kerato
horn (car) κλαξόν *klakson*
horse άλογο *alogho*
horse racing κούρσα
αλόγων *koorsa aloghon*
horse riding ιππασία
eepaseea
hose pipe λάστιχο
lasteekho
hospital νοσοκομείο
nosokomeeo
hospitality φιλοξενία
feelokseneea
hostel ξενώνας *ksenonas*
hot καυτός *kaftos*
hot spring θερμή/ιαματική
πηγή *thermee/*
eeamateekee peeghee
hot-water bottle
θερμοφόρα *thermofora*
hour ώρα *ora*
hourly ωριαία *oree-ea*
house σπίτι *speetee*
house wine χύμα κρασί
kheema krasee
housework δουλειά
του σπιτιού *dhooleea*
too speeteeoo
hovercraft αερολισθήρας
aerolistheeras
How? Πως; *Pos?*
How are you? Πως είσαι;
Pos eese?
How do you do?
Τι κάνεις; *Tee kanees*
How many? Πόσα; *Posa?*
How much is it? Πόσο
κάνει; *Poso kanee*
humid υγρασία *eeghraseea*
humour χιούμορ
kheeoomor
Hungarian (m)
Ουγγαρέζος *Oongarezos*

Hungarian (f) Ουγγαρέζα
Oongareza
Hungary Ουγγαρία
Oongareea
hungry πεινασμένος
peenasmenos
hunt κυνηγώ *keeneegho*
hunting permit άδεια
κυνηγού *adheea*
keeneeghoo
hurry (vb) βιάζομαι
veeazome
hurt (vb) πονάω *ponao*
hurts πονάει *ponaee*
husband άνδρας *andhras*
hydrofoil ιπτάμενο δελφίνι
eeptameno dhelfeenee
hypodermic needle
υποδερμική βελόνα
eepodhermeekee velona

I
I εγώ *egho*
ice πάγος *paghos*
ice cream παγωτό
paghoto
ice rink αίθουσα για
πατινάζ *ethoosa gheea*
pateenaz
ice skates παγοπέδιλα
paghopedheela
iced coffee παγωμένος
καφές *paghomenos kafes*
idea ιδέα *eedhea*
identity card ταυτότητα
taftoteeta
if εάν *ean*
if not εάν όχι *ean okhee*
ignition έναυσμα *enavsma*
ignition key κλειδί εκκίνησης του αυτοκινήτου
kleedhee ekeeneesees
too aftokeeneetoo
ill ασθενείς *asthenees*
illness ασθένεια, αρρώστεια *astheneea, arosteea*
immediately αμέσως
amesos

important σημαντικό
seemandeeko
impossible αδύνατο
adheenato
improve βελτιώνω
velteeono
in μέσα *mesa*
inch ίντσα *eentsa*
included συμπεριλαμ-
βανόμενος *seemberee-
lamvanomenos*
inconvenience ενόχληση
enokhleesee
incredible απίστευτο
apeestefto
Indian Ινδός *Eendhos*
indicator δείκτης *dheektees*
indigestion δυσπεψία
dheespepseea
indoor pool εσωτερική
πισίνα *esotereekee
peeseena*
indoors μέσα *mesa*
infection μόλυνση
moleensee
infectious κολλητικός,
μεταδοτικός *koleeteekos,
metadhoteekos*
inflammation ανάφλεξη
anafleksee
inflate φουσκώνω *fooskono*
informal ανεπίσημος
anepeeseemos
information πληροφορίες
pleeroforee-es
ingredients συστατικά
seestateeka
injection ένεση *enesee*
injured τραυματισμένος
travmateesmos
injury τραύμα *travma*
ink μελάνι *melanee*
in-laws πεθερικά
pethereeka
inn πανδοχείο
pandhokheeo
inner tube εσωτερικό
λάστιχο *esotereeko l
asteekho*

insect έντομο *endomo*
insect bite τσίμπημα
εντόμου *tseembeema
endomoo*
insect repellent
εντομοαπωθητικό
endomoapotheeteeko
inside μέσα *mesa*
insist επιμένω *epeemeno*
insomnia αϋπνία
aeepneea
inspect ελέγχω *elengkho*
instant coffee στιγμιαίος
καφές *steeghmee-eos
kafes*
instead αντί γι αυτό
andee ghee afto
insulin ινσουλίνη
eensooleenee
insurance ασφάλεια
asfaleea
intelligent ευφυής
efee-ees
intend σκοπεύω *skopevo*
interesting ενδιαφέρον
endheeaferon
international διεθνές
dhee-ethnes
interpreter διερμηνέας,
μεταφραστής *dhee-
ermeeneas, metafrastees*
intersection διασταύρωση
dheeastavrosee
interval διάλειμμα
dheealeema
into μέσα *mesa*
introduce συνιστώ
seeneesto
investigation έρευνα *erevna*
invitation πρόσκληση
proskleese
invite καλώ *kalo*
invoice τιμολόγιο
teemologheeo
Ireland Ιρλανδία
Eerlandheea
Irish, Irishman/woman
Ιρλανδός/Ιρλανδέζα
Eerlandhos/Eerlandheza

ENGLISH → GREEK

iron (appliance) σίδερο
seedhero
iron (metal) σίδηρος
seedheeros
ironing board σανίδα
σιδερώματος *saneedha
seedheromatos*
ironmonger's στου
σιδηροπώλη *stoo
seedheeropolee*
is είναι *eene*
island νησί *neesee*
it (direct object) αυτό
afto
it (indirect object) το *to*
it (subject) τούτο *tooto*
Italian Ιταλός/Ιταλίδα
Eetalos/Eetaleedha
Italian (language) Ιταλικά
Eetaleeka
Italy Ιταλία *Eetaleea*
itch (n) φαγούρα *faghoora*

J

jack (car) γρύλος *ghreelos*
jacket σακάκι, ζακέτα
sakakee, zaketa
jam μαρμελάδα
marmeladha
jammed στριμωγμένος
streemoghmenos
January Ιανουάριος
Eeanooareeos
jar βάζο *vazo*
jaundice ίκτερος *Eekteros*
jaw σαγόνι *saghonee*
jealous ζηλιάρης
zeeleearees
jelly ζελές *zeles*
jellyfish τσούχτρα, μέδουσα
tsookhtra, medhoosa
jersey φανέλα *fanela*
Jew, Jewish Ιουδαίος/
Ιουδαία, Εβραίος/Εβραία
*Eeoodheos/Eeoodhea,
Evreos/Evrea*
jeweller's στου
κοσμηματοπώλη *stoo
kosmeematopolee*

jewellery κοσμήματα
kosmeemata
job επάγγελμα *epangelma*
jog (vb) κάνω τζόγκιν *kano
tzogeen*
jog (n) τροχάδι *trokhadhee*
join ενώνω *enono*
joint κοινός *keenos*
joke αστείο *asteeo*
journey ταξίδι *takseedhee*
joy χαρά *khara*
judge δικαστής
dheekastees
jug κανάτα *kanata*
juice χυμός *kheemos*
July Ιούλιος *Eeooleeos*
jump (vb) πηδώ *peedho*
jump (n) πήδημα *peedheema*
jump leads καλώδια
μπαταρίας *kalodheea
batareeas*
jumper πουλόβερ *poolover*
junction συμβολή
seemvolee
June Ιούνιος *Eeooneeos*
just (fair) δίκαιος
dheekeos
just (only) μόνο *mono*

K

keep κρατάω *kratao*
Keep the change! Κράτα
τα ρέστα! *Krata ta resta*
kettle τσαγιερό *tsaghero*
key κλειδί *kleedhee*
key ring κλειδαριά
kleedhareea
kick κλωτσάω *klotsao*
kidney νεφρό *nefro*
kill φονεύω *fonevo*
kilo κιλό *keelo*
kilogram χιλιόγραμμο
kheeleeoghramo
kilometre χιλιόμετρο
kheeleeometro
kind είδος *eedhos*
king βασιλιάς *vaseeleeas*
kiosk περίπτερο
pereeptero

kiss (n) φιλί *fee*l*ee*
kiss (vb) φιλάω *fee*l*ao*
kitchen κουζίνα *kooz*ee*na*
kitchenette κουζινίτσα
  *kooz*een*ee*tsa
knee γόνατο *ghonato*
knickers κυλότα *keel*o*ta*
knife μαχαίρι *makh*e*ree*
knit πλέκω *pl*e*ko*
knitting needle βελόνα
  πλέξιματος *vel*o*na*
  *pleks*ee*matos*
knitwear πλεκτά *plek*t*a*
knock χτυπάω την πόρτα
  *khteep*ao* teen p*o*rta*
knock down χτυπώ και
  ρίχνω κάτω *khteep*o* ke*
  *r*ee*khno k*a*to*
knock over ρίχνω κάτω
  *r*ee*kno k*a*to*
know ξέρω, γνωρίζω
  *ks*e*ro, ghnor*ee*zo*

L
label ταμπέλα *tamb*e*la*
lace δαντέλα *dhant*e*la*
ladder σκάλα *sk*a*la*
ladies' toilet γυνεκείες
  τουαλέτες *gheenek*e*e-es*
  *tooal*e*tes*
ladies' wear γυνεκείος
  ρουχισμός *gheenek*e*e-os*
  *rookheesm*o*s*
lady κυρία *keer*e*a*
lager ξανθή μπύρα
  *ksanth*ee* b*ee*ra*
lake λίμνη *l*ee*mnee*
lamb αρνί *arn*ee*
lamp πορτατίφ *portat*ee*f*
land γη *ghee*
landlady σπιτονοικοκυρά
  *speetoneekokee*r*a*
landlord σπιτονοικοκύρης
  *speetoneekok*e*e*rees*
landslide καθίζηση
  *kath*ee*zeesee*
lane λωρίδα *lor*ee*dha*
language γλώσσα *ghl*o*sa*

language course
  μαθήματα γλώσσας
  *math*ee*mata ghl*o*sas*
large μεγάλος *megh*a*los*
last τελευταίος *teleft*e*os*
last night εχτές βράδυ
  *ekht*e*s vr*a*dhee*
late αργά *argh*a*
later αργώτερα *argh*o*tera*
Latvia Λάτβια *L*a*tveea*
laugh (vb) γελάω *ghel*a*o*
laugh (n) γέλιο *gh*e*leeo*
**launderette, Laundro-
  mat** πλυντήρια ρούχων
  *pleend*e*e*reea r*oo*khon*
laundry πλυντήρια
  *pleend*e*e*reea*
lavatory αποχωρητήριο
  *apokhoreet*e*e*reeo*
law νόμος *n*o*mos*
lawyer δικηγόρος
  *dheekeegh*o*ros*
laxative καθαρτικό
  *kathart*ee*ko*
lazy τεμπέλης *temb*e*lees*
lead (vb) οδηγώ *odheegh*o*
lead (n, metal) μόλυβδος
  *m*o*leevdhos*
lead-free αμόλυβδος
  *am*o*leevdhos*
leaf φύλλο *fee*l*o*
leaflet φυλλάδιο *feel*a*dheeo*
leak (n) διαρροή *dheearo*e*e*
leak (vb) διαρρέω *dheear*e*o*
learn μαθαίνω *math*e*no*
lease (n) εκμίσθωση
  *ekm*ee*sthosee*
lease (vb) μισθώνω
  *meesth*o*no*
leather δέρμα *dh*e*rma*
leave αφήνω, φεύγω
  *af*ee*no, f*e*vgho*
leek πράσο *pr*a*so*
left, to the left αριστερά,
  στα αριστερά *areest*e*ra,
  sta areest*e*ra*
left-hand drive οδήγηση
  στα αριστερά *odh*e*e-
  gheesee sta areest*e*ra*

left-handed αριστερό-
χειρας *areesterokheeras*
leg πόδι *podhee*
lemon λεμόνι *lemonee*
lemonade λεμονάδα
lemonadha
lend δανίζω, δανίζομαι
dhaneezo, dhaneezome
lens φακός *fakos*
lenses φακοί *fakee*
lentil φακές *fakes*
lesbian λεσβία *lesveea*
less λιγότερος *leeghoteros*
lesson μάθημα
matheemata
let (allow) επιτρέπω
epeetrepo
let (hire) ενοικιάζω
eneekeeazo
letter γράμμα *ghrama*
letterbox
γραμματοκιβώτιο
ghramatokeevoteeo
lettuce μαρούλι *maroolee*
level crossing ισόπεδη
διάβαση *eesopedhee
dheeavasee*
lever μοχλός *mokhlos*
library βιβλιοθήκη
veevleeotheekee
licence άδεια *adheea*
lid καπάκι *kapakee*
lie (vb, recline) ξαπλώνω
ksaplono
lie (vb, fib) ψεύδομαι
psevdhome
lie down ξαπλώνω κάτω
ksaplono kato
life ζωή *zoee*
life belt σωσίβιο *soseeveeo*
life insurance ασφάλεια
ζωής *asfaleea zoees*
life jacket σωσίβιο-
χιτώνας *soseeveeo-
kheetonas*
lifeguard σωματοφύλακας
somatofeelakas
lift (n) ασανσέρ *asanser*
lift (vb) ανυψώνω *aneepsono*

light (colour) ανοιχτό
aneektho
light (weight) ελαφρύ
elafree
light (n) φως *fos*
light (vb) φωτίζω *foteezo*
light bulb λάμπα *lamba*
lightning αστραπή
astrapee
like (vb) μου αρέσει *aresee*
like (adj) όμοιο *omeeo*
lime γλυκολέμονο
ghleekolemono
line γραμμή *ghramee*
linen σεντόνια *sendoneea*
lingerie γυνεκεία
εσώρουχα *gheenekeea
esorookha*
lion λιοντάρι *leeondaree*
lipstick κραγιόν *krageeon*
liqueur λικέρ *leeker*
list λίστα, κατάλογος
leesta, kataloghos
listen ακούω *akoo-o*
Lithuania Λιθουανία
Leethooaneea
litre λίτρο *leetro*
litter (n, rubbish)
σκουπίδια *skoopeedheea*
litter (n, puppies) γέννα
ghena
little μικρός *meekros*
live ζω *zo*
lively ζωντανός *zondanos*
liver συκώτι *seekotee*
living room καθημερινό
δωμάτιο *katheemereeno
dhomateeo*
loaf καρβέλι *karvelee*
lobby προθάλαμος
prothalamos
lobster αστακός *astakos*
local τοπικός *topeekos*
lock (n) κλειδαριά
kleedhareea
lock (vb) κλειδώνω
kleedhono
lock in κλειδώνω μέσα
kleedhono mesa

lock out κλειδώνω έξω
kleedhono ekso
locked in κειδωμένος μέσα
kleedhomenos mesa
locker ιματιοθήκη
eemateeotheekee
lollipop γλειφιτζούρι
ghleefeetzooree
long (adj) μακρύς *makrees*
long (vb) λαχταρώ *lakhtaro*
long-distance call
τηλεφώνημα μακράς
αποστάσεως *teelefon-
eema makras apostaseos*
look after φυλάω *feelao*
look at κοιτάω *keetao*
look for ψάχνω *psakhno*
look forward to
προσβλέπω *prosvlepo*
loose χαλαρός *khalaros*
lorry φορτηγό *forteegho*
lose χάνω *khano*
lost χαμμένος *khamenos*
lost property απολεσ-
θέντα αντικείμενα *apo-
lesthenda andeekeemena*
lot μοίρα *meera*
loud δυνατός *dheenatos*
lounge σαλόνι *salonee*
love (n) αγάπη *aghapee*
love (vb) αγαπάω *aghapao*
lovely όμορφος *omorfos*
low χαμηλός *khameelos*
low fat χαμηλών λιπαρών
khameelon leeparon
luck τύχη *teekhee*
luggage αποσκευές
aposkeves
luggage rack ράφι αποσκευών *rafee aposkevon*
luggage tag ταμπέλα
αποσκευών *tambela
aposkevon*
luggage trolley
καροτσάκι αποσκευών
karotsakee aposkevon
lump κομμάτι, σβόλος
komatee, svolos

lunch μεσημεριανό
meseemereeano
lung πνεύμονας *pnevmonas*
Luxembourg Λουξεμ-
βούργο *Looksemvoorgho*
luxury πολυτελείς
poleetelees

M
machine μηχανή
meekhanee
mad τρελός *trelos*
made φτιαγμένος
fteeaghmenos
magazine περιοδικό
pereeodheeko
maggot σκουλίκι
skooleekee
magnet μαγνήτης
maghneetees
magnifying glass
μεγενθυτικός φακός
meghentheeteekos fakos
maid υπηρέτρια
eepeeretreea
maiden name το γένος
to ghenos
mail (n) ταχυδρομείο
takheedhromeeo
mail (vb) ταχυδρομώ
takheedhromo
main κύριος *keereeos*
main course κύριο πιάτο
keereeo peeato
main post office κεντρικό
ταχυδρομείο *kendreeko
takheedhromeeo*
main road κεντρικός δρόμος
kendreekos dhromos
mains switch γενικός
διακόπτης *gheneekos
dheeakoptees*
make κάνω *kano*
male αρσενικός *arseneekos*
man άνδρας *andhras*
man-made fibre τεχνητή
ίνα *tekhneetee eena*
manager διευθυντής
dhee-eftheendees

ENGLISH → GREEK

manual εγχειρίδιο
  engkheereedheeo
many πολλά *pola*
map χάρτης *khartees*
marble μάρμαρο *marmaro*
March Μάρτιος *Marteeos*
market αγορά *aghora*
marmalade μαρμελάδα
  πορτοκαλιού *marmeladha*
  portokhaleeoo
married παντρεμένος
  pandremenos
marsh βάλτος *valtos*
mascara μάσκαρα
  maskara
mashed potatoes
  πουρές *poores*
mask μάσκα *maska*
Mass (rel) Θεία
  Λειτουργία *Theea*
  Leetoorgheea
mast κατάρτι *katartee*
match (sport) αγώνας
  aghonas
matches (for lighting)
  σπίρτα *speerta*
material ύφασμα *eefasma*
matter ύλη *eelee*
matter – it doesn't
  matter πειράζει – δεν
  πειράζει *peerazee –*
  dhen peerazee
mattress στρώμα *stroma*
May Μάιος *Maeeos*
may μπορώ *mboro*
maybe ίσως *eesos*
mayonnaise μαγιονέζα
  magheeoneza
me εγώ/εμένα *egho/emena*
meal γεύμα *ghevma*
mean (intend) εννοώ
  eno-o
mean (nasty) μίζερος
  meezeros
measles ιλαράς *eelaras*
measure (n) μέτρο *metro*
measure (vb) μετράω
  metrao
meat κρέας *kreas*

mechanic μηχανικός
  meekhaneekos
medical insurance
  ιατρική ασφάλεια
  eeatreekee asfaleea
medicine (drug)
  φάρμακο *farmako*
medicine (science)
  ιατρική *eeatreekee*
medieval μεσαίωνας
  meseonas
Mediterranean
  Μεσόγειος *Mesogheeos*
medium μέτριος *metreeos*
medium dry wine
  μέτριος ξηρός οίνος
  metreeos kseeros eenos
medium rare (meat)
  μέτριο προς σενιάν
  (κρέας) *metreeo pros*
  seneean (kreas)
medium sized μέτριο
  μέγεθος *metreeo*
  meghethos
meet συναντώ *seenando*
meeting συνάντηση,
  συνεδρίαση *seenan-*
  deesee, seenedhreeasee
melon πεπόνι *peponee*
melt λιώνω *leeono*
men άνδρες *andhres*
mend διορθώνω
  dheeorthono
meningitis μηνιγγίτιδα
  meeneengeeteedha
menswear ανδρικός
  ρουχισμός *andhreekos*
  rookheesmos
mention αναφέρω *anafero*
menu μενού *menoo*
meringue μαρέγκα
  marenga
message μήνυμα
  meeneema
metal μέταλλο *metalo*
meter μετρητής
  metreetees
metre μέτρο *metro*
metro μετρό *metro*

114

microwave oven
φούρνος μικροκυμάτων
foornos meekrokeematon
midday μεσημέρι
meseemeree
middle μεσαίος *meseos*
midnight μεσάνυχτα,
μεσονύχτι *mesaneekhta,*
mesoneekhtee
might (n) δύναμη *dheenamee*
migraine ημικρανία
eemeekraneea
mile μίλι *meelee*
milk γάλα *ghala*
minced meat κιμάς
keemas
mind νους *noos*
mineral water μεταλλικό
νερό *metaleeko nero*
minister υπουργός
eepoorghos
mint μέντα *menta*
minute λεπτό *lepto*
mirror καθρέπτης
kathreptees
Miss Δεσποινίδα
Dhespeeneedha
missing απολεσθείς
apolesthees
mist ομίχλη *omeekhlee*
mistake λάθος *lathos*
misunderstanding
παρεξήγηση
parekseegheesee
mix μίγμα *meeghma*
mix-up μπέρδεμα
mberdhema
mix up ανακατεύω
anakatevo
mobile phone κινητό
τηλέφωνο *keeneeto*
teelefono
moisturizer υδατική κρέμα
eedhateekee krema
moment στιγμή
steeghmee
monastery μονή,
μοναστήρι *monee,*
monasteeree

Monday Δευτέρα *Dheftera*
money λεπτά, χρήματα
lefta, kreemata
money order ταχυδρομική
επιταγή *takheedhro-*
meekee epeetaghee
month μήνας *meenas*
monthly μηνιαία
meenee-ea
monument μνημείο
mneemeeo
moon φεγγάρι *fengaree*
mooring αγκυροβόλιο
angeerovoleeo
more περισσότερος
pereesoteros
morning πρωί *proee*
mosque τζαμί *dzamee*
mosquito κουνούπι
koonoopee
most ο περισσότερος
o pereesoteros
mostly περισσότερο
pereesotero
moth σκώρος *skoros*
mother μητέρα *meetera*
mother-in-law πεθερά
pethera
motor κινητήρας
keeneeteeras
motorbike μοτοσικλέτα
motoseekleta
motorboat βενζινάκατος
venzeenakatos
motorway
αυτοκινητόδρομος
aftokeeneetodhromos
mountain βουνό *voono*
mountain rescue
διάσωση ορειβατών
dheeasosee oreevaton
mountaineering
ορειβασία *oreevaseea*
mouse ποντίκι *pondeekee*
moustache μουστάκι
moostakee
mouth στόμα *stoma*
mouth ulcer πληγή στο
στόμα *pleeghee sto stoma*

ENGLISH → GREEK

115

mouthwash στοματικό
διάλυμα *stomateeko*
dheealeema
move κινούμαι, μετακινώ
keenoome, metakeeno
move house μετακομίζω
metakomeezo
Mr κύριος *keereeos*
Mrs κυρία *keereea*
Ms δεσποινίδα
dhespeeneedha
much πολύ *polee*
mud λάσπη *laspee*
mug κούπα *koopa*
mugged κακοποιημένος
kakopee-eemenos
mumps μαγουλάδες
maghooladhes
muscle μυς *mees*
museum μουσείο
mooseeo
mushroom μανιτάρι
maneetaree
musician μουσικός
mooseekos
Muslim Μουσουλμάνος
Moosoolmanos
mussel μύδι *meedhee*
must πρέπει *prepee*
mustard μουστάρδα
moostardha
mutton αρνίσιο κρέας
arneeseeo kreas
my δικό μου *dheeko moo*
myself ο εαυτός μου
o eaftos moo

N

nail νύχι *neekhee*
nail brush βούρτσα νυχιών
voortsa neekheeon
nail file λίμα νυχιών *leema*
neekheeon
nail polish/varnish
βερνίκι νυχιών *verneekee*
neekheeon
nail polish remover
ασετόν *aseton*

nail scissors ψαλλίδι
νυχιών *psaleedhee*
neekheeon
name όνομα *onoma*
nanny νταντά, παραμάνα
dada, paramana
napkin πετσέτα *petseta*
nappy πάνα *pana*
narrow στενό *steno*
nasty μοχθηρός
mokhteeros
national εθνικός
ethneekos
nationality εθνικότητα
ethneekoteeta
natural φυσικός *feeseekos*
nature φύση *feesee*
nature reserve εθνικό
πάρκο *ethneeko parko*
nausea ναυτία *nafteea*
navy ναυτικό *nafteeko*
navy blue σκούρο μπλε
skooro ble
near (adv) κοντά *konda*
near (vb) κοντεύω *kondevo*
nearby (adv) κοντινός,
εδώ κοντά *kondeenos,*
edho konda
nearly σχεδόν *skhedhon*
necessary αναγκαίος
anangeos
neck λαιμός *lemos*
necklace κολιέ *kolee-e*
need (vb) χρειάζομαι
khreeazome
need (n) ανάγκη *anangee*
needle βελόνα *velona*
negative (photo)
αρνητικό *arneeteeko*
neighbour γείτονας
gheetonas
neither ... nor μείτε ...
μείτε *meete...meete*
nephew ανηψιός
aneepseeos
nest φωλιά *foleea*
net δίχτυ *dheekhtee*
Netherlands Ολλανδία
Olandheea

never ποτέ *pote*
new νέο *neo*
New Year Νέο Έτος
　Neo Etos
New Year's Eve Παρα-
　μονή Πρωτοχρονιάς *Para-*
　monee Protokhroneeas
New Zealand, New
　Zealander Νεα
　Ζηλανδία, Νεοζηλανδός,
　Νεοζηλανδή *Nea Zee-*
　landheea, Neozeelandhos,
　Neozeelandhee
news ειδήσεις, νέα
　eedheesees, nea
news stand
　εφημεριδοπώλης
　efeemereedhopolees
newspaper εφημερίδα
　efeemereedha
next επόμενος *epomenos*
nice ωραίος *oreos*
niece ανηψιά *aneepseea*
night, last night βράδυ,
　χθες βράδυ *vradhee,*
　khthes vradhee
nightdress νυχτικό
　neekhteeko
no όχι *okhee*
nobody κανείς *kanees*
noise φασαρία *fasareea*
noisy θορυβώδης
　thoreevodhees
non-alcoholic μη-αλκοολικό
　mee-alko-oleeko
non-smoking
　μη-καπνιστών
　mee-kapneeston
none κανένας, καθόλου
　kanenas, katholoo
north βορράς *voras*
North Sea Βόρεια
　Θάλασσα *Voreea*
　Thalassa
Northern Ireland
　Βόρεια Ιρλανδία
　Voreea Eerlandheea
Norway Νορβηγία
　Norveegheea

Norwegian (m) Νορβηγός
　Norveeghos
Norwegian (f) Νορβηγίδα,
　Norveegheedha
nose μύτη *meetee*
not όχι *okhee*
note σημείωμα *seemeeoma*
notebook σημειωματάριο
　seemeeomatareeo
notepaper χαρτί
　σημειώματος *khartee*
　seemeeomatos
nothing τίποτα *teepota*
nothing else τίποτε άλλο
　teepote alo
noticeboard πίνακας
　ανακοινώσεων *peenakas*
　anakeenoseon
novel νουβέλα,
　μυθιστόρημα *noovela,*
　meetheestoreema
November Νοέμβριος
　Noemvrios
now τώρα *tora*
nudist beach παραλία
　γυμνιστών *paraleea*
　gheemneeston
number αριθμός
　areethmos
number plate πινακίδα
　peenakeedha
nurse νοσοκόμα *nosokoma*
nursery (plants) φυτώριο
　feetoreeo
nursery school
　νηπιαγωγείο
　neepeeaghogheeo
nursery slope πλαγιά για
　αρχάριους *plagheea gheea*
　arkhareeoos
nut καρύδι *kareedhee*
nut (for bolt) παξιμάδι
　pakseemadhee

O
oak βαλανιδιά
　valaneedheea
oar κουπί *koopee*
oats βρώμη *vromee*

ENGLISH → GREEK

obtain λαμβάνω, αποκτώ
lamvano, apokto
occasionally σποραδικά,
πότε–πότε, κάπου–κάπου
*sporadheeka, pote-pote,
kapoo-kapoo*
occupation επάγγελμα
epangelma
occupied (e.g. toilet)
κατειλημμένος
kateeleemenos
ocean ωκεανός *okeanos*
October Οκτώβριος
Oktovreeos
odd (number) μονός
monos
odd (strange) περίεργος
peree-erghos
of του/της *too/tees*
off σβηστός *sveestos*
office γραφείο *ghrafeeo*
often συχνά *seekhna*
oil λάδι *ladhee*
ointment αλοιφή *aleefee*
OK όλα καλά *ola kala*
old (object) παλαιό *paleo*
old (person) ηλικιωμένος
eeleekeeomenos
old-age pensioner
συνταξιούχος
seendakseeookhos
old-fashioned ντεμοντέ
ndemode
olive ελιά *eleea*
olive oil ελαιόλαδο
eleoladho
omelette ομελέτα *omeleta*
on (top) επάνω *epano*
on (switched on)
αναμένος *anamenos*
once μιά φορά *meea fora*
one ένα *ena*
one-way street δρόμος
μιάς κατευθύνσεως
*dhromos meeas
kaftheenseos*
onion κρεμμύδι
kremeedhee
only (adj) μόνος *monos*

only (adv) μόνον *monon*
open ανοιχτός *aneekhtos*
open ticket ανοιχτό
εισιτήριο *aneekhto
eeseeteereeo*
opening times ώρες
ανοίγματος *ores
aneeghmatos*
opera όπερα *opera*
operation εγχείρηση
engkheereesee
operator (phone)
τηλεφωνητής
teelefoneetees
ophthalmologist
οφθαλμίατρος
ofthalmeeatros
opposite αντίθετος
andeethetos
optician οπτικός *opteekos*
or ή *ee*
orange πορτοκάλι
portokalee
orange juice χυμός
πορτοκαλιού *kheemos
portokaleeoo*
orchestra ορχήστρα
orkheestra
order (vb) παραγγέλνω
parangelno
order (n) παραγγελεία
parangeleea
organic vegetables
οργανικά λαχανικά
orghaneeka lakhaneeka
other άλλος *allos*
otherwise αλλοιώς *aleeos*
our δικά μας *dheeka mas*
out έξω *ekso*
out of order εκτός
λειτουργίας *ektos
leetoorgheeas*
outdoors ύπαιθρος
eepethros
outside έξω *ekso*
outskirts περίχωρα
pereekhora
oven φούρνος *foornos*

ovenproof κατάλληλο
για το φούρνο *kataleelo
ghee*a *to foorno*
over πάνω από *pano apo*
over here εδώ πέρα
edho pera
over there εκεί πέρα
ekee pera
overcharge υπερχρεώνω
eeperkhreono
overcoat παλτό *palto*
overdone παραψημένο
parapseemeno
overheat παραζεσταμένο
parazestameno
overnight αποβραδίς
apovradhees
overtake προσπερνώ
prosperno
owe χρωστάω *khrostao*
owl κουκουβάγια
kookoovagheea
owner ιδιοκτήτης
eedheeokteetees

P

pacemaker ηλεκτρικός
βηματοδότης *eelektreekos
veematodhotees*
pacifier κατευναστής,
πιπίλα *katevanastees,
peepeela*
pack (vb) συσκευάζω
seeskevazo
package πακέτο *paketo*
package holiday
οργανωμένη εκδρομή
orghanomenee ekdhromee
packet δέμα, πακέτο *dhema,
paketo*
padlock λουκέτο *looketo*
page σελίδα *seleedha*
paid πληρωμένος
pleeromenos
pail κουβάς *koovas*
pain πόνος *ponos*
painful οδυνηρός
odheeneeros

painkiller παυσίπονο
pafseepono
paint (vb) βάφω *vafo*
paint (n) μπογιά *bogheea*
painting ζωγραφική, πίνακας
zoghrafeekee, peenakas
pair ζευγάρι *zevgharee*
palace παλάτι *palatee*
pale χλωμός *khlomos*
pan τηγάνι *teeghanee*
pancake τηγανίτα
teeghaneeta
panties κιλότα *keelota*
pants παντελόνι *pandelonee*
pantyhose καλτσόν *kaltson*
paper χαρτί *khartee*
paper napkins χαρτο–
πετσέτες *khartopetsetes*
parcel δέμα *dhema*
Pardon? Συγγνώμη?
Seenghnomee
parents γονείς *ghonees*
parents-in-law πεθερικά
pethereeka
park (n) πάρκο *parko*
park (vb) παρκάρω *parkaro*
parking meter παρκόμετρο
parkometro
parking ticket κλήση
για παράνομη στάθμευση
*kleesee gheea paranomee
stathmefsee*
part μέρος *meros*
partner (companion)
σύντροφος *seendrofos*
partner (business)
συνέταιρος *seeneteros*
party (celebration) πάρτυ
partee
party (political) κόμμα *koma*
pass (vb) προσπερνώ
prosperno
pass control έλεγχος
διάβασης *elengkhos
dheeavasees*
passenger επιβάτης
epeevatees
passport διαβατήριο
dheeavateereeo

119

ENGLISH → GREEK

past παρελθόν *parelthon*
pastry πάστα, γλυκό *pasta, ghleeko*
path μονοπάτι, δρόμος *monopatee, dhromos*
patient (n) ασθενείς *asthenees*
patient (adj) υπομονετικός *eepomoneteekos*
pattern σχέδιο *skhedheeo*
pavement πεζοδρόμιο *pezodhromeeo*
pay πληρώνω *pleerono*
payment πληρωμή *pleeromee*
payphone τηλέφωνο για το κοινό *teelefono ghee to keeno*
pea (dry) μπιζέλι *mbeezelee*
pea (green) αρακάς *arakas*
peach ροδάκινο *rodhakeeno*
peak κορυφή *koreefee*
peak rate κορυφαία τιμή *koreefea teemee*
peanut φυστίκι *feesteekee*
pear αχλάδι *akhladhee*
pearl μαργαριτάρι *marghareetaree*
peculiar παράξενος *paraksenos*
pedal πηδάλιο, πεντάλ *peedhaleeo, pedal*
pedestrian πεζός *pezos*
pedestrian crossing διάβαση πεζών *dheeavasee pezon*
peel (n) φλούδι *floodhee*
peel (vb) ξεφλουδίζω *ksefloodheezo*
peg μανταλάκι *mandalakee*
pen πένα *pena*
pencil μολύβι *moleevee*
penfriend φίλος δι'αλληλογραφίας *feelos dhee'aleeloghrafeeas*
peninsula ακρωτήρι *akroteeree*
people άνθρωποι *anthropee*

pepper (vegetable) πιπεριά *peepereea*
pepper (spice) πιπέρι *peeperee*
per ανά, κατά *ana, kata*
perfect τέλειος *teleeos*
performance εκπλήρωση *ekpleerosee*
perfume άρωμα *aroma*
perhaps πιθανόν *peethanon*
period περίοδος *pereeodhos*
perm περμανάντ *permanand*
permit (n) άδεια *adheea*
permit (vb) επιτρέπω *epeetrepo*
person άνθρωπος *anthropos*
pet κατοικίδιο ζώο *kateekeedheeo zo-o*
petrol βενζίνη *venzeenee*
petrol can δοχείο βενζίνης *dhokheeo venzeenees*
petrol station βενζινάδικο *venzeenadheeko*
pharmacist φαρμακοποιός *farmakopeeos*
pharmacy φαρμακείο *farmakeeo*
phone booth τηλεφωνικός θάλαμος *teelefoneekos thalamos*
phone card τηλεφωνοκάρτα *teelefonokarta*
phone number αριθμός τηλεφώνου *areethmos teelefonoo*
photo φωτογραφία *fotoghrafeea*
photocopy (n) φωτοτυπία *fototeepeea*
photograph (vb) φωτο-γραφίζω *fotoghrafeezo*
photograph (n) φωτο-γραφία *fotoghrafeea*
phrase book βιβλίο διαλόγων *veevleeo dheealoghon*
piano πιάνο *peeano*
pickpocket πορτοφολάς *portofolas*

picnic πικνίκ *peekn**ee**k*
picture εικόνα, φωτογραφία
  *eek**o**na, fotoghraf**ee**a*
picture frame κορνίζα
  *korn**ee**za*
pie πίτα *p**ee**ta*
piece κομμάτι *kom**a**tee*
pig γουρούνι *ghoor**oo**nee*
pill χάπι *kh**a**pee*
pillow μαξιλάρι *maks**ee**lar**ee*
pillowcase μαξιλαροθήκη
  *makselaroth**ee**kee*
pilot πιλότος *peel**o**tos*
pin καρφίτσα *karf**ee**tsa*
pin number προσωπικός
  αριθμός αναγνώρισης
  *prosopeek**os** areethm**os**
  *anaghn**o**reesees*
pineapple ανανάς *anan**as***
pink ροζ *roz*
pipe (plumbing) σωλήνας
  *sol**ee**nas*
pipe (smoking) πίπα,
  τσιμπούκι *p**ee**pa,
  tseemb**oo**kee*
pity, It's a pity! κρίμα, τι
  κρίμα! *kr**ee**ma, tee kr**ee**ma*
place μέρος *m**e**ros*
plain (n) πεδιάδα
  *pedhee**a**dha*
plain (adj) σαφής ***safees***
plait κοτσίδα, πλεξούδα
  *kots**ee**dha, pleks**oo**dha*
plane επίπεδο, αεροπλάνο
  *ep**ee**pedho, aeropl**a**no*
plant (vb) φυτεύω *feet**e**vo*
plant (n) φυτό *feet**o***
plaster έμπλαστρο *e**mblastro*
plastic πλαστικό *plasteek**o***
plastic bag πλαστική
  σακούλα *plasteek**ee** sak**oo**la*
plate πιάτο *pee**a**to*
platform αποβάθρα
  *apov**a**thra*
play (vb) παίζω *p**e**zo*
play (n) παιχνίδι
  *pekhn**ee**dhee*
playground παιδική χαρά
  *pedheek**ee** khar**a***

please παρακαλώ *parakal**o***
pleased ευχαριστημένος
  *efkhareesteem**e**nos*
Pleased to meet you!
  Χάρηκα που σας γνώρισα!
  *Kh**a**reeka poo sas
  ghn**o**reesa*
plenty πολλά *pol**a***
pliers πένσα *p**e**nsa*
plug (bath) τάπα *t**a**pa*
plug (elec) πρίζα *pr**ee**za*
plum δαμάσκηνο
  *dham**a**skeeno*
plumber υδραυλικός
  *eedhravleek**os***
p.m. (after noon)
  μετά μεσημβρίας *met**a**
  meseemvr**ee**as*
poached ποσέ *pos**e***
pocket τσέπη *ts**e**pee*
point (vb) δείχνω *dh**ee**khno*
point (n) σημείο *seem**ee**o*
points (car) πλατίνες
  *plat**ee**nes*
poison δηλητήριο
  *dheeleet**ee**reeo*
poisonous δηλητηριώδης
  *dheeleeteeree**o**dhees*
Poland Πολωνία *Polon**ee**a*
Pole, Polish Πολωνός
  *Polon**os***
police αστυνομία
  *asteenom**ee**a*
police station αστυνομικό
  τμήμα *asteenomeek**o**
  tm**ee**ma*
policeman/woman αστυ-
  νομικός *asteenomeek**os***
polish (vb) γυαλίζω,
  λουστράρω *gheeal**ee**zo,
  loostr**a**ro*
polish (n) βερνίκι, λούστρο
  *vern**ee**kee, l**oo**stro*
polite ευγενικός
  *evgheneek**os***
polluted μολυσμένος
  *moleesm**e**nos*
pool πισίνα *pees**ee**na*

121

poor (impecunious)
φτωχός *ftokhos*
poor (quality) κακός *kakos*
poppy παπαρούνα
paparoona
popular (of the people)
λαϊκός *laeekos*
popular (famous)
δημοφιλής *dheemofeelees*
population πληθυσμός
pleetheesmos
pork χοιρινό *kheereeno*
port (harbour) λιμάνι
leemanee
port (wine) πορτό *porto*
porter θυρωρός *theeroros*
portion μερίδα *mereedha*
portrait πορτραίτο *portreto*
Portugal Πορτογαλία
Portoghaleea
Portuguese (m)
Πορτογάλος *Portoghalos*
Portuguese (f) Πορτο-
γαλίδα *Portoghaleedha*
posh σικ, φίνος *seek, feenos*
possible δυνατός, πιθανός
dheenatos, peethanos
post (n, position) θέση
thesee
post (n, mail) πόστο *posto*
post (vb) ταχυδρομώ
takheedhromo
post office ταχυδρομείο
takheedhromeeo
post office box ταχυδρομική θυρίδα *takheedhro-
meekee theereedha*
postage ταχυδρομικά τέλη
takheedhromeeka telee
postage stamp γραμματόσημο *ghramatoseemo*
postal code ταχυδρομικός
κώδικας/τομέας
*takheedhromeekos
kodheekas/tomeas*
postbox ταχυδρομικό κουτί
takheedhromeeko kootee
postcard καρτ ποστάλ
kart postal

poster αφίσα *afeesa*
postman/postwoman
ταχυδρόμος *takheedhromos*
postpone αναβάλλω *anavalo*
potato πατάτα *patata*
pothole λακκούβα *lakoova*
pottery κεραμική
kerameekee
pound (weight) λίβρα *leevra*
pound (currency) λίρα *leera*
pour χύνω, ρίχνω *kheeno,
reekhno*
powder σκόνη *skonee*
powdered milk γάλα
σε μορφή σκόνης *ghala
se morfee skonees*
power cut διακοπή
ρεύματος *dheeakopee
revmatos*
practice πρακτική, πράξη
prakteekee, praksee
practise εξασκούμαι,
γυμνάζομαι *eksaskoome,
gheemnazome*
pram καροτσάκι μωρού
karotsakee moroo
prawn γαρίδα *ghareedha*
pray προσεύχομαι
prosefkhome
prefer προτιμώ *proteemo*
pregnant έγκυος *engeeos*
prescription συνταγή
γιατρού *seendaghee
gheeatroo*
present (now) παρόν *paron*
present (gift) δώρο *dhoro*
present (vb) παρουσιάζω
parooseeazo
pressure πίεση *pee-esee*
pretty όμορφος *omorfos*
price τιμή *teemee*
priest παπάς, ιερέας
papas, ee-ereas
prime minister πρωθυ-
πουργός *protheepoorghos*
print (vb) εκτυπώνω
ekteepono
printed matter έντυπο
υλικό *endeepo eeleeko*

prison φυλακή *feelakee*
private ιδιωτικός
eedheeoteekos
prize βραβείο *vraveeo*
probably πιθανόν *peethanon*
problem πρόβλημα
provleema
programme, program
πρόγραμμα *proghrama*
prohibited απαγορευμένος
apaghorevmenos
promise (vb) υπόσχομαι
eeposkhome
promise (n) υπόσχεση
eeposkhesee
pronounce προφέρω *profero*
properly καθώς πρέπει,
σωστά *kathos prepee, sosta*
Protestant Διαμαρτυρόμενος
Dheeamarteeromenos
public δημόσιος
dheemoseeos
public holiday επίσημη
αργία *epeeseemee argheea*
pudding πουτίγκα *pooteenga*
pull τραβώ *travo*
pullover πουλόβερ *poolover*
pump (n) αντλία *andleea*
puncture σκάσιμο, τρύπημα
σε λάστιχο *skaseemo,
treepeema se lasteekho*
puppet show κουκλοθέατρο
kooklotheatro
purple πορφυρός, βυσσινίς
porfeeros, veeseenees
purse πορτοφόλι *portofolee*
push σπρώχνω *sprokhno*
pushchair παιδικό αμαξάκι
pedheeko amaksakee
put βάζω *vazo*
put up with ανέχομαι
anekhome
pyjamas πυτζάμες
peetzames

Q
quality ποιότητα *peeoteeta*
quantity ποσότητα *posoteeta*

quarantine καραντίνα
karandeena
quarrel (n) καυγάς *kavghas*
quarrel (vb) καυγαδίζω
kavghadheezo
quarter τέταρτο *tetarto*
quay προκυμαία *prokeemea*
queen βασίλισσα *vaseeleesa*
question ερώτηση *eroteesee*
queue (n) ουρά *oora*
queue (vb) μπαίνω σε ουρά
mbeno se oora
quickly γρήγορα *ghreeghora*
quiet ήσυχος *eeseekhos*
quilt πάπλωμα *paploma*
quite αρκετά *arketa*

R
rabbit κουνέλι *koonelee*
rabies λύσσα *leesa*
race (people) γένος, φυλή
ghenos, feelee
race (sport) κούρσα *koorsa*
race course ιπποδρόμιο
eepodromeeo
racket (noise) φασαρία
fasareea
racket (sport) ρακέτα *raketa*
radiator ψυγείο *pseegheeo*
radio ραδιόφωνο
radheeofono
radish ραπανάκι *rapanakee*
rag κουρέλι *koorelee*
railway σιδηρόδρομος
seedheerodhromos
railway station
σιδηροδρομικός σταθμός
*seedheerodhromeekos
stathmos*
rain βροχή *vrokhee*
raincoat αδιάβροχο
adheeavrokho
raisin σταφίδα *stafeedha*
rake τσουγκράνα *tsoongrana*
rape (n) βιασμός *veeasmos*
rape (vb) βιάζω *veeazo*
rare σπάνιος *spaneeos*
rash εξάνθημα *eksantheema*
raspberry σμέουρο *smeooro*

123

ENGLISH → GREEK

rat αρουραίος *aroor@os*
rate (of exchange)
συνάλλαγμα *seenalaghma*
raw ωμός *omos*
razor ξυράφι *kseerafee*
razor blade ξυριστική
λεπίδα *kseereesteekee
lepeedha*
read διαβάζω *dheeavazo*
ready έτοιμος *eteemos*
real αληθινός *aleetheenos*
realize αντιλαμβάνομαι
andeelamvanome
really πραγματικά
praghmateeka
rear-view mirror
καθρέφτης οδηγήσεως
kathreftees odheegheeseos
reasonable λογικός
logheekos
receipt απόδειξη
apodheeksee
receiver (tax) φορολογική
απόδειξη *forologheekee
apodheeksee*
receiver (telephone)
δέκτης *dheektees*
recently πρόσφατος
prosfatos
reception ρεσεψιόν
resepseeon
receptionist ρεσεψιονίστας
resepseeoneestas
recharge επαναφορτώνω
epanafortono
recipe συνταγή *seendaghee*
recognize αναγνωρίζω
anaghnoreezo
recommend προτείνω
proteeno
record (legal) αρχείο
arkheeo
record (music) δίσκος
dheeskos
red κόκκινο *kokeeno*
red wine κόκκινο κρασί
kokeeno krasee
reduce μειώνω *meeono*
reduction μείωση *meeosee*

refund (n) επιστροφή
χρημάτων *epeestrofee
khreematon*
refund (vb) επιστρέφω
χρήματα *epeestrefo
khreemata*
refuse (vb) αρνούμαι
arnoome
refuse (n) απορρίμματα
aporeemata
region περιοχή *pereeokhee*
register (n) κατάλογος,
μητρώο *kataloghos,
meetro-o*
register (vb) δηλώνω,
εγγράφω *dheelono, engrafo*
registered mail συστημένο
γράμμα *seesteemeno
ghrama*
registration form έντυπο/
φόρμα εγγραφής *endeepo/
forma engrafees*
registration number
αριθμός μητρώου
areethmos meetro-oo
relative, relation σχετικός,
σχέση *skheteekos, skhesee*
remain απομένω *apomeno*
remember θυμάμαι
theemame
rent (vb) νοικιάζω
neekeeazo
repair (vb) επισκευάζω
epeeskevazo
repair (n) επισκευή
epeeskevee
repeat επαναλαμβάνω
epanalamvano
reply (vb) απαντώ *apando*
reply (n) απάντηση
apandeesee
report (vb) αναφέρω *anafero*
report (n) αναφορά *anafora*
request (n) παράκληση
parakleesee
request (vb) κάνω παράκληση *kano parakleesee*
require χρειάζομαι
khreeazome

rescue (vb) διασώζω
  dheeasozo
rescue (n) διάσωση
  dheeasosee
reservation κράτηση
  krateesee
reserve κρατώ *krato*
resident κάτοικος *kateekos*
resort θέρετρο *theretro*
rest (relax) αναπαύομαι
  anapavome
rest (remainder) υπόλοιπο
  eepoleepo
retired συνταξιούχος
  seendakseeookhos
return επιστροφή
  epeestrofee
return ticket εισιτήριο μετ'
  επιστροφής *eeseeteereeo
  met'epeestrofees*
reverse (n) αντίστροφος,
  αντίθετος *andeestrofos,
  andeethetos*
reverse (vb) αντιστρέφω
  andeestrefo
reverse gear όπισθεν
  opeesthen
reverse-charge call
  τηλεφώνημα με χρέωση του
  καλούμενου *teelefoneema
  me khreosee too
  kaloomenoo*
revolting αποτροπιαστικός
  apotropeeasteekos
rheumatism ρευματισμός
  revmateesmos
rib πλευρό *plevro*
ribbon κορδέλα *kordhela*
rice ρύζι *reezee*
rich πλούσιος *plooseeos*
ride καβαλικεύω *kavaleekevo*
ridiculous γελοίος *gheleeos*
right σωστός *sostos*
right-hand drive οδήγηση
  από τα δεξιά *odheegheesee apo ta dhekseea*
ring (n, on finger)
  δαχτυλίδι *dhakhteeleedhee*

ring (n, sound) κουδούνισμα
  koodhooneesma
ring road κυκλικός δρόμος
  keekleekos dhromos
rip-off αποσπώ *aospo*
ripe ώριμος *oreemos*
river ποταμός *potamos*
road δρόμος *dhromos*
road accident τροχαίο ατύχημα *trokheo ateekheema*
road map οδικός χάρτης
  odheekos khartees
road sign σήμα κυκλοφορίας
  seema keekloforeeas
road works οδικά έργα
  odheeka ergha
roll κυλώ *keelo*
roof στέγη *steghee*
roof-rack σχάρα *skhara*
room δωμάτιο *dhomateeo*
rope σχοινί *skheenee*
rose (flower) τριαντάφυλλο
  treeandafeelo
rotten σάπιος *sapeeos*
rough σκληρά *skleera*
roughly τραχιά *trakheea*
round γύρω *gheero*
roundabout περιφραστικός
  pereefrasteekos
row (n, line) σειρά *seera*
row (n, noise) φασαρία
  fasareea
royal βασιλικός *vaseeleekos*
rubber λάστιχο *lasteekho*
rubbish σκουπίδια
  skoopeedheea
rudder πηδάλιο *peedhaleeo*
rug χαλάκι *khalakee*
ruin καταστροφή *katastrofee*
ruler (for measuring)
  χάρακας *kharakas*
rum ρούμι *roomee*
run τρέχω *trekho*
rush σπεύδω *spevdho*
rusty σκουριασμένος
  skooreeasmenos
rye bread σικάλινο ψωμί
  sikaleeno psomee

125

S

sad θλιμμένος *thleemenos*
saddle σέλα *sela*
safe (adj, cautious)
  ασφαλής *asfalees*
safe (adj, sure) προσεκτικός *prosekteekos*
safety belt ζώνη ασφαλείας
  zonee asfaleeas
safety pin παραμάνα
  paramana
sail πλέω *pleo*
sailing ιστιοπλοΐα
  eesteeoploeea
salad σαλάτα *salata*
salad dressing αρτύμια
  της σαλάτας *arteemea
  tees salatas*
sale πώληση *poleesee*
sales representative
  αντιπρόσωπος πωλήσεων
  andeeprosopos poleeseon
salesperson πωλητής (m),
  πωλήτρια (f) *poleetees (m),
  poleetreea (f)*
salmon σολομός *solomos*
salt αλάτι *alatee*
same ίδιος *eedheeos*
sand άμμος *amos*
sandals σανδάλια, πέδιλα
  sandhaleea, pedheela
sandwich σάντουιτς
  sadooeets
sanitary pads σερβιέττες
  servee-etes
Saturday Σάββατο *Savato*
sauce σάλτσα *saltsa*
saucer πιατάκι *peeatakee*
sausage λουκάνικο
  lookaneeko
save (rescue) σώζω *sozo*
save (money) αποταμιεύω
  apotamee-evo
savoury πικάντικος
  peekandeekos
say λέω *leo*
scales λέπια *lepeea*
scarf κασκόλ, φουλάρι
  kaskol, foolaree

scenery τοπεία *topeea*
school σχολείο *skholeeo*
scissors ψαλίδι *psaleedhee*
Scot, Scottish Σκωτσέζος
  Skotsezos
Scotland Σκωτία *Skoteea*
scrambled eggs αυγά
  σφουγγάτο *avgha sfoongato*
scratch (n) γρατσούνισμα
  ghratsooneesma
scratch (vb) γρατσουνίζω
  ghratsooneezo
screen παραβάν *paravan*
screw βίδα *vheedha*
screwdriver κατσαβίδι
  katsaveedhee
scrubbing brush αγριόβουρτσα *aghreeovoortsa*
scuba diving υποβρύχια
  κατάδυση *eepovreekheea
  katadheesee*
sea θάλασσα *thalasa*
seagull γλάρος *ghlaros*
seasickness ναυτία *nafteea*
seaside παραλία *paraleea*
season εποχή *epokhee*
season ticket διαρκές
  εισιτήριο *dheearkes
  eeseeteereeo*
seasoning καρύκευμα
  kareekevma
seat κάθισμα *katheesma*
seatbelt ζώνη καθίσματος
  zonee katheesmatos
seaweed φύκι *feekee*
secluded απομονωμένος
  apomonomenos
second (order) δεύτερος
  dhefteros
second (time)
  δευτερόλεπτο *dhefterolepto*
second-class δεύτερης
  κατηγορίας *dhefterees
  kateeghoreeas*
second-hand μεταχειρισμένο, από δεύτερο χέρι
  *metakheereesmeno, apo
  dheftero kheree*

secretary γραμματέας _ghramateas_
security guard φύλακας, φρουρός _feelakas, frooros_
see βλέπω _vlepo_
self-catering ανεξάρτητος _aneksarteetos_
self-employed αυτοαπασχολούμενος _aftoapaskholoomenos_
self-service σελφ– σέρβις, αυτοεξυπηρέτηση _self-servees, aftoekseepeereteesee_
sell πουλάω _poolao_
sell-by date ημερομηνία λήξης _eemeromeeneea leeksees_
send στέλνω _stelno_
senior citizen συνταξιούχος _seendakseeookhos_
sentence (grammar) πρόταση _protasee_
sentence (law) ποινή _peenee_
separate (vb) χωρίζω _khoreezo_
separate (adj) χωριστός _khoreestos_
September Σεπτέμβριος _Septemvreeos_
septic σηπτικός _seepteekos_
septic tank σηπτικός βόθρος _seepteekos vothros_
serious σοβαρός _sovaros_
service υπηρεσία _eepeereseea_
service charge ποσοστό υπηρεσίας _pososto eepeereseeas_
serviette χαρτοπετσέτα _khartopetseta_
set menu καθορισμένο μενού _kathoreesmeno menoo_
several πολλοί, αρκετοί _polee, arketee_
sew ράβω _ravo_
sex (gender) φύλο _feelo_

sex (intercourse) σεξ _seks_
shade σκιάζω _skeeazo_
shake κουνώ _koono_
shallow ρηχός _reekhos_
shame ντροπή _ndropee_
shampoo and set λούσιμο και χτένισμα _looseemo ke khteneesma_
share (n) μερίδα _mereedha_
share (vb) μοιράζομαι _meerazome_
sharp μυτερός, κοφτερός _meeteros, kofteros_
shave ξυρίζομαι _kseereezome_
she αυτή _aftee_
sheep πρόβατο _provato_
sheet σεντόνι _sendonee_
shelf ράφι _rafee_
shellfish θαλασσινά _thalaseena_
sheltered προστατευμένος _prostatevomenos_
shine λάμπω _lambo_
shingle κροκάλι _krokalee_
shingles έρπης ζωστήρας _erpees zosteeras_
ship πλοίο _pleeo_
shirt πουκάμισο _pookameeso_
shock absorber αμορτισέρ _amorteeser_
shoe παπούτσι _papootsee_
shoelace κορδόνι παπουτσιών _kordhonee papootseeon_
shop μαγαζί _maghazee_
shop assistant υπάλληλος _eepaleelos_
shop window βιτρίνα _veetreena_
shopping centre εμπορικό κέντρο _emboreeko kendro_
shore ακτή _aktee_
short κοντός _kondos_
short-cut συντομότερος τρόπος _seendomoteros tropos_
short-sighted μυωπικός _meeopeekos_

127

shorts κοντό παντελόνι, σορτς *kondo pantelonee, sorts*
should θα έπρεπε *tha eprepe*
shoulder ώμος *omos*
shout (vb) φωνάζω *fonazo*
shout (n) κραυγή *kravghee*
show (n) θέαμα *theama*
show (vb) δείχνω *dheekno*
shower ντούς *ndoos*
shrimp γαρίδα *ghareedha*
shrink συρρικνούμαι, μπαίνω *seereeknoome, mbeno*
shut κλείνω *kleeno*
shutter παντζούρι *pantzooree*
shy ντροπαλός *ndropalos*
sick, I'm going to be sick! άρρωστος, θα κάνω εμετό! *arostos, tha kano emeto*
side πλευρά *plevra*
side dish συμπληρωματικό φαγητό *seemblee-romateeko fagheeto*
sidewalk πεζοδρόμιο *pezodhromeeo*
sieve κόσκινο *kokeeno*
sight όραση *orasee*
sightseeing επίσκεψη στα αξιοθέατα *epeeskepsee sta akseeotheata*
sign (n) ταμπέλα *tambela*
sign (vb) υπογράφω *eepoghrafo*
signal σήμα *seema*
signature υπογραφή *eepoghrafee*
signpost πινακίδα *peenakeedha*
silence σιωπή, σιγή *seeopee, seeghee*
silk μετάξι *metaksee*
silly ανόητος *anoeetos*
silver αργυρός, ασήμι *argheeros, aseemee*
similar όμοιος *omeeos*
simple απλός *aplos*
sing τραγουδάω *traghoodhao*

singer τραγουδιστής *traghoodheestees*
single μόνος *monos*
single bed μονό κρεββάτι *mono krevatee*
single room μονόκλινο δωμάτιο *monokleeno dhomateeo*
single ticket μονό εισιτήριο *mono eeseeteereeo*
sink νεροχύτης *nerokheetees*
sister αδελφή *adhelfee*
sister-in-law (brother's wife) νύφη *neefee*
sister-in-law (wife's sister) κουνιάδα *kooneeadha*
sit κάθομαι *kathome*
size μέγεθος *meghethos*
skate (gear) παγοπέδιλο *paghopedheelo*
skate (fish) σαλάχι *salakhee*
skating rink παγοδρόμιο *paghodhromeeo*
ski σκι *skee*
ski boot μπότα του σκι *mbota too skee*
ski jump άλμα με σκι *alma me skee*
ski slope πλαγιά για σκι *plagheea gheea skee*
skiing σκι *skee*
skin δέρμα *dherma*
skirt φούστα *foosta*
sky ουρανός *ooranos*
sledge έλκηθρο *elkeethro*
sleep κοιμάμαι *keemame*
sleeper, sleeping car κλινάμαξα *kleenamaksa*
sleeping bag υπνοσάκος *eepnosakos*
sleeping pill υπνωτικό χάπι *eepnoteeko khapee*
sleepy νυσταλέος *neestaleos*
slice φέτα *feta*
slide (n) διολίσθηση *dheeoleestheesee*
slide (vb) γλιστρώ *ghleestro*
slip τσουλήθρα *tsooleethra*

slippers παντόφλες
  pandofles
slippery γλιστερός
  ghleesteros
Slovak Σλοβακινός
  Slovakeenos
Slovak Republic
  Δημοκρατία της Σλοβακίας
  *Dheemokrateea tees
  Slovakeeas*
slow αργός *arghos*
slowly αργά *argha*
small μικρός *meekros*
smell μυρίζομαι *meereezome*
smile (vb) χαμογελώ
  khamoghelo
smoke (n) καπνός *kapnos*
smoke (vb) καπνίζω
  kapneezo
smoked salmon καπνιστός
  σολομός *kapneestos
  solomos*
snack μεζές, κολατσό
  mezes, kolatso
snake φίδι *feedhee*
sneeze φταρνίζομαι
  ftarneezome
snore ροχαλίζω *rokhaleezo*
snorkel αναπνευστικός
  σωλήνας *anapnefsteekos
  soleenas*
snow, it is snowing χιόνι,
  χιονίζει *kheeonee,
  kheeoneezee*
soaking solution υγρό
  συντήρησης φακών επαφής
  *eeghro seendeereesees
  fakon epafees*
soap σαπούνι *sapoonee*
soap powder απορρυ–
  παντικό *aporeepandeeko*
sober νηφάλιος *neefaleeos*
socket (elec) πρίζα *preeza*
socks κάλτσες *kaltses*
soda σόδα *sodha*
soft μαλακός *malakos*
soft drink αναψυκτικό
  anapseekteeko
sole (fish) γλώσσα *ghlosa*

sole (shoe) πέλμα *pelma*
soluble διαλυτός *dheealeetos*
some μερικός *mereekos*
someone, somebody
  κάποιος *kapeeos*
something κάτι *katee*
sometimes κάποτε *kapote*
somewhere κάπου *kapoo*
son γιός *gheeos*
son-in-law γαμπρός
  ghambros
song τραγούδι *traghoodhee*
soon σύντομα *seendoma*
sore πονεμένος *ponemenos*
sore, it's sore πονάει
  ponaee
sore throat πονόλαιμος
  ponolemos
Sorry! Λυπάμαι! *Leepame!*
sort είδος *eedhos*
soup σούπα *soopa*
sour ξινός *kseenos*
south νότιος *noteeos*
South Africa Νότια Αφρική
  Noteea Afreekee
South African (m)
  Νοτιοαφρικάνος
  Noteeoafreekanos
South African (f)
  Νοτιοαφρικάνα
  Noteeoafreekana
souvenir ενθύμιο
  entheemeeo
spade φτυάρι *fteearee*
Spain Ισπανία *Eespaneea*
Spaniard, Spanish
  Ισπανός *Eespanos*
spanner γαλλικό κλειδί
  ghaleeko kleedhee
spare part ανταλλακτικό
  adalakteeko
spare tyre ρεζέρβα *rezerva*
spark plug μπουζί *boozee*
sparkling αφρώδης
  afrodhees
speak μιλώ *meelo*
speciality ειδικότητα
  eedheekoteeta

ENGLISH → GREEK

spectacles γυαλιά
gheealeea
speed ταχύτητα *takheeteeta*
speed limit όριο ταχύτητας
oreeo takheeteetas
speedometer ταχύμετρο,
κοντέρ *takheemetro, konder*
spell συλλαβίζω, ορθογραφώ
seelaveezo, orthoghrafo
spend (money) ξοδεύω
ksodhevo
spend (time) διαθέτω χρόνο
dheeatheto khrono
spice μπαχαρικό
mbakhareeko
spider αράχνη *arakhnee*
spill χύνω *kheeno*
spin-dryer στεγνωτήριο
steghnoteereeo
spinach σπανάκι *spanakee*
spine σπονδυλική στήλη
spondheeleekee steelee
spirit (soul) πνεύμα *pnevma*
spirits (drink)
οινοπνευματώδη ποτά
eenopnevmatodhee pota
splinter θραύσμα *thravsma*
spoil χαλώ *khalo*
spoke (of wheel) αχτίνα
τροχού *akhteena trokhoo*
sponge σφουγγάρι
sfoongaree
sponge cake παντεσπάνι
pandespanee
spoon κουτάλι *kootalee*
sprain (vb) στραμπουλίζω
strambooleezo
sprain (n) εξάρθρωση
eksarthrosee
spring (season) άνοιξη
aneeksee
square τετράγωνος
tetraghonos
stadium στάδιο *stadheeo*
stain λεκές *lekes*
stairs σκαλιά *skaleea*
stale μπαγιάτικος
bagheeateekos

stall υπαίθριο μαγαζί,
περίπτερο *eepethreeo*
maghazee, pereeptero
stamp χτυπώ κάτω (τα
πόδια) *khteepo kato (ta*
podheea)
staple (n) συδεντήρας
seendheteeras
staple (adj) βασικός
vaseekos
star αστέρι *asteree*
start αρχή *arkhee*
starter (car) μίζα *meeza*
station σταθμός *stathmos*
stationer's στου χαρτοπώλη
stoo khartopolee
stationery χαρτικά, γραφική
ύλη *kharteeka, ghrafeekee*
eelee
statue άγαλμα *aghalma*
stay παραμονή *paramonee*
steal κλέβω *klevo*
steam ατμός *atmos*
steer διευθύνω *dee-eftheeno*
steering wheel τιμόνι
teemonee
step σκαλί *skalee*
stepfather πατρυιός
patreeos
stepmother μητριά
meetreea
stew (with tomato) γιαχνί
gheeakhnee
stew (with onions)
στιφάδο *steefadho*
stick (n) βέργα *vergha*
sticking plaster
λευκοπλάστης *lefkoplastees*
still (yet) ακόμη *akomee*
still (quiet) ήσυχος
eeseekhos
sting κεντρί *kendree*
sting τσούκημο *tsookseemo*
sting κεντρίζω *kendreezo*
stitch ράμμα *rama*
stock (soup) ζωμός *zomos*
stocking κάλτσα *kaltsa*
stolen κλεμμένος *klemenos*
stomach στομάχι *stomakhee*

stomachache κοιλόπονος
keeloponos
stone πέτρα _petra_
stop σταματάω _stamatao_
stop sign σήμα στοπ
seema stop
stopover στάση _stasee_
store (n) αποθήκη
apotheekee
store (vb) αποθηκεύω
apotheekevo
storey όροφος _orofos_
storm θύελλα _thee-ella_
straight ίσιος, ευθύς
eeseeos, efthees
straight on ευθεία _eftheea_
straightaway κατ'ευθείαν
kat'eftheean
strange παράξενος,
περίεργος _paraksenos,
peree-erghos_
strange, stranger ξένος
ksenos
strap λουρίδα _looreedha_
straw (drinking) καλαμάκι
kalamakee
straw (hay) άχυρο _akheero_
strawberry φράουλα _fraoola_
stream χείμαρρος _kheemaros_
street δρόμος _dhromos_
street map οδικός χάρτης
odheekos khartees
strike (n) απεργία _apergheea_
string σπάγγος _spangos_
stroke (caress) χαϊδεύω
khaeedhevo
stroke (illness) εγκεφαλική
συμφόρηση _engefaleekee
seemforeesee_
strong δυνατός _dheenatos_
stuck κολλημένος
koleemenos
student (tertiary) φοιτητής
feeteetees
student (school) μαθητής
matheetees
student discount
φοιτητική έκπτωση
feeteeteekee ekptosee

stuffed γεμιστός _ghemeestos_
stupid βλάκας _vlakas_
subtitle υπότιτλος
eepoteetlos
suburb προάστειο _proasteeo_
subway υπόγειος
σιδηρόδρομος _eepogheeos
seedheerodhromos_
suddenly ξαφνικά _ksafneeka_
suede καστόρι _kastoree_
sugar ζάχαρη _zakharee_
sugar-free χωρίς ζάχαρη
khorees zakharee
suit κοστούμι _kostoomee_
suitcase βαλίτσα _valeetsa_
summer καλοκαίρι _kalokeree_
summit κορυφή _koreefee_
sun ήλιος _eeleeos_
sunblock αντιηλιακό
andee-eeleeako
sunburn κάψιμο από τον ήλιο
kapseemo apo ton eeleeo
Sunday Κυριακή _Keereeakee_
sunglasses γυαλιά ηλίου
gheealeea eeleeoo
sunny ηλιόλουστος
eeleeoloostos
sunrise ανατολή του ηλίου
anatolee too eeleeoo
sunroof τζαμένια σκέπη
tzameneea skepee
sunset δύση του ηλίου
dheesee too eeleeoo
sunshade ομπρέλα ηλίου
ombrela eeleeoo
sunshine λιακάδα _leeakadha_
sunstroke ηλίαση _eeleeasee_
suntan ηλιοθεραπία
eeleeotherapeea
suntan lotion λάδι
ηλιοθεραπίας _ladhee
eeleeotherapeeas_
supper δείπνο _dheepno_
supplement συμπλήρωμα
seembleeroma
sure σίγουρος _seeghooros_
surfboard σανίδα
κυματοδρομίας _saneedha
keematodhromeeas_

ENGLISH → GREEK

surgery (doctor's rooms) ιατρείο *eeatreeo*
surgery (procedure) χειρουργική *keeroorgheekee*
surname επώνυμο *eponeemo*
surrounded περικυκλωμένος *pereekeeklomenos*
swallow (vb) καταπίνω *katapeeno*
swear (an oath) ορκίζομαι *orkeezome*
swear (curse) βρίζω *vreezo*
swear word βρισιά *vreeseea*
sweat (vb) υδρώνω *eedhrono*
sweat (n) υδρώτας *eedhrotas*
sweater μάλλινη μπλούζα *maleenee blooza*
Sweden Σουιδία *Sooeedheea*
Swedish, Swede Σουιδός (m), Σουιδέζα (f) *sooeedhos (m), sooeedheza (f)*
sweet γλυκός *ghleekos*
swell φουσκώνω, πρίζομαι *fooskono, preezome*
swelling πρίξιμο *preekseemo*
swim κολυμπώ *koleembo*
swimming costume μαγιό *magheeo*
swing κούνια *kooneea*
Swiss Ελβετός *Elvetos*
Swiss-German Ελβετογερμανός *Elvetoghermanos*
switch διακόπτης *dheeakoptees*
switch off σβήνω *sveeno*
switch on ανάβω *anavo*
Switzerland Ελβετία *Elveteea*
swollen πρισμένος *preesmenos*
synagogue συναγωγή *seenaghoghee*

T
table τραπέζι *trapezee*
table wine επιτραπέζιος οίνος *epeetrapezeeos eenos*
tablecloth τραπεζομάντηλο *trapezomandeelo*
tablespoon κουτάλα σερβιρίσματος *kootala serveereesmatos*
tailor ράφτης *raftees*
take παίρνω *perno*
take-away food φαγητό σε πακέτο *fagheeto se paketo*
talcum powder πούδρα *poodhra*
talk μιλώ *meelo*
tall ψηλός *pseelos*
tampon ταμπόν *tampon*
tangerine μανταρίνι *mandareenee*
tank δεξαμενή *dheksamenee*
tape ταινία *teneea*
tape measure μετροταινία *metroteneea*
tape recorder μαγνητόφωνο *maghneetofono*
taste (n) γεύση *ghefsee*
tax φόρος *foros*
taxi ταξί *taksee*
taxi driver οδηγός ταξί *odheeghos taksee*
taxi rank σταθμός ταξί *stathmos taksee*
tea τσάι *tsaee*
tea bag ατομικό φακελάκι με τσάι *atomeeko fakelakee me tsaee*
teach διδάσκω *dheedhasko*
teacher δάσκαλος *dhaskalos*
team ομάδα *omadha*
teapot τσαγιερό *tsagheero*
tear (n) δάκρυ *dhakree*
tear (vb) σκίζω *skeezo*

teaspoon κουταλάκι του
τσαγιού *kootalakee too
tsagheeoo*

teat (bottle) ρώγα *rogha*

teeth δόντια *dhondeea*

telephone τηλέφωνο
teelefono

telephone call τηλεφώνημα
teelefoneema

telephone directory
τηλεφωνικός κατάλογος
teelefoneekos kataloghos

television τηλεόραση
teeleorasee

tell λέω *leo*

temperature θερμοκρασία
thermokraseea

temple ναός *naos*

temporary προσωρινός
prosoreenos

tendon τένοντας *tenondas*

tennis τένις *tenees*

tennis court γήπεδο του
τένις *gheepedho too tenees*

tennis racket ρακέτα του
τένις *raketa too tenees*

tent σκηνή *skeenee*

tent peg παλούκι σκηνής
palookee skeenees

terminal (airport) αερολιμένας *aeroleemenas*

terminal (bus, train)
τέρμα *terma*

thank ευχαριστώ *efkhareesto*

that αυτό *afto*

the το *to*

theatre θέατρο *theatro*

theft κλοπή *klopee*

there εκεί *ekee*

thermometer θερμόμετρο
thermometro

they αυτοί *aftee*

thick χοντρός *khondros*

thief κλέφτης *kleftees*

thigh μπούτι *bootee*

thin λιγνός *leeghnos*

thing πράγμα *praghma*

think σκέπτομαι
skeptome

third-party insurance
ασφάλεια για χρήση από
τρίτους *asfaleea gheea
khreesee apo treetoos*

thirsty διψασμένος
dheepsasmenos

this τούτο *tooto*

this morning σήμερα το
πρωί *seemera to proee*

this way από 'δώ *apo'dho*

this week αυτή την
εβδομάδα *aftee teen
evdhomadha*

thorn αγκάθι *angathee*

those αυτά *afta*

thousand χίλια *kheeleea*

thread κλωστή *klostee*

throat λαιμός *lemos*

throat lozenges παστίλιες
για το λαιμό *pasteelee-es
gheea to lemo*

through δια μέσου
dheea mesoo

throw πετώ *peto*

thumb αντίχειρας
andeekheeras

thunder βροντή *vrondee*

thunderstorm καταιγίδα,
θύελλα *kateegheedha,
thee-ela*

Thursday Πέμπτη *Pemptee*

ticket εισιτήριο
eeseeteereeo

ticket collector ελεγκτής
elengtees

ticket office γραφείο έκδοσης εισιτηρίων *ghrafeeo
ekdhosees eeseeteereeon*

tide, low tide, high tide
παλίρροια, άμπωτη,
πλημμυρίδα _paleereea,
ambotee, pleemeereedha_
tie δένω _dheno_
tie γραβάτα _ghravata_
tight στενός _stenos_
tights καλτσόν _kaltson_
till (cash register) ταμείο
tameeo
till (until) έως ότου
eos otoo
time ώρα _ora_
timetable ωρολόγιο
πρόγραμμα _orologheeo
proghrama_
tin τενεκές _tenekes_
tin opener ανοιχτήρι
aneekhteeree
tinfoil ασημόχαρτο
aseemokharto
tiny μικροσκοπικός
meekroskopeekos
tip άκρη _akree_
tired κουρασμένος
koorasmenos
tissue λεπτό ύφασμα
lepto eefasma
to προς _pros_
toad βάτραχος _vatrakhos_
today σήμερα _seemera_
toe δάχτυλο ποδιού
dhakhteelo podheeoo
together μαζί _mazee_
toilet τουαλέτα _tooaleta_
tolerate ανέχομαι
anekhome
toll, toll road διόδια
dheeodheea
tomato ντομάτα _domata_
tomato juice χυμός ντομάτας _kheemos domatas_
tomorrow αύριο _avreeo_

**tomorrow morning/after-
noon/evening** αύριο
το πρωί/απόγευμα/
βράδυ _avreeo to proee/
apoghevma/vradhee_
tongue γλώσσα _ghlosa_
tonight απόψε _apopse_
tonsillitis αμυγδαλίτιδα
ameeghdhaleeteedha
too επίσης _epeesees_
too much πάρα πολύ
para polee
tool εργαλείο _erghaleeo_
toolkit κουτί με εργαλεία
kootee me erghaleea
tooth δόντι _dhondee_
toothache πονόδοντος
ponodhondos
toothbrush οδοντόβουρτσα
odhondovoortsa
toothpick οδοντογλυφίδα
odhondoghleefeedha
top κορυφή _koreefee_
top floor πάνω πάτωμα
pano patoma
topless γυμνόστηθη
gheemnosteethee
torch δάδα _dhadha_
torn σκισμένος
skeesmenos
total σύνολο _seenolo_
tough σκληρός _skleeros_
tour περιήγηση
peree-eegheesee
tour guide τουριστικός
συνοδός _tooreesteekos
seenodhos_
tour operator οργανωτής
εκδρομών _orghanotees
ekdhromon_
tow ρυμουλκώ _reemoolko_
towel πετσέτα _petseta_
tower πύργος _peerghos_
town πόλη _polee_

town hall δημαρχείο *dheemarkh<u>ee</u>o*

toy παιχνίδι *pekhn<u>ee</u>dhee*

tracksuit φόρμα *f<u>o</u>rma*

traffic κίνηση *k<u>ee</u>neesee*

traffic jam κυκλοφοριακή συμφόρηση *keekloforee- ak<u>ee</u> seemf<u>o</u>reesee*

traffic light φωτεινός σηματοδότης *feteen<u>o</u>s seematodh<u>o</u>tees*

trailer (for goods) ρυμούλκα *reem<u>oo</u>lka*

trailer (caravan) τροχόσπιτο *trokh<u>o</u>speeto*

train τραίνο *tr<u>e</u>no*

tram τράμ *tram*

tranquillizer ηρεμιστικό φάρμακο *eeremeesteek<u>o</u> f<u>a</u>rmako*

translate μεταφράζω *metafr<u>a</u>zo*

translation μετάφραση *metafrasee*

translator μεταφραστής *metafrast<u>ee</u>s*

trash σκουπίδια *skoop<u>ee</u>dheea*

travel ταξιδεύω *takseedh<u>e</u>vo*

travel agent ταξιδιωτικός πράκτορας *takseedh<u>ee</u>o- teek<u>o</u>s pr<u>a</u>ktoras*

travel documents έγγραφα ταξιδιώτη *<u>e</u>ngrafa taksee- dhe<u>o</u>tee*

travel sickness διάρροια, ναυτία *dhee<u>e</u>areea, naft<u>ee</u>a*

traveller's cheque ταξι- διωτική επιταγή *taksee- dhee<u>o</u>teek<u>ee</u> epeetagh<u>ee</u>*

tray δίσκος *dh<u>e</u>eskos*

tree δέντρο *dh<u>e</u>ndro*

trolley καροτσάκι *karots<u>a</u>kee*

trouble φασαρία, σκοτούρα *fasar<u>ee</u>a, skot<u>oo</u>ra*

trousers παντελόνι *pantel<u>o</u>nee*

trout πέστροφα *p<u>e</u>strofa*

truck φορτηγό *forteegh<u>o</u>*

true αληθινός *aleetheen<u>o</u>s*

trunk (of car) πορτ- μπαγκάζ *port-bag<u>a</u>z*

try προσπαθώ *prospath<u>o</u>*

try on δοκιμάζω *dhokeem<u>a</u>zo*

tube σωλήνας *sol<u>ee</u>nas*

tuna τόνος *t<u>o</u>nos*

tunnel τούνελ *t<u>oo</u>nel*

turkey γαλοπούλα *ghalop<u>oo</u>la*

Turkey Τουρκία *Toork<u>ee</u>a*

Turkish, Turk Τούρκος (m), Τουρκάλα (f) *T<u>oo</u>rkos (m), Toork<u>a</u>la (f)*

turn στροφή *strof<u>ee</u>*

turn around αντιστρέφω *andeestr<u>e</u>fo*

turn off σβήνω *sv<u>ee</u>no*

turquoise τουρκουάζ *toork<u>oo</u>az*

tweezers τσιμπιδάκι *tseembeedh<u>a</u>kee*

twice δύο φορές *dh<u>e</u>eo for<u>e</u>s*

twin beds δύο μονά κρεββά- τια *dh<u>e</u>eo mon<u>a</u> krevat<u>e</u>ea*

twins δίδυμα *dh<u>e</u>edheema*

type τύπος *t<u>e</u>epos*

typical χαρακτηριστικός *kharakteereesteek<u>o</u>s*

tyre λάστιχο αυτοκινήτου *lasteekho aftokeen<u>ee</u>too*

tyre pressure η πίεση στα λάστιχα *ee p<u>e</u>e-esee sta l<u>a</u>steekha*

U

ugly άσχημος *<u>a</u>skheemos*

ulcer έλκος, πληγή *<u>e</u>lkos, pleegh<u>ee</u>*

ENGLISH → GREEK

umbrella ομπρέλα *ombrela*
uncle θείος *theeos*
uncomfortable άβολος, όχι άνετος *avolos, okhee anetos*
unconscious αθέλητος, αναίσθητος *atheleetos, anestheetos*
under κάτω από *kato apo*
underdone όχι καλά ψημένο *okhee kala pseemeno*
underground υπέδαφος *eepedhafos*
underground (subway) υπόγειος σιδηρόδρομος, μετρό *eepogheeos seedheerodhromos, metro*
underpants σώβρακο *sovrako*
understand καταλαβαίνω *katalaveno*
underwear εσώρουχα *esorookha*
unemployed άνεργος *anerghos*
United Kingdom Ηνωμένο Βασίλειο *Eenomeno Vaseeleeo*
United States Ηνωμένες Πολιτείες *Eenomenes Poleetee-es*
university πανεπιστήμιο *panepeesteemeeo*
unleaded petrol αμόλυβδη βενζίνη *amoleevdhee venzeenee*
unlimited απεριόριστος *apereeoreestos*
unlock ξεκλειδώνω *ksekleedhono*
unpack ξεπακετάρω *ksepaketaro*
unscrew ξεβιδώνω *kseveedhono*
until μέχρι *mekhree*

unusual ασυνήθης *aseeneethees*
up επάνω *epano*
up-market ακριβός *akreevos*
upside down ανάποδος *anapodhos*
upstairs επάνω *epano*
urgent επείγων *epeeghon*
us εμείς *emees*
use χρησιμοποιώ *khreeseemopeeo*
useful χρήσιμος *khreeseemos*
usual συνήθης *seeneethees*
usually συνηθισμένα *seeneetheesmena*

V
vacancy διαθέσιμο δωμάτιο/διαμέρισμα *dheeathseemo dhomateeo/dheeamereesma*
vacation διακοπές *dheeakopes*
vaccine εμβόλιο *emvoleeo*
vacuum cleaner ηλεκτρική σκούπα *eelektreekee skoopa*
valid έγκυρος *engeeros*
valley κοιλάδα *keeladha*
valuable πολύτιμος *poleeteemos*
value αξία *akseea*
valve βαλβίδα *valveedha*
van (for goods) φορτηγάκι *forteeghakee*
van (home-on-wheels) τροχόσπιτο *trokhospeeto*
VAT φόρος προστιθέμενης αξίας *foros prosteethemenees akseeas*
veal μοσχάρι *moskharee*

vegetables λαχανικά, χορταρικά *lakhaneeka, khortareeka*

vegetarian χορτοφάγος *khortofaghos*

vehicle όχημα της ξηράς *okheema tees kseeras*

vein φλέβα *fleva*

vending machine αυτόματος πωλητής *aftomatos poleetees*

venereal disease αφροδίσιο νόσημα *afrodheeseeo noseema*

very πολύ *polee*

vest εσωτερική φανέλα *esotereekee fanela*

veterinarian κτηνίατρος *kteeneeatros*

via μέσω *meso*

Vienna Βιέννη *Vee-enee*

view όψη, θέα *opsee, thea*

village χωριό *khoreeo*

vinegar ξίδι *kseedhee*

vineyard αμπέλι *ambelee*

violet βιολετί *veeoletee*

virus ιός *eeos*

visa θεώρηση (διαβατηρίου), βίζα *theoreesee (dhee-avateereeoo), veeza*

visit επισκέπτομαι *epeeskeptome*

visiting hours ώρες επισκέψεως *ores epeeskepseos*

visitor επισκέπτης *epeeskeptees*

voice φωνή *fonee*

volcano ηφαίστειο *eefesteeo*

voltage βολτάζ, τάση *voltaz, tasee*

vomit κάνω εμετό *kano emeto*

voucher κουπόνι *kooponee*

W

wage μεροκάματο *merokamato*

waist μέση *mesee*

waistcoat γιλέκο *gheeleko*

wait περιμένω *pereemeno*

waiter/waitress σερβιτόρος/σερβιτόρα *serveetoros/serveetora*

waiting room αίθουσα αναμονής *ethoosa anamonees*

wake up ξυπνάω *kseepnao*

wake-up call τηλεφώνημα για ξύπνημα *teelefoneema ghea kseepneema*

Wales Ουαλία *Ooaleea*

walk περπατώ *perpato*

wall τοίχος *teekhos*

wallet πορτοφόλι *portofolee*

walnut καρύδι *kareedhee*

want θέλω *thelo*

war πόλεμος *polemos*

ward (hospital) θάλαμος *thalamos*

wardrobe γκαρνταρόμπα *gardaromba*

warehouse αποθήκη *apotheekee*

warm ζεστός *zestos*

wash πλένω *pleno*

washbasin νιπτήρας *neepteeras*

washing powder απορρυπαντικό *aporeepandeeko*

washing-up liquid υγρό για τα πιάτα *eeghro ghea ta peeata*

wasp σφήκα *sfeeka*

waste απορρίμματα *aporeemata*

waste bin κάλαθος αχρήστων *kalathos akhreeston*

watch (timepiece) ρολόι *roloee*

watch (vb) παρακολουθώ *parakolootho*

watch strap λουράκι ρολο– γιού *loorakee rologheeoo*

water νερό *nero*

watermelon καρπούζι *karpoozee*

waterproof υδατοστεγής *eedhatosteghees*

water-skiing θαλάσσιο σκι *thalaseeo skee*

wave κύμα *keema*

we εμείς *emees*

weak αδύνατος *adheenatos*

wear χρήση *khreesee*

weather καιρός *keros*

weather forecast δελτίο καιρού *dhelteeo keroo*

web ιστός *eestos*

wedding γάμος *ghamos*

wedding present γαμήλιο δώρο *ghameeleeo dhoro*

wedding ring βέρα *vera*

Wednesday Τετάρτη *Tetartee*

week εβδομάδα *evdhomadha* **last week** την περασμένη εβδομάδα *teen perasmenee evdhomadha;* **this week** αυτή την εβδομάδα *aftee teen evdhomadha;* **next week** την επόμενη εβδομάδα *teen epomenee evdhomadha;* **a week ago** πρίν από μία εβδομάδα *preen apo meea evdhomadha*

weekday μέσα στην εβδομάδα *mesa steen evdhomadha*

weekend σαββατοκύριακο *savatokeereeako*

weekly εβδομαδιαίος *evdhomadhee-eos*

weigh ζυγίζω *zeegheezo*

weight βάρος *varos*

weird παράξενος *paraksenos*

welcome ευπρόσδεκτος *efprosdhektos*

well καλά *kala*

Welsh, Welshman, Welsh- woman Ουαλός (m) *Ooalos,* Ουαλή (f) *Ooalee*

were ήταν *eetan*

west δύση *dheesee*

wet υγρός *eeghros*

wetsuit στολή υποβρύχιου ψαρέματος *stolee eepo- vreekheeoo psarematos*

What? Τι; *Tee?*

What is wrong? Τι συμ- βαίνει; *Tee seemvenee?*

What's the matter? Τι τρέχει; *Tee trekhee?*

What's the time? Τι ώρα είναι; *Tee ora eene?*

wheel ρόδα *rodha*

wheelchair αναπηρική πολυθρόνα *anapeereekee poleethrona*

When? Πότε; *Pote?*

Where? Που; *Poo?*

Which? Ποιά; *Peea?*

while ενώ *eno*

whipped cream σαντιγύ *sandeeghee*

white λευκός, άσπρος *lefkos, aspros*

Who? Ποιός; *Peeos?*

whole (entire) ολόκληρος *olokleeros*

whole (healthy) σώος *so-os*

wholemeal bread ψωμί με ακοσκίνιστο αλεύρι *psomee me akoskeeneesto alevree*

Whose? Τίνος; *Teenos?*

Why? Γιατί; *Gheeatee?*
wide φαρδύς, πλατύς
  fardhees, platees
widower, widow χήρος,
  χήρα *kheeros, kheera*
wife γυναίκα *gheeneka*
wig περούκα *perooka*
win κερδίζω *kerdheezo*
wind αέρας *aeras*
window παράθυρο
  paratheero
window seat θέση κοντά
  στο παράθυρο *thesee
  konda sto paratheero*
windscreen παρμπρίζ
  parbreez
windscreen wiper
  καθαριστήρας του
  παρμπρίζ *kathareesteeras
  too parbreez*
windy ανεμώδης
  anemodhees
wine κρασί *krasee*
wine glass ποτήρι του
  κρασιού *kraseeoo*
winter χειμώνας *kheemonas*
wire σύρμα *seerma*
wish εύχομαι *efkhome*
with με *me*
without χωρίς *khorees*
witness μάρτυρας
  marteeras
wolf λύκος *leekos*
woman γυναίκα *gheeneka*
wood ξύλο *kseelo*
wool μαλλί *malee*
word λέξη *leksee*
work δουλεύω *dhoolevo*
world κόσμος *kosmos*
worried ανήσυχος
  aneeseekhos
worse χειρότερος
  kheeroteros
worth αξίας *akseeas*

wrap up κλείνω, ολοκηρώνω
  kleeno, olokleerono
wrapping paper χαρτί
  τυλίγματος *khartee
  teeleeghmatos*
wrinkles ρυτίδες *reeteedhes*
wrist καρπός του χεριού
  karpos too khereeo
write γράφω *ghrafo*
writing paper χαρτί
  αλληλογραφίας *khartee
  aleeloghrafeeas*

X
X-ray ακτίνες Χ,
  ακτινογραφία *akteenes
  Khee, akteenoghrafeea*

Y
yacht γιωτ, κότερο
  yheeot, kotero
year έτος, χρόνος
  etos, khronos
yellow κίτρινος *keetreenos*
yellow pages Χρυσός Οδηγός *Khreesos Odheeghos*
yes ναι *ne*
yesterday χθες *khthes*
yolk κρόκος *krokos*
you εσύ *esee*
young νέος *neos*
your δικό σου *dheeko soo*
youth hostel ξενώνας
  νεότητας *ksenonas
  neoteetas*

Z
zero μηδέν *meedhen*
zipper, zip fastener
  φερμουάρ *fermooar*
zone ζώνη *zonee*
zoo ζώο *zo-o*

A

άβολος **avolos**
uncomfortable

άγαλμα **aghalma** statue

αγαπάω **aghapao** love (vb)

αγάπη **aghapee** love (n)

αγαπητός **aghapeetos** dear

Αγγλία **Angleea** England

Αγγλικά **Angleeka** English
(language)

Άγγλος, Αγγλίδα **Anglos,
Angleedha** English,
Englishman/woman

αγγούρι **angooree**
cucumber

αγελάδα **agheladha** cow

αγκάθι **angathee** thorn

αγκυροβόλιο **angee-
rovoleeo** mooring

αγκώνας **angonas** elbow

αγορά **aghora** market

αγοράζω **aghorazo** buy

αγόρι **aghoree** boy

αγριόβουρτσα **aghreeo-
voortsa** scrubbing brush

αγριόχοιρος **aghree-
okheeros** boar

αγροικία **aghreekeea**
farmhouse

αγρός **aghros** field

αγρότης **aghrotees** farmer

αγώνας **aghonas** match
(sport)

αγώνας ποδοσφαίρου
aghonas podhosferoo
football match

άδεια **adheea** licence,
permit (n)

άδεια αλιείας **adheea
alee-eeas** fishing permit

άδεια κυνηγού **adheea
keeneeghoo** hunting
permit

άδεια μπαταρία **adheea
batareea** flat battery

άδεια οδήγησης **adheea
odheegheesees** driving
licence

άδειος **adheeos** empty

αδελφή **adhelfee** sister

αδελφός **adhelfos** brother

αδιάβροχο **adheeavrokho**
raincoat

αδύνατο **adheenato**
impossible

αδύνατος **adheenatos**
weak

αέρας **aeras** air, wind

αέριο **aereeo** gas

αεροδρόμιο **aerodhromeeo**
airport

αερολιμένας **aerolee-
menas** terminal (airport)

αερολισθήρας **aerolis-
theeras** hovercraft

αεροπλάνο **aeroplano**
plane, aeroplane

αεροπορικό εισιτήριο **aeroporeeko eeseeteereeo**
air ticket

αεροπορικώς **aeroporee-
kos** airmail

αετός **aetos** eagle

αθέλητος **atheleetos**
unconscious

αίθουσα **ethoosa** hall

αίθουσα αναμονής **ethoosa
anamonees** waiting room

αίθουσα για πατινάζ
**ethoosa gheea
pateenaz** ice rink

αίμα **ema** blood

αισθάνομαι **esthanome** feel

αισιόδοξα **eseeodhoksa**
hopefully

αιώνας **eonas** century

ακολουθώ **akolootho** follow

ακόμη **akomee** still (yet)

ακόμη και **akomee ke**
even (adv)

ακουστικά **akoosteeka**
earphones, headphones

ακουστικό βαρυκοΐας
**akoosteeko varee-
koeeas** hearing aid

ακούω **akoo-o** hear, listen

άκρη **akree** edge, tip

GREEK → ENGLISH

ακριβής *akreevees*
  accurate
ακριβός *akreevos*
  expensive, up-market
ακριβώς *akreevos* exactly
ακροατήριο *akroateereeo*
  audience
ακρωτήρι *akroteeree*
  peninsula
ακτή *aktee* coast, shore
ακτίνες Χ *akteenes Khee*
  X-ray
ακτινογραφία *akteeno-
  ghrafeea* X-ray
ακτοφύλακας *aktofeelakas*
  coastguard
ακυρώνω *akeerono* cancel
ακύρωση *akeerosee*
  cancellation
αλάτι *alatee* salt
αλεπού *alepoo* fox
αλεύρι *alevree* flour
αληθινός *aleetheenos* real,
  true
αλλά *ala* but
αλλάζω *alazo* change
  (clothes)
αλλεργική καταρροή
  alergheekee kataroee
  hay fever
αλλοιώς *aleeos* otherwise
άλλος *allos* another, other
άλμα με σκι *alma me skee*
  ski jump
άλογο *alogho* horse
αλοιφή *aleefee* ointment
αμαξάκι *amaksakee* buggy
αμβλύς *amvlees* blunt
άμεσος *amesos* direct (adj)
αμέσως *amesos*
  immediately
άμμος *amos* sand
αμόλυβδη βενζίνη *amol-
  eevdhee venzeenee*
  unleaded petrol
αμόλυβδος *amoleevdhos*
  lead-free
αμορτισέρ *amorteeser*
  shock absorber
αμπέλι *ambelee* vineyard

αμπραγιάζ *abragheeaz*
  clutch (car)
άμπωτη *ambotee* low tide
αμυγδαλίτιδα *ameeghdha-
  leeteedha* tonsillitis
αμύγδαλο *ameeghdhalo*
  almond
αν και *an ke* although
ανά *ana* per
αναβάλλω *anavalo*
  postpone
ανάβω *anavo* switch on
αναγκαίος *anangeos*
  necessary
ανάγκη *anangee*
  emergency
αναγνωρίζω *anaghno-
  reezo* recognize
αναζήτηση αποσκευών
  *anazeeteesee apos-
  kevon* baggage reclaim
αναισθητικό *anesthee-
  teeko* anaesthetic
αναίσθητος *anestheetos*
  unconscious
ανακαλύπτω *anakaleepto*
  discover
ανακατεύω *anakatevo*
  mix up
αναμένος *anamenos*
  switched on
ανάμεσα *anamesa* among
ανανάς *ananas* pineapple
ανάγκη *anangee* need (n)
αναπαύομαι *anapavome*
  rest (relax)
αναπηρική πολυθρόνα *ana-
  peereekee poleethrona*
  wheelchair
ανάπηρος *anapeeros*
  disabled, handicapped
αναπνευστικός σωλήνας
  *anapnefsteekos
  soleenas* snorkel
αναπνέω *anapneo* breathe
ανάποδος *anapodhos*
  upside down
αναπτήρας *anapteeras*
  cigarette lighter

GREEK → ENGLISH

αναπτύσσω *anapteeso* develop

αναστολή *anastolee* suspension

ανατολή *anatolee* east

ανατολή του ηλίου *anatolee too eeleeoo* sunrise

αναφέρω *anafero* mention, report (vb)

ανάφλεξη *anafleksee* inflammation

αναφορά *anafora* report (n)

αναχώρηση *anakhoreesee* departure

αναχωρώ *anakhoro* depart

αναψυκτικό *anapseekteeko* soft drink

άνδρας *andhras* husband, man

άνδρες *andhres* men

ανδρικός ρουχισμός *andhreekos rookheesmos* menswear

ανεβαίνω *aneveno* get on

ανεμοβλογιά *anemovlogheea* chicken pox

ανεμοπορία *anemoporeea* hang-gliding

ανεμώδης *anemodhees* windy

ανεξάρτητος *aneksarteetos* self-catering

ανεπίσημος *anepeeseemos* informal

άνεργος *anerghos* unemployed

άνετος *anetos* comfortable

ανέχομαι *anekhome* put up with, tolerate

ανήσυχος *aneeseekhos* worried

ανηψιά *aneepseea* niece

ανηψιός *aneepseeos* nephew

ανθοπώλης *anthopolees* florist

ανθρακούχο *anthrakookho* fizzy

άνθρωποι *anthropee* folk, people

άνθρωπος *anthropos* person

ανόητος *anoeetos* silly

άνοιξη *aneeksee* spring (season)

ανοιχτήρι *aneekhteeree* can opener, tin opener, bottle opener

ανοιχτό *aneekhtho* light (colour)

ανοιχτό εισιτήριο *aneekhtho eeseeteereeo* open ticket

ανοιχτός *aneekhtos* open

ανταλλακτικό *adalakteeko* spare part

αντί γι αυτό *andee ghee afto* instead

αντίγραφο *andeeghrafo* copy

αντιηλιακό *andee-eeleeako* sunblock

αντίθετος *andeethetos* opposite, reverse (n)

αντιλαμβάνομαι *andeelamvanome* realize

αντίο *andeeo* goodbye

αντιοξύ *andeeoksee* antacid

αντιπρόσωπος πωλήσεων *andeeprosopos poleeseon* sales representative

αντιστρέφω *andeestrefo* reverse (vb), turn around

αντίστροφος *andeestrofos* reverse (n)

αντισυλληπτικό *andeeseeleepteeko* contraceptive

αντίχειρας *andeekheeras* thumb

αντλία *andleea* pump (n)

ανυψώνω *aneepsono* lift (vb)

αξία *akseea* value

αξίας *akseeas* worth

απαγορευμένος **apaghorevmenos** forbidden, prohibited

απαίσιο **apeseeo** awful

απάντηση **apandeesee** answer, reply (n)

απαντώ **apando** reply (vb)

απαραίτητος **apareteetos** essential

απασχολημένος **apaskholeemenos** busy

απεργία **aperghea** strike (n)

απεριόριστος **apereeoreestos** unlimited

απίστευτο **apeestefto** incredible

απλός **aplos** simple

από **apo** by, from

από δεύτερο χέρι **apo dheftero kheree** second-hand

από 'δω **apo'dho** this way

από κάτω **apo kato** below, at the bottom

αποβάθρα **apovathra** platform

αποβραδίς **apovradhees** overnight

απόγευμα **apoghevma** afternoon

απογοητευμένος **apoghoeetevmenos** disappointed

απόδειξη **apodheeksee** receipt

αποθηκεύω **apotheekevo** store (vb)

αποθήκη **apotheekee** barn, store (n), warehouse

αποκάλυψη **apokaleepsee** exposure

αποκλείω **apokleeo** exclude

αποκτώ **apokto** obtain

απολαμβάνω **apolamvano** enjoy

απολεσθείς **apolesthees** missing

απολεσθέντα αντικείμενα **apolesthenda andeekeemena** lost property

απολυμαντικός **apoleemandeekos** disinfectant

απόλυτα **apoleeta** absolutely

απομένω **apomeno** remain

απομίμηση **apomeemeesee** fake (adj)

απομονωμένος **apomonomenos** secluded

απορρίμματα **aporeemata** refuse (n), waste

απορρυπαντικό **aporeepandeeko** detergent, soap powder, washing powder

αποσκευές **aposkeves** baggage, luggage

αποσπώ **apospo** rip-off

απόσταση **apostasee** distance

απόστημα **aposteema** abscess

αποσυνδεμένος **aposendhemenos** disconnected

αποταμιεύω **apotameeevo** save (money)

αποτροπιαστικός **apotropeeasteekos** revolting

απόφαση **apofasee** decision

αποφασίζω **apofaseezo** decide

αποφέρω **apofero** bring in

αποφεύγω **apofevgho** avoid

αποχωρητήριο **apokhoreeteereeo** lavatory

απόψε **apopse** tonight

αρακάς **arakas** green pea

αράχνη **arakhnee** spider

αργά **argha** late, slowly

αργός **arghos** slow

αργυρός **argheeros** silver

αργώτερα **arghotera** later

αριθμός **areethmos** number

GREEK → ENGLISH

αριθμός μητρώου **areethmos meetro-oo** registration number

αριθμός τηλεφώνου **areethmos teelefonoo** phone number

αριστερά, στα αριστερά **areestera, sta areestera** left, to the left

αριστερόχειρας **areesterokheeras** left-handed

αρκετά **arketa** quite

αρκετοί **arketee** several

αρκετός **arketos** enough

αρνητικό **arneeteeko** negative (photo)

αρνί **arnee** lamb

αρνίσιο κρέας **arneeseeo kreas** mutton

αρνούμαι **arnoome** refuse (vb)

αρουραίος **arooreos** rat

αρραβωνιασμένος **aravoneeasmenos** engaged (to be married)

αρραβωνιαστικιά **aravoneeasteekeea** fiancée

αρραβωνιαστικός **aravoneeasteekos** fiancé

αρρώστεια **arosteea** disease, illness

άρρωστος, θα κάνω εμετό! **arostos, tha kano emeto!** sick, I'm going to be sick!

αρσενικός **arseneekos** male

άρτιος **arteeos** even (number)

αρτύμια της σαλάτας **arteemeea tees salatas** salad dressing

αρχαίο **arkheo** ancient

αρχάριος **arkhareeos** beginner

αρχείο **arkheeo** record (legal)

αρχή **arkhee** start

αρχιμάγειρας **arkheemagheeras** chef

άρωμα **aroma** perfume

ασανσέρ **asanser** lift (n), elevator

ασανσέρ αναπηρικής πολυθρώνας **asanser anapeereekees poleethronas** chair lift

ασετόν **aseton** nail polish remover

ασήμι **aseemee** silver

ασημόχαρτο **aseemokharto** tinfoil

ασθένεια **astheneea** illness

ασθενείς **asthenees** ill, patient (n)

ασθενοφόρο **asthenoforo** ambulance

άσπρος **aspros** white

αστακός **astakos** lobster

αστείο **asteeo** funny, joke

αστέρι **asteree** star

αστράγαλος **astraghalos** ankle

αστραπή **astrapee** flash of lightning

αστυνομία **asteenomeea** police

αστυνομικό τμήμα **asteenomeeko tmeema** police station

αστυνομικός **asteenomeekos** policeman/woman

ασυνήθης **aseeneethees** unusual

ασφάλεια **asfaleea** insurance

ασφάλεια **asfaleea** fuse

ασφάλεια αυτοκινήτων **asfaleea aftokeeneeton** car insurance

ασφάλεια για χρήση από τρίτους **asfaleea gheea khreesee apo treetoos** third-party insurance

ασφάλεια ζωής **asfaleea zoees** life insurance

ασφαλής **asfalees** safe
(adj, cautious)
ασφαλώς **asfalos**
certainly
άσχημος **askheemos**
bad, ugly
ατμός **atmos** steam
ατομικό φακελάκι με τσάι
**atomeeko fakelakee
me tsaee** tea bag
ατύχημα **ateekheema**
accident
αυγά σφουγγάτο **avgha
sfoongato** scrambled
eggs
αυγή **avghee** dawn
αυγό **avgho** egg
αϋπνία **aeepneea**
insomnia
αύριο **avreeo** tomorrow
αύριο το πρωί/απόγευμα/
βράδυ **avreeo to proee/
apoghevma/vradhee**
tomorrow morning/
afternoon/evening
αυτά **afta** those
αυτή **aftee** her, she
αυτή την εβδομάδα **aftee
teen evdhomadha**
this week
αυτί **aftee** ear
αυτό **afto** it (direct object),
that
αυτοαπασχολούμενος
aftoapaskholoomenos
self-employed
αυτοεξυπηρέτηση
aftoekseepeereteesee
self-service
αυτοί **aftee** they
αυτοκίνητο **aftokeeneeto**
car
αυτοκινητόδρομος
aftokeeneetodhromos
motorway
αυτοκόλλητη ταινία
aftokoleetee teneea
adhesive tape

αυτόματος διανομέας
χρημάτων **aftomatos
dheanomeas khree-
maton** cash dispenser
αυτόματος πωλητής
aftomatos poleetees
vending machine
αυτός **aftos** he, him
αυτουνού **aftoonoo** his
αφαιρώ **afero** deduct,
subtract
αφήνω **afeeno** leave
άφιξη **afeeksee** arrival
αφίσα **afeesa** poster
αφορολόγητος **aforo-
logheetos** duty-free
αφροδίσιο νόσημα **afro-
dheeseeo noseema**
venereal disease
αφρώδης **afrodhees**
sparkling
αχλάδι **akhladhee** pear
αχρωματοψία **akhroma-
topseea** colour blind
αχτίνα τροχού **akhteena
trokhoo** spoke (of wheel)
άχυρο **akheero** straw (hay)

Β

βαγιόφυλο **vagheeofeelo**
bay leaf
βαγόνι **vaghonee**
compartment
βαγόνι του μπουφέ
vaghonee too boofe
buffet car
βάζο **vazo** jar
βάζω **vazo** put
βαθμός **vathmos** degree
(measurement)
βαθύς **vathees** deep
βαλανιδιά **valaneedheea**
oak
βαλβίδα **valveedha** valve
βαλίτσα **valeetsa** suitcase
Βαλτική Θάλασσα **Valtee-
kee Thalassa** Baltic Sea
βάλτος **valtos** marsh

GREEK → ENGLISH

GREEK → ENGLISH

βαμβακερή κλωστή **vamvakeree klostee** cotton
βαμβάκι **vamvakee** cotton wool
βαρέλι **varelee** barrel
βάρος **varos** weight
βαρύς **varees** heavy
βασικός **vaseekos** staple (adj)
βασιλιάς **vaseeleeas** king
βασιλικός **vaseeleekos** royal
βασίλισσα **vaseeleesa** queen
βαστώ **vasto** carry
βατραχοπέδιλα **vatrakhopedheela** flippers
βάτραχος **vatrakhos** frog, toad
βαφή **vafee** dye (n)
βαφτιστικό όνομα **vafteesteeko onoma** Christian name
βάφω **vafo** paint, dye (vb)
βέβαιος **veveos** certain
Βέλγιο **Velgheeo** Belgium
Βέλγος **Velghos** Belgian
βελόνα **velona** needle
βελόνα πλεξίματος **velona plekseematos** knitting needle
βελτιώνω **velteeono** improve
βενζινάδικο **venzeenadheeko** garage, petrol station
βενζινάκατος **venzeenakatos** motorboat
βενζίνη **venzeenee** petrol
βέρα **vera** wedding ring
βέργα **vergha** stick (n)
βερνίκι **verneekee** polish (n)
βερνίκι νυχιών **verneekee neekheeon** nail polish/ nail varnish
βήχας **veekhas** cough (n)
βήχω **veekho** cough (vb)
βιάζομαι **veeazome** hurry (vb)

βιάζω **veeazo** rape (vb)
βιασμός **veeasmos** rape (n)
βιβλίο **veevleeo** book
βιβλίο διαλόγων **veevleeo dheealoghon** phrase book
βιβλίο επιταγών **veevleeo epeetaghon** cheque book
βιβλιοθήκη **veevleeotheekee** library
βιβλιοπωλείο **veevleeopoleeo** bookshop
βίδα **vheedha** screw
Βιέννη **Vee-enee** Vienna
βίζα **veeza** visa
βιολετί **veeoletee** violet
βιτρίνα **veetreena** shop window
βλάβη **vlavee** fault
βλάβη αυτοκινήτου **vlavee aftokeeneetoo** breakdown (of car)
βλάκας **vlakas** stupid
βλέπω **vlepo** see
βοδινό **vodheeno** beef
βοήθεια **voeetheea** help
Βοήθεια! **Voeetheea!** Help!
βολβός **volvos** bulb (plant)
βολικός **voleekos** convenient
βολτάζ **voltaz** voltage
Βόρεια Θάλασσα **Voreea Thalassa** North Sea
Βόρεια Ιρλανδία **Voreea Eerlandheea** Northern Ireland
βορράς **voras** north
βότανα **votana** herbs
βουνό **voono** mountain
βούρτσα **voortsa** brush, hairbrush
βούρτσα νυχιών **voortsa neekheeon** nail brush
βούτυρο **vooteero** butter
βραβείο **vraveeo** prize
βράδυ **vradhee** evening

βράδυ, χθες βράδυ *vradhee,*
   khthes vradhee night,
   last night
βράζω *vrazo* boil (vb)
βραχιόλι *vrakheeolee*
   bracelet
βρεφικός σταθμός *vrefee-*
   kos stathmos crèche
βρίζω *vreezo* swear, curse
βρισιά *vreeseea* swear
   word
βρίσκω *vreesko* find
βρογχίτιδα *vronkhee-*
   teedha bronchitis
βροντή *vrondee* thunder
βροχή *vrokhee* rain
Βρυξέλλες *Vreekseles*
   Brussels
βρύση *vreesee* fountain
βρώμη *vromee* oats
βρώμικος *vromeekos* dirty
   (adj), filthy
βυσσινίς *veeseenees*
   purple

Γ
γάλα *ghala* milk
γάλα σε μορφή σκόνης
   ghala se morfee
   skonees powdered milk
γαλάζιο *ghalazeeo* blue
Γαλλία *Ghaleea* France
γαλλικό κλειδί *ghaleeko*
   kleedhee spanner
Γάλλος, Γαλλίδα *Ghalos,*
   Ghaleedha French,
   Frenchman/woman
γαλόνι *ghalonee* gallon
γαλοπούλα *ghalopoola*
   turkey
γαμήλιο δώρο *ghameeleeo*
   dhoro wedding present
γάμος *ghamos* wedding
γαμπρός *ghambros*
   bridegroom, brother-in-law,
   son-in-law
γάντια *ghandeea* gloves
γαρίδα *ghareedha* prawn,
   shrimp

γάτα *ghata* cat
γαύγισμα *ghavgheesma*
   bark (n, of dog)
γείτονας *gheetonas*
   neighbour
γελάω *ghelao* laugh (vb)
γέλιο *gheleeo* laugh (n)
γελοίος *gheleeos* ridiculous
γεμάτος *ghematos* full,
   crowded
γεμίζω *ghemeezo* fill, fill up
γέμιση *ghemeesee* filling
   (sandwich)
γεμιστός *ghemeestos*
   stuffed
Γενεύη *Ghenevee* Geneva
γένια *gheneea* beard
γενικός *gheneekos* general
γενικός διακόπτης *ghenee-*
   kos dheeakoptees
   mains switch
γέννα *ghena* litter (n,
   puppies)
γενναιόδωρος *ghene-*
   odhoros generous
γεννέθλια *ghenethleea*
   birthday
γεννημένος *gheneemenos*
   born
γέννηση *gheneesee* birth
γεννήτρια *gheneetreea*
   dynamo
γένος *ghenos* race (people)
Γερμανία *Ghermaneea*
   Germany
Γερμανίδα *Ghermaneedha*
   German (f)
Γερμανός *Ghermanos*
   German (m)
γεύμα *ghevma* meal
γεύση *ghefsee* flavour,
   taste (n)
γεφύρι *ghefeeree* bridge
γη *ghee* earth, land
γήπεδο γκολφ *gheepedho*
   golf golf course
γήπεδο του τένις
   gheepedho too tenees
   tennis court

για *gheea* for
για παράδειγμα *gheea paradheeghma* for example
γιαγιά *gheeagheea* grandmother
Γιατί; *Gheeatee?* Why?
γιατρός *gheeatros* doctor
γιαχνί *gheeakhnee* stew (with tomato)
γιλέκο *gheeleko* waistcoat
γιός *gheeos* son
γιώτ *yheeot* yacht
γκάζι *gazee* accelerator
γκαζόν *gazon* grass
γκαλερί *galeree* gallery
γκαράζ *garaz* garage
γκαρνταρόμπα *gardaromba* wardrobe
γκέι *ge-ee* gay
γκέι μπαρ *ge-ee bar* gay bar
γκρεμός *gremos* cliff
γκρίζος *greezos* grey
γλάρος *ghlaros* seagull
γλειφιτζούρι *ghleefeetzooree* lollipop
γλιστερός *ghleesteros* slippery
γλιστρώ *ghleestro* slide (vb)
γλυκά *ghleeka* candy
γλυκό *ghleeko* pastry
γλυκολέμονο *ghleekolemono* lime
γλυκός *ghleekos* sweet
γλώσσα *ghlosa* language, tongue, sole (fish)
γνήσιο *ghneeseeo* genuine
γνωρίζω *ghnoreezo* know
γόνατο *ghonato* knee
γονείς *ghonees* parents
Γοτθικός *Ghottheekos* Gothic
γούνα *ghoona* fur
γούνινο παλτό *ghooneeno palto* fur coat
γουρούνι *ghooroonee* pig
γοφός *ghofos* hip
γραβάτα *ghravata* tie

γράμμα *ghrama* letter
γραμμάριο *ghramareeo* gram
γραμματέας *ghramateas* secretary
γραμματική *ghramateekee* grammar
γραμματοκιβώτιο *ghramatokeevoteeo* letterbox
γραμματόσημο *ghramatoseemo* postage stamp
γραμμή *ghramee* line
γρασίδι *ghraseedhee* grass
γρατσουνίζω *ghratsooneezo* scratch (vb)
γρατσούνισμα *ghratsooneesma* scratch (n)
γραφείο *ghrafeeo* desk, office
γραφείο έκδοσης εισιτηρίων *ghrafeeo ekdhosees eeseeteereeon* ticket office
γραφείο συναλλάγματος *ghrafeeo seenalaghmatos* bureau de change
γραφική ύλη *ghrafeekee eelee* stationery
γράφω *ghrafo* write
γρήγορα *ghreeghora* quickly
γρήγορος *ghreeghoros* fast
γρίπη *ghreepee* flu
γρύλος *ghreelos* jack (car)
γυαλιά *gheealeea* glasses, spectacles, goggles
γυαλιά ηλίου *gheealeea eeleeoo* sunglasses
γυαλίζω *gheealeezo* polish (vb)
γυμνάζομαι *gheemnazome* practise
γυμναστήριο *gheemnasteereeo* gym
γυμνόστηθη *gheemnosteethee* topless
γυναίκα *gheeneka* wife, woman

γυνεκεία εσώρουχα **gheenekeea esorookha** lingerie

γυνεκείες τουαλέτες **gheenekee-es tooaletes** ladies' toilet

γυνεκείος ρουχισμός **gheenekee-os rookheesmos** ladies' wear

γύρω **gheero** round

γωνία **ghoneea** corner

Δ

δαγκώνω **dhangono** bite (vb)

δάδα **dhadha** torch

δάκρυ **dhakree** tear (n)

δαμάσκηνο **dhamaskeeno** plum

Δανία **Dhaneea** Denmark

δανίζομαι **dhaneezome** borrow

δανίζω **dhaneezo** borrow

δανίζω, δανίζομαι **dhaneezo, dhaneezome** lend

δαντέλα **dhantela** lace

δάσκαλος **dhaskalos** teacher

δάσος **dhasos** forest

δαχτυλίδι **dhakhteeleedhee** ring (n, on finger)

δάχτυλο **dhakhteelo** finger

δάχτυλο ποδιού **dhakhteelo podheeoo** toe

δείκτης **dheektees** indicator

δείκτης πετρελαίου **dheektees petreleoo** fuel gauge

δείπνο **dheepno** dinner, supper

δείχνω **dheekhno** point (vb), show

δεκανίκια **dhekaneekeea** crutches

δεκαπενθήμερο **dhekapentheemero** fortnight

Δεκέμβριος **Dhekemvrios** December

δέκτης **dheektees** receiver (telephone)

δελτίο επιβίβασης **dhelteeo epeeveevasees** boarding card

δελτίο καιρού **dhelteeo keroo** weather forecast

δέμα **dhema** packet, parcel

δεν θα μπορούσα **dhen tha mboroosa** couldn't

δεν μπορώ **dhen boro** can't

δέντρο **dhendro** tree

δένω **dheno** tie

δεξαμενή **dheksamenee** cistern, tank

δέρμα **dherma** leather, skin

Δεσποινίδα **Dhespeeneedha** Miss, Ms

Δευτέρα **Dheftera** Monday

δεύτερης κατηγορίας **dhefterees kateeghoreeas** second-class

δευτερόλεπτο **dhefterolepto** second (time)

δεύτερος **dhefteros** second (order)

δέχομαι **dhekhome** accept

δηλητήριο **dheeleeteereeo** poison

δηλητηριώδης **dheeleeteereeodhees** poisonous

δηλώνω **dheelono** register (vb)

δημαρχείο **dheemarkheeo** town hall

Δημοκρατία της Σλοβακίας **Dheemokrateea tees Slovakeeas** Slovak Republic

Δημοκρατία της Τσεχίας **Dheemokrateea tees Tsekheeas** Czech Republic

δημόσιος **dheemoseeos** public

δημοφιλής **dheemofeelees** popular (famous)

δια μέσου **dheea mesoo** through

GREEK → ENGLISH

διαβάζω *dheeav<u>a</u>zo*
read

διάβαση *dhee<u>a</u>vasee*
crossing

διάβαση πεζών
dhee<u>a</u>vasee pez<u>o</u>n
pedestrian crossing

διαβατήριο *dheeavat<u>ee</u>-
reeo* passport

διαβητικός *dheeaveetee-
k<u>o</u>s* diabetic (adj)

διαδρομή *dheeadhrom<u>ee</u>*
course

διάδρομος *dhee<u>a</u>dhromos*
aisle, corridor

διαθέσιμο *dheeath<u>e</u>seemo*
available

διαθέσιμο δωμάτιο/
διαμέρισμα *dheeath<u>e</u>seemo
dhom<u>a</u>teeo/dheea-
m<u>e</u>reesma* vacancy

διαθέτω χρόνο *dheeath<u>e</u>to
khr<u>o</u>no* spend time

δίαιτα *dh<u>ee</u>-eta* diet

διακοπές *dheeakop<u>e</u>s*
holidays, vacation

διακοπή ρεύματος
dheeakop<u>ee</u> r<u>e</u>vmatos
power cut

διακόπτης *dheeak<u>o</u>ptees*
switch

διαλέγω *dheal<u>e</u>gho*
choose

διάλειμμα *dhee<u>a</u>leema*
interval

διαλυτός *dheealeet<u>o</u>s*
soluble

διαμάντι *dheeam<u>a</u>ndee*
diamond

Διαμαρτυρόμενος
Dheeamarteer<u>o</u>menos
Protestant

διαμέρισμα *dheeamer-
<u>ee</u>sma* apartment

διαμονή *dheeamon<u>ee</u>*
accommodation

διαμονή και πρωινό *dheea-
mon<u>ee</u> ke proeen<u>o</u>*
bed & breakfast

διαρκές εισιτήριο *dhee-
ark<u>e</u>s eeseet<u>ee</u>reeo*
season ticket

διαρρέω *dheear<u>e</u>o* leak (vb)

διάρρηξη *dheear<u>ee</u>ksee*
break-in, burglary

διαρροή *dheear<u>o</u>ee* leak (n)

διάρροια *dhee<u>a</u>reea*
diarrhoea, travel sickness

διάσειση *dhee<u>a</u>seesee*
concussion

διάσημος *dhee<u>a</u>seemos*
famous

διασκέδαση *dheeask<u>e</u>d-
hasee* fun (to have)

διάσκεψη *dhee<u>a</u>skepsee*
conference

διασταύρωση *dheea-
st<u>a</u>vrosee* crossroads,
intersection

διασώζω *dheeas<u>o</u>zo*
rescue (vb)

διάσωση *dhee<u>a</u>sosee*
rescue (n)

διάσωση ορειβατών
dhee<u>a</u>sosee oreevat<u>o</u>n
mountain rescue

διαφεύγω *dheeaf<u>e</u>vgho*
escape (vb)

διαφήμηση *dheeaf<u>ee</u>-
meesee* advertisement

διαφορά *dheeafor<u>a</u>*
difference

διαφορετικός *dheeafore-
teek<u>o</u>s* different

διδάσκω *dheedh<u>a</u>sko*
teach

δίδυμα *dh<u>ee</u>dheema* twins

διεθνές *dhee-ethn<u>e</u>s*
international

διερμηνέας *dhee-
ermeen<u>e</u>as* interpreter

διευθύνω *dee-efth<u>ee</u>no*
steer

διευθυντής *dhee-
efth<u>ee</u>ndees* manager

δικά μας *dheek<u>a</u> mas* our

δίκαια *dh<u>ee</u>kea* fairly

150

δικαιολογία *dheekeolo-**gheea*** excuse (n)

δίκαιος *dheekeos* fair, just

δικαστής *dheekastees* judge

δικηγόρος *dheekeeghoros* lawyer

δικό μου *dheeko moo* my

δικό σου *dheeko soo* your

δικό του *dheeko too* his

δίνω *dheeno* give

δίνω πίσω *dheeno peeso* give back

διόδια *dheeodheea* toll, toll road

διολίσθηση *dheeolees-**theesee*** slide (n)

διορθώνω *dheeorthono* fix, mend

δίπλα *dheepla* beside

διπλό δωμάτιο *dheeplo **dhomateeo*** double room

διπλό κρεββάτι *dheeplo **krevatee*** double bed

διπλός *dheeplos* double

δίσκος *dheeskos* disk, record (music), tray

δίχτυ *dheekhtee* net

διψασμένος *dheepsas-**menos*** thirsty

δοκιμάζω *dhokeemazo* try on

δοκιμαστήριο *dhokeemas-**teereeo*** fitting room, changing room

δόλωμα *dholoma* bait

δόντι *dhondee* tooth

δόντια *dhondeea* teeth

δουλειά του σπιτιού *dhooleea too **speeteeoo*** housework

δουλεύω *dhoolevo* work

δοχείο *dhokheeo* bin

δοχείο βενζίνης *dhokheeo **venzeenees*** petrol can

δοχείο ψύξης *dhokheeo **pseeksees*** cool box

δραπετεύω *dhrapetevo* escape (vb)

δρόμος *dhromos* path, road, street

δρόμος μιάς κατευθύνσεως *dhromos meeas katef-**theenseos*** one-way street

δροσερό *dhrosero* cool

δύναμη *dheenamee* might (n)

δυνατός *dheenatos* loud, possible, strong

δύο μονά κρεββάτια *dheeo **mona krevateea*** twin beds

δύο φορές *dheeo fores* twice

δύση *dheesee* west

δύση του ηλίου *dheesee **too eeleeoo*** sunset

δυσκοίλιος *dheeskeeleeos* constipated

δύσκολος *dheeskolos* difficult

δυσπεψία *dheespepseea* indigestion

δυστύχημα *dheestee-**kheema*** crash (n)

δωδεκάδα *dhodhekadha* dozen

δωμάτιο *dhomateeo* room

δωρεάν *dhorean* free (cost)

δώρο *dhoro* gift, present

δώρο γεννεθλίων *dhoro **ghenethleeon*** birthday present

E

εάν *ean* if

εάν όχι *ean okhee* if not

εβδομάδα *evdhomadha* week

εβδομαδιαίος *evdhoma-**dhee-eos*** weekly

Εβραίος, Εβραία *Evreos, Evrea* Jew, Jewish

εγγονή *engonee* granddaughter

εγγονός *engonos* grandson

GREEK → ENGLISH

έγγραφα ταξιδιώτη **engrafa takseedheeotee** travel documents

έγγραφο **engrafo** document (n)

εγγράφω **engrafo** register (vb)

εγγύηση **engee-eesee** guarantee

εγκεφαλική συμφόρηση **engefaleekee seemforeesee** stroke (illness)

έγκλημα **engleema** crime

έγκυος **engeeos** pregnant

έγκυρος **engeeros** valid

εγχείρεση **engkheereesee** operation

εγχειρίδιο **engkheereedheeo** manual

έγχρωμο φιλμ **engkhromo feelm** colour film

εγώ **egho** I, me

έδαφος **edhafos** ground

εδώ **edho** here

εδώ κοντά **edho konda** nearby (adv)

εδώ πέρα **edho pera** over here

έθιμο **etheemo** custom

εθνική οδός **ethneekee odhos** freeway

εθνικό πάρκο **ethneeko parko** nature reserve

εθνικός **ethneekos** national

εθνικότητα **ethneekoteeta** nationality

είδη κιγκαλερίας **eedhee keengalereeas** hardware shop

ειδήσεις **eedheesees** news

ειδικότητα **eedheekoteeta** speciality

είδος **eedhos** kind, sort

εικόνα **eekona** picture

ειλικρινής **eeleekreenees** honest

είμαι **eeme** be, am, I am

είναι **eene** are, is

εισιτήριο **eeseeteereeo** fare, ticket

εισιτήριο μετ' επιστροφής **eeseeteereeo met'epeestrofees** return ticket

είσοδος **eesodhos** entrance, admission fee

είτε ... είτε **eete ... eete** either ... or

εκατοντάβαθμο **ekatondavathmo** Centigrade

εκατοστό **ekatosto** centimetre

εκδρομή **ekdhromee** excursion

εκδρομή με τουριστικό οδηγό **ekdhromee me tooreesteeko odheegho** guided tour

εκδρομικό **ekdhromeeko** backpack

εκεί **ekee** there

εκεί πέρα **ekee pera** over there

έκθεση **ekthesee** exhibition

εκκλησία **ekleeseea** church

εκμίσθωση **ekmeesthosee** lease (n)

εκπίπτω **ekpeepto** deduct (discount)

εκπληκτικός **ekpleekteekos** astonishing

εκπλήρωση **ekpleerosee** performance

έκπτωση **ekptosee** discount

έκρηξη **ekreeksee** explosion

έκταση **ektasee** area

εκτός από **ektos apo** except

εκτός λειτουργίας **ektos leetoorgheeas** out of order

έκτρωση **ektrosee** abortion

εκτυπώνω **ekteepono** print (vb)

ελαιόλαδο **eleoladho** olive oil

152

ελαστικός **elasteekos** elastic

ελάττωμα **elatoma** flaw

ελαφρύ **elafree** light (weight)

Ελβετία **Elveteea** Switzerland

Ελβετογερμανός **Elvetoghermanos** Swiss-German

Ελβετός **Elvetos** Swiss

ελεγκτής **elengtees** ticket collector

έλεγχος διάβασης **elengkhos dheeavasees** pass control

ελέγχω **elengkho** check, inspect

ελεύθερος **eleftheros** free

ελιά **eleea** olive

ελικόπτερο **eleekoptero** helicopter

έλκηθρο **elkeethro** sledge

έλκος **elkos** ulcer

Ελλάδα **Eladha** Greece

Έλληνας **Eleenas** Greek (m)

Ελληνίδα **Eleeneedha** Greek (f)

Ελληνικό **Eleeneeko** Greek (n)

ελπίζω **elpeezo** hope

εμβόλιο **emvoleeo** vaccine

εμείς **emees** us, we

εμένα **emena** me

έμπειρος **embeeros** experienced

έμπλαστρο **emblastro** plaster

εμπορικό κέντρο **emboreeko kendro** shopping centre

εμποροπανήγυρη **emboropaneegheeree** fair, fête

ένα **ena** one

εναντίον **enandeeon** against

έναυσμα **enavsma** ignition

ενδιαφέρον **endheeaferon** interesting

ενήλικας **eneeleekas** adult

ενθύμιο **entheemeeo** souvenir

ένεση **enesee** injection

εννοώ **eno-o** mean (intend)

ενοικιαζόμενα αυτοκίνητα **eneekeeazomena aftokeeneeta** car hire

ενοικιάζω **eneekeeazo** let, hire

ενόχληση **enokhleesee** inconvenience

ενοχλώ **enokhlo** annoy, disturb

εντάξι **endaksee** all right

έντομο **endomo** insect

εντομοαπωθητικό **endomoapotheeteeko** insect repellent

έντυπο **enteepo** form (document)

έντυπο υλικό **endeepo eeleeko** printed matter

έντυπο/φόρμα εγγραφής **endeepo/forma engrafees** registration form

ενώ **eno** while

ενώνω **enono** join

εξ'αιτίας **eks'eteeas** because of

εξ'ολοκλήρου **eks'olokleeroo** completely

εξαγωγή **eksaghoghee** export

εξάδελφος **eksadhelfos** cousin

εξαιρετικός **eksereteekos** extraordinary

εξάνθημα **eksantheema** rash

εξαντλημένος **eksandleemenos** exhausted

εξάρθρωση **eksarthrosee** sprain (n)

εξαρτήματα αυτοκινήτου **eksarteema aftokeeneetoo** car parts

εξασκούμαι **eksaskoome** practise

εξάτμιση **eks_atmeesee**
exhaust pipe

εξαφανίζομαι **eksafa-
neezome** disappear

εξέδρα καταδύσεων
**eks_edhra katadhee-
seon** diving board

εξέταση **eks_etasee**
examination

εξηγώ **eks_eegho** explain

έξοδα **eksodha** expenses

έξοδος **eksodhos** exit

έξοδος ανάγκης **eksodhos
anangees** emergency
exit

έξοδος κινδύνου **eksodhos
keendheenoo** fire exit

εξοπλισμός **eksopleesmos**
equipment

έξυπνος **eks_eepnos** clever

έξω **ekso** out, outside

εξωτερικό **eksotereek_o**
abroad

εξωτερικός **eksotereekos**
foreign (country)

επάγγελμα **epangelma**
job, occupation

επαναλαμβάνω **epana-
lamvano** repeat

επαναφορτώνω **epana-
fortono** recharge

επάνω **epano** on top, up,
upstairs

επαφή **epafee** contact

επείγων **epeeghon**
urgent

επειδή **epeedhee**
because

επέκταση **epektasee**
extension

επεξεργασία φιλμ **epek-
serghas_eea feelm**
film processing

επέτειος **epeteeos**
anniversary

επιβάτης **epeev_atees**
passenger

επιβεβαιώνω **epeeveve-
_ono** confirm

επιβεβαίωση **epeeveveo-
see** confirmation

επιβλαβές **epeevlav_es**
faulty

επίδεσμος **epeedhesmos**
bandage, dressing

επιδόρπιο **epeedh_orpeeo**
dessert

επίθεση **epeethesee**
attack (n)

επικίνδυνος **epeek_een-
dheenos** dangerous

επιληπτικός **epeeleep-
teekos** epileptic

επιληψία **epeeleepseea**
epilepsy

επιμένω **epeemeno** insist

επίπεδο **epeepedho** plane

επίπεδος **epeepedhos**
flat (adj)

έπιπλα **epeepla** furniture

επιπλωμένο **epeeplomeno**
furnished

επίσημη αργία
epeeseemee argheea
public holiday

επίσημος **epeeseemos**
formal

επίσης **epeesees** also, too

επισκέπτης **epeesk_eptees**
visitor

επισκέπτομαι **epee-
skeptome** visit

επισκευάζω **epeeskevazo**
repair (vb)

επισκευή **epeeskev_ee**
repair (n)

επίσκεψη στα αξιοθέατα
**epeeskepsee sta ak-
seeotheata** sightseeing

επιστάτης **epeest_atees**
caretaker

επιστρέφω **epeestrefo**
come back

επιστρέφω χρήματα
epeestrefo khreemata
refund (vb)

επιστροφή **epeestrofee**
return

επιστροφή χρημάτων *epeestrofee khreematon* refund (n)

επιταγή *epeetaghee* cheque

επιτίθεμαι *epeeteetheme* attack, charge (vb)

επιτραπέζιος οίνος *epeetrapezeeos eenos* table wine

επιτρέπω *epeetrepo* allow, let, permit (vb)

επιχείρηση *epeekheereesee* business

επόμενος *epomenos* next

εποχή *epokhee* season

επώνυμο *eponeemo* surname

εργαλεία μαγειρικής *erghaleea magheereekees* cooking utensils

εργαλείο *erghaleeo* tool

εργοστάσιο *erghostaseeo* factory

έρευνα *erevna* investigation

έρημος *ereemos* desert

έρπης ζωστήρας *erpees zosteeras* shingles

ερυθρά *ereethra* German measles

έρχομαι *erkhome* come

ερώτηση *eroteesee* question

Εστονία *Estoneea* Estonia

εσύ *esee* you

εσώρουχα *esorookha* underwear

εσωτερική πισίνα *esotereekee peeseena* indoor pool

εσωτερική φανέλα *esotereekee fanela* vest

εσωτερικό λάστιχο *esotereeko lasteekho* inner tube

ετήσιος *eteeseeos* annual

έτοιμος *eteemos* ready

έτος *etos* year

ευγενικός *evgheneekos* polite

ευγνώμων *evghnomon* grateful

ευθεία *eftheea* straight on

εύθραυστος *efthrafstos* breakable

ευθύς *efthees* straight

εύκολο *efkolo* easy

ευπρόσδεκτος *efprosdhektos* welcome

Ευρωπαϊκή Ένωση *Evropaeekee Enosee* EU

Ευρωπαϊκό Συμβούλιο *Evropaeeko Seemvooleeo* EC

Ευρωπαίος *Evropeos* European

Ευρώπη *Evropee* Europe

ευτυχώς *efteekhos* fortunately

ευφραδής *effradhees* fluent

ευφυής *efee-ees* intelligent

ευχαριστημένος *efkhareesteemenos* pleased

ευχαριστώ *efkhareesto* thank

εύχομαι *efkhome* wish

εφημερίδα *efeemereedha* newspaper

εφημεριδοπώλης *efeemereedhopolees* news stand

εχτές βράδυ *ekhtes vradhee* last night

έχω *ekho* have

έως ότου *eos otoo* till, until

Z

ζακέτα *zaketa* jacket, cardigan

ζαλισμένος *zaleesmenos* dizzy

ζαμπόν *zambon* ham

ζάρι *zaree* die (n)

ζάρια *zareea* dice

ζάχαρη *zakharee* sugar

ζαχαροπλαστείο **zakharoplasteeo**
bakery, cake shop

ζελές **zeles** jelly

ζέστη **zestee** heat

ζεστός **zestos** warm

ζευγάρι **zevgharee** couple, pair

ζηλιάρης **zeleearees** jealous

ζημιά **zeemeea** damage

ζήτηση πληροφοριών **zeeteesee pleeroforeon** enquiry

ζητώ **zeeto** ask

ζυγίζω **zeegheezo** weigh

ζυθοποιείο **zeethopee-eeo** brewery

ζω **zo** live

ζωγραφιά **zoghrafeea** drawing

ζωγραφική **zoghrafeekee** painting

ζωή **zoee** life

ζωμός **zomos** stock (soup)

ζώνη **zonee** belt, zone

ζώνη ασφαλείας **zonee asfaleeas** safety belt

ζώνη καθίσματος **zonee katheesmatos** seatbelt

ζωντανός **zondanos** lively

ζώο **zo-o** animal, zoo

Η

ή **ee** or

η πίεση στα λάστιχα **ee pee-esee sta lasteekha** tyre pressure

ήδη **eedhee** already

ηλεκτρική σκούπα **eelektreekee skoopa** vacuum cleaner

ηλεκτρική σύνδεση **eelektreekee seendhesee** connection (elec)

ηλεκτρικός **eelektreekos** electric

ηλεκτρικός βηματοδότης **eelektreekos veematodhotees** pacemaker

ηλεκτρικός φακός **eelektreekos fakos** flashlight

ηλεκτρισμός **eelektreesmos** electricity

ηλεκτρολόγος **eelektrologhos** electrician

ηλίαση **eeleeasee** sunstroke

ηλικία **eeleekeea** age

ηλικιωμένος **eeleekeeomenos** old (person)

ηλιοθεραπία **eeleeotherapeea** suntan

ηλιόλουστος **eeleeoloostos** sunny

ήλιος **eeleeos** sun

ημέρα **eemera** day

ημερολόγιο **eemerologheeo** diary

ημερομηνία **eemeromeeneea** date (of year)

ημερομηνία γεννήσεως **eemeromeeneea gheneeseos** date of birth

ημερομηνία λήξης **eemeromeeneea leeksees** sell-by date

ημικρανία **eemeekraneea** migraine

Ηνωμένες Πολιτείες **Eenomenes Poleetee-es** United States

Ηνωμένο Βασίλειο **Eenomeno Vaseeleeo** United Kingdom

ηρεμιστικό φάρμακο **eeremeesteeko farmako** tranquillizer

ήρεμος **eeremos** calm

ήσυχος **eeseekhos** quiet, still

ήταν **eetan** were

ηφαίστειο **eefesteeo** volcano

GREEK → ENGLISH

Θ

θα έπρεπε *tha eprepe* should

Θα μπορούσα; *Tha mboroosa?* Could I?

θάλαμος *thalamos* ward (hospital)

θάλαμος ατυχημάτων *thalamos ateekheematon* casualty department

θάλασσα *thalasa* sea

θαλασσινά *thalaseena* shellfish

θαλάσσιο σκι *thalaseeo skee* water-skiing

θάμνος *thamnos* bush

θάνατος *thanatos* death

θαυμαστής *thavmastees* fan

θέα *thea* view

θέαμα *theama* show (n)

θέατρο *theatro* theatre

θεία *theea* aunt

Θεία Λειτουργία *Theea Leetoorgheea* Mass (rel)

θείος *theeos* uncle

θέλω *thelo* want

Θεός *Theos* God

θέρετρο *theretro* resort

θερμαινόμενος *thermenomenos* heating

θερμάστρα *thermastra* heater

θερμή *thermee* hot spring

θερμοκρασία *thermokraseea* temperature

θερμόμετρο *thermometro* thermometer

θερμοφόρα *thermofora* hot-water bottle

θέση *thesee* post (n, position)

θέση κοντά στο παράθυρο *thesee konda sto paratheero* window seat

θεώρηση (διαβατηρίου) *theoreesee (dheeavateereeoo)* visa

θηλυκός *theeleekos* female

θλιμμένος *thleemenos* sad

θορυβώδης *thoreevodhees* noisy

θραύσμα *thravsma* splinter

θύελλα *thee-ella* storm, thunderstorm

θυμάμαι *theemame* remember

θυμωμένος *theemomenos* angry, cross (adj)

θυρωρός *theeroros* doorman, porter

Ι

ιαματική πηγή *eeamateekee peeghee* hot spring

Ιανουάριος *Eeanooareeos* January

ιατρείο *eeatreeo* surgery (doctor's rooms)

ιατρική *eeatreekee* medicine (science)

ιατρική ασφάλεια *eeatreekee asfaleea* medical insurance

ιδέα *eedhea* idea

ιδιαιτέρως *eedhee-eteros* especially

ιδιοκτήτης *eedheeokteetees* owner

ίδιος *eedheeos* same

ιδιωτικός *eedheeoteekos* private

ιερέας *ee-ereas* priest

ιερός *ee-eros* holy

ικανός *eekanos* fit (healthy)

ίκτερος *Eekteros* jaundice

ιλαράς *eelaras* measles

ιματιοθήκη *eemateeotheekee* locker

Ινδός *Eendhos* Indian

ινσουλίνη *eensooleenee* insulin

ινστιτούτο καλλονής *eensteetooto kallonees* beauty salon

ίντσα *eentsa* inch

ιός *eeos* virus

157

GREEK → ENGLISH

καθαριστήρας του παρμπρίζ
**_kathareesteeras too
parbreez_** windscreen
wiper

καθαριστικό διάλυμα
**_kathareesteeko dhee-
aleema_** cleaning solution

καθαρός **_katharos_**
clean (adj)

καθαρτικό **_katharteeko_**
laxative

κάθε **_kathe_** each, every

κάθε τι **_kathe tee_** everything

καθεδρικός ναός **_kathe-
dhreekos naos_** cathedral

καθένας **_kathenas_** everyone

καθημερινά **_kathee-
mereena_** daily

καθημερινό δωμάτιο
**_katheemereeno
dhomateeo_** living room

καθίζηση **_katheezeesee_**
landslide

κάθισμα **_katheesma_** seat

κάθισμα κοντά στο διάδρομο
**_katheesma konda sto
dheeadhromo_** aisle seat

κάθισμα παιδιού **_kathees-
ma pedheoo_** child car
seat

Καθολικός **_Katholeekos_**
Catholic

καθόλου **_katholoo_** none

κάθομαι **_kathome_** sit

καθορισμένο μενού
kathoreesmeno menoo
set menu

καθρέπτης **_kathreptees_**
mirror

καθρέφτης οδηγήσεως
**_kathreftees odhee-
gheeseos_** rear-view
mirror

καθυστέρηση **_kathees-
tereesee_** delay

καθώς πρέπει **_kathos
prepee_** properly

και **_ke_** and

Ιουδαίος, Ιουδαία
Eeoodheos, Eeoodhea
Jew, Jewish

Ιούλιος **_Eeooleeos_** July

Ιούνιος **_Eeooneeos_** June

ιππασία **_eepaseea_** horse
riding

ιπποδρόμιο **_eepo-
dhromeeo_** race course

ιπτάμενο δελφίνι
eeptameno dhelfeenee
hydrofoil

Ιρλανδία **_Eerlandheea_**
Ireland

Ιρλανδός/Ιρλανδέζα **_Eer-
landhos/Eerlandheza_**
Irish, Irishman/woman

ίσιος **_eeseeos_** straight

ισόγειο **_eesogheeo_** ground
floor

ισόπεδη διάβαση
**_eesopedhee dhee-
avasee_** level crossing

Ισπανία **_Eespaneea_** Spain

Ισπανός **_Eespanos_**
Spaniard, Spanish

ιστιοπλοΐα **_eesteeoploeea_**
sailing

ιστορία **_eestoreea_** history

ιστορικός **_eestoreekos_**
historic

ιστός **_eestos_** web

ίσως **_eesos_** maybe

Ιταλία **_Eetaleea_** Italy

Ιταλικά **_Eetaleeka_** Italian
(language)

Ιταλός/Ιταλίδα **_Eetalos/
Eetaleedha_** Italian

Κ

κάβα **_kava_** cellar

καβαλικεύω **_kavaleekevo_**
ride

καβούρι **_kavooree_** crab

καγκελόπορτα **_kangelo-
porta_** gate

καθαρίζω **_kathareezo_**
clean (vb)

και οι δύο **ke ee dh<u>ee</u>o** both

καιρός **ker<u>os</u>** weather

καίω **k<u>e</u>o** burn

κακάο **kak<u>a</u>o** cocoa

κακοποιημένος **kakopee-eem<u>e</u>nos** mugged

κακός **k<u>a</u>kos** bad, poor (quality)

καλά **kal<u>a</u>** well

καλάθι **kal<u>a</u>thee** basket

κάλαθος αχρήστων **k<u>a</u>lathos akhr<u>ee</u>ston** waste bin

καλαμάκι **kalam<u>a</u>kee** straw (drinking)

καλάμι ψαρέματος **kal<u>a</u>mee psar<u>e</u>matos** fishing rod

καλεσμένος **kalesm<u>e</u>nos** guest

καλή μέρα **kal<u>ee</u> mera** good day, good morning

καλή νύχτα **kal<u>ee</u> n<u>ee</u>khta** good night

καλή τύχη **kal<u>ee</u> t<u>ee</u>khee** good luck

Καλή Χρονιά! **Kal<u>ee</u> Khron<u>ea</u>!** Happy New Year!

καλλιτέχνης **kalee-t<u>e</u>khnees** artist

καλό απόγευμα **kal<u>o</u> ap<u>o</u>-ghevma** good afternoon

καλό βράδυ **kal<u>o</u> vr<u>a</u>dhee** good evening

Καλό Πάσχα! **Kal<u>o</u> P<u>a</u>skha!** Happy Easter!

καλόγερος **kal<u>o</u>gheros** boil (n)

καλόδιο επέκτασης **kal<u>o</u>-dheeo epekt<u>a</u>sees** extension lead

καλοκαίρι **kalok<u>e</u>ree** summer

καλός **kal<u>os</u>** fine (adj), good

κάλτσα **k<u>a</u>ltsa** stocking

κάλτσες **k<u>a</u>ltses** socks

καλτσόν **kalts<u>on</u>** pantyhose, tights

κάλυμμα παπλώματος **k<u>a</u>leema papl<u>o</u>matos** duvet cover

καλύτερος **kal<u>ee</u>teros** better

καλώ **kal<u>o</u>** invite

καλώ τον αριθμό (τηλεφώνου) **kal<u>o</u> ton areethm<u>o</u> (teelef<u>o</u>noo)** dial (vb)

καλώδια μπαταρίας **kal<u>o</u>dheea batar<u>ee</u>as** jump leads

καμαριέρα **kamaree-<u>e</u>ra** chambermaid

καμπάνα **kamb<u>a</u>na** bell

καμπίνα **kamb<u>ee</u>na** cabin

Καναδάς **Kanadh<u>as</u>** Canada

κανάλι **kan<u>a</u>lee** canal, channel

Κανάλι της Αγγλίας **Kan<u>a</u>lee tees Angl<u>ee</u>as** English Channel

καναπές **kanap<u>es</u>** couch

κανάτα **kan<u>a</u>ta** jug

κανείς **kan<u>ee</u>s** nobody

κανένα **kan<u>e</u>na** none

κανό **kan<u>o</u>** canoe

κανονίζω **kanon<u>ee</u>zo** arrange

καντράν **kandr<u>an</u>** dial (n)

κάνω **k<u>a</u>no** do, make

κάνω εμετό **k<u>a</u>no emet<u>o</u>** vomit

κάνω παράκληση **k<u>a</u>no parakl<u>ee</u>see** request (vb)

κάνω τζόγκιν **k<u>a</u>no tz<u>o</u>geen** jog (vb)

καούρα **ka<u>oo</u>ra** heartburn

καπάκι **kap<u>a</u>kee** lid

καπέλο **kap<u>e</u>lo** hat

καπνίζω **kapn<u>ee</u>zo** smoke (vb)

καπνιστός σολομός **kapneest<u>os</u> solom<u>os</u>** smoked salmon

καπνοδόχος **kapno-dh<u>o</u>khos** chimney

καπνός **kapn<u>os</u>** smoke (n)

GREEK → ENGLISH

καπό *kapo* bonnet, hood (car)

κάποιος *kapeeos* someone, somebody

κάποτε *kapote* sometimes

κάπου *kapoo* somewhere

κάπου-κάπου *kapoo-kapoo* occasionally

καραμέλες *karameles* candy

καραντίνα *karandeena* quarantine

καρβέλι *karvelee* loaf

κάρβουνο *karvoono* charcoal, coal

καρδιά *kardheea* heart

καρδιακή προσβολή *kardheeakee prosvolee* heart attack

καρέκλα *karekla* chair

καρκίνος *karkeenos* cancer

καρμπυρατέρ *karbeerater* carburettor

καρότο *karoto* carrot

καρότσα *karotsa* carriage

καροτσάκι *karotsakee* trolley

καροτσάκι αποσκευών *karotsakee aposkevon* luggage trolley

καροτσάκι μωρού *karotsakee moroo* pram

καρπός του χεριού *karpos too khereeo* wrist

καρπούζι *karpoozee* watermelon

καρτ ποστάλ *kart postal* postcard

κάρτα *karta* card

κάρτα γεννεθλίων *karta ghenethleeon* birthday card

κάρτα λογαριασμού επιταγών *karta loghareeasmoo epeetaghon* cheque card

καρύδα *kareedha* coconut

καρύδι *kareedhee* nut, walnut

καρύκευμα *kareekevma* dressing (salad), seasoning

καρφίτσα *karfeetsa* brooch, pin

κασέτα *kaseta* cassette

κασκόλ *kaskol* scarf

κάστανο *kastano* chestnut

καστόρι *kastoree* suede

κάστρο *kastro* castle

κατά *kata* per

κατά τη διάρκεια *kata tee dheearkeea* during

κάταγμα *kataghma* fracture

καταδύομαι *katadheeome* dive

καταθέτω *katatheto* deposit

καταιγίδα *kategheedha* thunderstorm

καταλαβαίνω *katalaveno* understand

κατάλληλο για το φούρνο *kataleelo ghea to foorno* ovenproof

κατάλογος *kataloghos* list, register (n)

καταπίνω *katapeeno* swallow (vb)

καταπληκτικό *katapleekteeko* amazing

καταρρέω *katareo* collapse

κατάρτι *katartee* mast

κατασκηνώνω *kataskeenono* camp (vb)

κατασκήνωση *kataskeenosee* camp site

κατάσταση *katastasee* condition

κατάστημα κατασκευαστικών υλικών *katasteema kataskevasteekon eeleekon* DIY shop

κατάστημα σιδηροπωλείο *katasteema seedheeropoleeo* hardware shop

κατάστημα τροφίμων *katasteema trofeemon* food shop

κατάστημα υγιεινών τροφών **katasteema eghee- eenon trofon** health food shop

καταστροφή **katastrofee** disaster, ruin

κατάψυξη **katapseeksee** freezer

κατεβαίνω **kateveno** get off

κατειλλημένος **kateelee- menos** engaged, occupied (e.g. toilet)

κατ'ευθείαν **kat'eftheean** straightaway

κατεύθυνση **katfetheensee** direction

κατευθύνω **kateftheeno** direct (vb)

κατευναστής **kate- vanastees** pacifier

κατηγορώ **kateegoro** charge

κατηφόρα **kateefora** downhill

κάτι **katee** something

κατοικίδιο ζώο **katee- keedheeo zo-o** pet

κάτοικος **kateekos** resident

κατόπιν **katopeen** afterwards

κατσαβίδι **katsaveedhee** screwdriver

κατσαρίδα **katsareedha** cockroach

κατσαρός **katsaros** curly

κατσίκι **katseekee** goat

κάτω **kato** downstairs

κάτω από **kato apo** under

καυγαδίζω **kavghadheezo** quarrel (vb)

καυγάς **kavghas** quarrel, fight (n)

καύσιμο **kafseemo** fuel

καυτός **kaftos** hot

καφές **kafes** coffee

καφετί **kafetee** brown

κάψιμο από τον ήλιο **kapseemo apo ton eeleeo** sunburn

κειδωμένος μέσα **kleedho- menos mesa** locked in

κέικ **ke-eek** cake

κελάρι **kelaree** cellar

κεντρί **kendree** sting

κεντρίζω **kendreezo** sting

κεντρική θέρμανση **ken- dreekee thermansee** central heating

κεντρικό κλείδωμα **ken- dreeko kleedhoma** central locking

κεντρικό ταχυδρομείο **ken- dreeko takheedhro- meeo** main post office

κεντρικός δρόμος **kendree- kos dhromos** main road

κέντρο **kendro** centre

κέντρο της πόλης **kendro tees polees** city centre

κεραμική **kerameekee** pottery

κερασάκι **kerasakee** cherry

κέρατο **kerato** horn (animal)

κερδίζω **kerdheezo** win

κερί **keree** candle

κέρμα **kerma** coin

κεφάλαιο **kefaleo** capital (money)

κεφάλι **kefalee** head

κέφι **kefee** fun (to have)

κεχριμπάρι **kekhreem- baree** amber

κηδεία **keedheea** funeral

κήλη **keelee** hernia

κήπος **keepos** garden

κιάλια **keealeea** binoculars

κιβώτιο ταχυτήτων **keevoteeo takhee- teeton** gearbox

κιθάρα **keethara** guitar

κιλό **keelo** kilo

κιμάς **keemas** minced meat

Κίνα **Keena** China

κίνδυνος **keendheenos** danger

κινηματογραφώ **keenee- matoghrafo** film (vb)

κίνηση **keeneesee** traffic

GREEK → ENGLISH

κινητήρας *keeneeteeras* motor

κινητό τηλέφωνο *keeneeto teelefono* mobile phone

κινούμαι *keenoome* move

κίτρινος *keetreenos* yellow

κλαίω *kleo* cry

κλαξόν *klakson* horn (car)

κλέβω *klevo* steal

κλειδαριά *kleedhareea* key ring, lock (n)

κλειδί *kleedhee* key

κλειδί εκκίνησης του αυτο- κινήτου *kleedhee ekee- neesees too aftokeen- eetoo* ignition key

κλειδιά αυτοκινήτου *klee- dheea aftokeeneetoo* car keys

κλειδώνω *kleedhono* lock (vb)

κλειδώνω έξω *kleedhono ekso* lock out

κλειδώνω μέσα *kleedhono mesa* lock in

κλείδωση του ώμου *kleedhosee too omoo* collarbone

κλείνω *kleeno* shut, wrap up

κλείνω το τηλέφωνο *kleeno to teelefono* hang up (phone)

κλειστό *kleesto* closed

κλεμμένος *klemenos* stolen

κλέφτης *kleftees* burglar, thief

κλήση για παρόνομη στάθ- μευση *kleesee ghea paranomee stath- mefsee* parking ticket

κλίμα *kleema* climate

κλιματισμός *kleematees- mos* air conditioning

κλινάμαξα *kleenamaksa* sleeper, sleeping car

κλινική *kleeneekee* clinic

κλινοσκεπάσματα *kleeno- skepasmata* bed linen

κλοπή *klopee* theft

κλωστή *klostee* thread

κλωστή για καθάρισμα ανάμεσα στα δόντια *klostee ghea katha- reesma anamesa sta dhonteea* dental floss

κλωτσάω *klotsao* kick

κόβω *kovo* cut

κοιλάδα *keeladha* valley

κοιλόπονος *keeloponos* stomachache

κοιμάμαι *keemame* sleep

κοιμητήριο *keemeetee- reeo* cemetery

κοινός *keenos* joint

κοιτάω *keetao* look at

Κόκα Κόλα *Koka Kola* Coke

κόκαλο *kokalo* bone

κοκκινάδι *kokeenadhee* blusher

κόκκινο *kokeeno* red

κόκκινο κρασί *kokeeno krasee* red wine

κόλα *kola* glue

κολάρο *kolaro* collar

κολατσό *kolatso* snack

κολιέ *kolee-e* necklace

κολλημένος *koleemenos* stuck

κολλητικός *koleeteekos* infectious

κόλπος *kolpos* bay

κολυμπώ *koleembo* swim

κόμμα *koma* party (political)

κομμάτι *komatee* bit, lump, piece

κομματιάζω *komateeazo* chop

κομπιουτεράκι *kombee- ooterakee* calculator

κονιάκ *koneeak* brandy

κοντά *konda* by, near (adv)

κοντέρ *konder* speedometer

κοντεύω *kondevo* near (vb)

κοντινός *kondeenos* nearby (adv)

κοντό παντελόνι **kondo pantelonee** shorts
κοντός **kondos** short
κορδέλα **kordhela** ribbon
κορδόνι παπουτσιών **kordhonee papootseeon** shoelace
κόρη **koree** daughter
κορίτσι **koreetsee** girl
κορνίζα **korneeza** picture frame
κορυφαία τιμή **koreefea teemee** peak rate
κορυφή **koreefee** peak, summit, top
κόσκινο **kokeeno** sieve
κοσμήματα **kosmeemata** jewellery
κόσμος **kosmos** world
κόστος **kostos** cost
κοστούμι **kostoomee** suit
κότερο **kotero** yacht
κοτόπουλο **kotopoolo** chicken
κοτσίδα **kotseedha** plait
κουβάς **koovas** bucket, pail
κουβέρ **koover** cover charge
κουβέρτα **kooverta** blanket
κουδούνι **koodhoonee** bell
κουδούνι πόρτας **koodhoonee portas** doorbell
κουδούνισμα **koodhooneesma** ring (n, sound)
κουζίνα **koozeena** cooker, kitchen
κουζινίτσα **koozeeneetsa** kitchenette
κουκέτα **kooketa** couchette
κούκλα **kookla** doll
κουκλοθέατρο **kooklotheatro** puppet show
κουκουβάγια **kookoovagheea** owl
κουκούλα **kookoola** hood (garment)
κουλούρα σχοινιού **kooloora skeeneeoo** coil (rope)

κουμπί **koobee** button
κουνέλι **koonelee** rabbit
κούνια **kooneea** swing
κουνιάδα **kooneeadha** sister-in-law (wife's sister)
κουνιάδος **kooneeadhos** brother-in-law
κουνούπι **koonoopee** mosquito
κουνουπίδι **koonoopeedhee** cauliflower
κουνώ **koono** shake
κούπα **koopa** mug
κουπί **koopee** oar
κουπόνι **kooponee** voucher
κουρασμένος **koorasmenos** tired
κουρείο **kooreeo** barber's shop
κουρέλι **koorelee** rag
κούρεμα **koorema** haircut
κούρσα **koorsa** race (sport)
κούρσα αλόγων **koorsa aloghon** horse racing
κουρτίνα **koorteena** curtain
κουρυφή **koreefee** crown (anat)
κουτάλα σερβιρίσματος **kootala serveereesmatos** tablespoon
κουταλάκι του τσαγιού **kootalakee too tsagheeoo** teaspoon
κουτάλι **kootalee** spoon
κουτί **kootee** box
κουτί με εργαλεία **kootee me erghaleea** toolkit
κουφός **koofos** deaf
κοφτερός **kofteros** sharp
κραγιόν **kragheeon** lipstick
κράμπα **kramba** cramp
κράνος **kranos** helmet, crash helmet
κρασί **krasee** wine
Κράτα τα ρέστα! **Krata ta resta** Keep the change!

GREEK → ENGLISH

κρατάω **kratao** hold, keep
κράτηση **krateesee** reservation
κρατώ **krato** reserve
κραυγή **kravghee** shout (n)
κρέας **kreas** meat
κρεββατάκι μωρού **krevatakee moroo** cot
κρεββάτι **krevatee** bed
κρέμα **krema** cream, custard
κρεμαστάρι **kremastaree** coat hanger
κρεμάστρα **kremastra** hanger
κρεμμύδι **kremeedhee** onion
κρίμα, τι κρίμα! **kreema, tee kreema** pity, It's a pity!
κροκάλι **krokalee** shingle
κρόκος **krokos** yolk
κρουαζιέρα **krooazee-era** cruise
κρύβω **kreevo** hide
κρύο **kreeo** cold
κτηματομεσίτης **kteematomeseetees** estate agent
κτηνίατρος **kteeneeatros** veterinarian
κυβέρνηση **keeverneesee** government
κυκλική κούρσα **keekleekee koorsa** cycle track
κυκλικός δρόμος **keekleekos dhromos** ring road
κύκλος **keeklos** circle, cycle (shape)
κυκλοφοριακή συμφόρηση **keekloforeeakee seemforeesee** traffic jam
κυλιόμενη σκάλα **keeleeomenee skala** escalator
κυλότα **keelota** knickers, panties
κυλώ **keelo** roll
κύμα **keema** wave
κυνηγώ **keeneegho** hunt

κυρία **keereea** lady, Mrs
Κυριακή **Keereeakee** Sunday
κύριο πιάτο **keereeo peeato** main course
κύριος **keereeos** main, Mr
κύστη **keestee** cyst
κυστίτιδα **keesteeteedha** cystitis
κώδικας **kodheekas** code
κωδικός αριθμός **kodheekos areethmos** dialling code
κωμμοτής **komotees** hairdresser
κωμωδία **komodheea** comedy

Λ
λαδερό **ladhero** greasy
λάδι **ladhee** oil
λάδι ηλιοθεραπίας **ladhee eeleeotherapeeas** suntan lotion
λάθος **lathos** error, mistake
λαϊκός **laeekos** popular (of the people)
λαιμός **lemos** neck, throat
λακκούβα **lakoova** pothole
λαμβάνω **lamvano** obtain
λάμπα **lamba** light bulb
λαμπρό **lambro** bright
λάμπω **lambo** shine
λάσπη **laspee** mud
λαστιχένια (φουσκωτή) βάρκα **lasteekheneea (fooskotee) varka** dinghy
λάστιχο **lasteekho** hose pipe, rubber
λάστιχο αυτοκινήτου **lasteekho aftokeeneetoo** tyre
Λάτβια **Latveea** Latvia
λαχανικά **lakhaneeka** vegetables
λάχανο **lakhano** cabbage
λαχταρώ **lakhtaro** long (vb)
λείπει **leepee** away

λεκάνη **lekanee** bowl
λεκές **lekes** stain
λεμονάδα **lemonadha** lemonade
λεμόνι **lemonee** lemon
λέξη **leksee** word
λεξικό **lekseeko** dictionary
λέπια **lepeea** scales
λεπτό **lepto** minute
λεπτό ύφασμα **lepto eefasma** tissue
λεπτομέρειες **lepto-meree-es** details
λερώνω **lerono** dirty (vb)
λεσβία **lesveea** lesbian
λέσχη γκολφ **leskhee golf** golf club (place)
λευκαντικό **lefkandeeko** bleach (n)
λευκοπλάστης **lefko-plastees** sticking plaster
λευκός **lefkos** white
λεφτά **lefta** money
λέω **leo** say, tell
λεωφορείο **leoforeeo** bus
λεωφόρος **leoforos** avenue
λήγω **leegho** expire
λιακάδα **leeakadha** sunshine
λίβρα **leevra** pound (weight)
λίγα **leegha** a few
λιγνός **leeghnos** thin
λιγότερος **leeghoteros** less
Λιθουανία **Leethooaneea** Lithuania
λικέρ **leeker** liqueur
λίμα **leema** file (tool)
λίμα νυχιών **leema neekheeon** nail file
λιμάνι **leemanee** port, harbour
λίμνη **leemnee** lake
λιοντάρι **leeondaree** lion
λιπαρός **leeparos** fatty
λιποθυμώ **leepotheemo** faint (vb)
λίρα **leera** pound (currency)
λίστα **leesta** list
λίτρο **leetro** litre

λιώνω **leeono** melt
λογαριασμός **loghareeasmos** account, bill
λογικός **logheekos** reasonable
λοσιόν αφαίρεσης καλλυν-τικών ματιού **loseeon aferesees kaleendee-kon mateeoo** eye make-up remover
λοσιόν καθαρισμού **loseeon kathareesmoo** cleansing lotion
λουκάνικο **lookaneeko** sausage
λουκέτο **looketo** padlock
λουκουμάς **lookoomas** doughnut
λουλούδι **looloodhee** flower
Λουξεμβούργο **Looksem-voorgho** Luxembourg
λουράκι ρολογιού **loorakee rologheeoo** watch strap
λουρί του βεντιλατέρ **looree too vendeelater** fanbelt
λουρίδα **looreedha** strap
λούσιμο και χτένισμα **looseemo ke khten-eesma** shampoo and set
λουστράρω **loostraro** polish (vb)
λούστρο **loostro** polish (n)
λύκος **leekos** wolf
Λυπάμαι! **Leepame!** Sorry!
λύση **leesee** answer, solution
λύσσα **leesa** rabies
λωρίδα **loreedha** lane

Μ

μα **ma** but
μαγαζί **maghazee** shop
μάγειρας **magheeras** cook (n)
μαγειρεύω **magheerevo** cook (vb)
μαγιό **magheeo** swimming costume
μαγιονέζα **magheeoneza** mayonnaise

μαγνήτης *maghneetees*
magnet

μαγνητόφωνο *maghneeto-fono* tape recorder

μαγουλάδες *maghoola-dhes* mumps

μάγουλο *maghoolo* cheek

μαζεύω *mazevo* collect

μαζί *mazee* together

μαθαίνω *matheno* learn

μάθημα *matheema*
lesson

μαθήματα γλώσσας *matheemata ghlosas* language course

μαθητής *matheetees*
student (school)

Μάιος *Maeeos* May

μακρυά *makreea* far (adv)

μακρυνός *makreenos*
far (adj)

μακρύς *makrees* long (adj)

μακρύτερα *makreetera*
further

μαλακός *malakos* soft

μαλλί *malee* wool

μαλλιά *maleea* hair

μάλλινη μπλούζα *malee-nee blooza* sweater

μαλώνω *malono* fight (vb)

μανικετόκουμπα *manee-ketokoomba* cufflinks

μανιτάρι *maneetaree*
mushroom

μανταλάκι *mandalakee*
peg, clothes peg

μανταρίνι *mandareenee*
tangerine

μαντίλι *mandeelee*
handkerchief

μαξιλάρι *makseelaree*
cushion, pillow

μαξιλαροθήκη *makselarotheekee*
pillowcase

μαραγκός *marangos*
carpenter

μαργαριτάρι *margharee-taree* pearl

μαρέγκα *marenga*
meringue

μάρκα *marka* brand

μάρμαρο *marmaro* marble

μαρμελάδα *marmeladha*
jam

μαρμελάδα πορτοκαλιού *marmeladha porto-khaleeoo* marmalade

μαρούλι *maroolee* lettuce

Μάρτιος *Marteeos* March

μάρτυρας *marteeras*
witness

μασέλα *masela* dentures

μάσκα *maska* mask

μάσκαρα *maskara*
mascara

μάτι *matee* eye

ματώνω *matono* bleed

μαύρη σταφίδα *mavree stafeedha* blackcurrant

μαύρος *mavros* black

μαχαίρι *makheree* knife

μαχαιροπήρουνα *makhero-peeroona* cutlery

με *me* with

Με συγχωρείτε! *Me seengkhoreete!*
Excuse me!

Μεγάλη Βρετανία *Meghalee Vretaneea* Great Britain

Μεγάλη Παρασκευή *Meghalee Paraskevee* Good Friday

μεγαλοπρεπής *meghalo-prepees* grand

μεγάλος *meghalos* big, great, grand, large

μέγεθος *meghethos* size

μεγένθυση *meghen-theesee* enlargement

μεγεθυντικός φακός *meghentheeteekos fakos* magnifying glass

μέδουσα *medhoosa*
jellyfish

μεζές *mezes* snack

μεθυσμένος *methees-menos* drunk (adj)

μείτε ... μείτε **meete... meete** neither ... nor
μειώνω **meeono** reduce
μείωση **meeosee** reduction
μελαγχολικός **melangkholeekos** gloomy
μελάνι **melanee** ink
μελανιά **melaneea** bruise (n)
μέλι **melee** honey
μέλισσα **meleesa** bee
μέλλον **melon** future
μενού **menoo** menu
μέντα **menta** mint
μερίδα **mereedha** portion, share (n)
μερικά **mereeka** few
μερικός **mereekos** some
μεροκάματο **merokamato** wage
μέρος **meros** part, place
μέσα **mesa** in, indoors, inside, into
μέσα στην εβδομάδα **mesa steen evdhomadha** weekday
μεσαίος **meseos** middle
μεσαίωνας **meseonas** medieval
μεσάνυχτα **mesaneekhta** midnight
μέση **mesee** waist
μεσημέρι **meseemeree** midday
μεσημεριανό **meseemereeano** lunch
Μεσόγειος **Mesogheeos** Mediterranean
μεσονύχτι **mesoneekhtee** midnight
μέσος όρος **mesos oros** average
μέσω **meso** via
μετά μεσημβρίας **meta meseemvreeas** p.m. (after noon)
μεταδοτικός **metadhoteekos** infectious

μετακινώ **metakeeno** move
μετακομίζω **metakomeezo** move house
μεταλλικό νερό **metaleeko nero** mineral water
μέταλλο **metalo** metal
μετάξι **metaksee** silk
μεταξύ **metaksee** among
μετασχηματιστής **metaskheemateestees** adapter
μεταφράζω **metafrazo** translate
μετάφραση **metafrasee** translation
μεταφραστής **metafrastees** interpreter, translator
μεταχειρισμένο **metakheereesmeno** second-hand
μετράω **metrao** measure (vb)
μετρητά **metreeta** cash
μετρητής **metreetees** meter
μέτριο μέγεθος **metreeo meghethos** medium sized
μέτριο προς σενιάν (κρέας) **metreeo pros seneean (kreas)** medium rare (meat)
μέτριος **metreeos** medium
μέτριος ξηρός οίνος **metreeos kseeros eenos** medium dry wine
μέτρο **metro** measure (n), metre
μετρό **metro** metro, subway, underground
μετροταινία **metroteneea** tape measure
μέτωπο **metopo** forehead
μέχρι **mekhree** until
μη-αλκοολικό **mee-alkooleeko** non-alcoholic
μηδέν **meedhen** zero
μη-καπνιστών **meekapneeston** non-smoking

GREEK → ENGLISH

μηλίτης *meeleetees* cider
μήνας *meenas* month
μήνας του μέλιτος
   meenas too meleetos
   honeymoon
μηνιαία *meenee-ea*
   monthly
μηνιγγίτιδα *meeneen-geeteedha* meningitis
μήνυμα *meeneema*
   message
μητέρα *meetera* mother
μητριά *meetreea*
   stepmother
μητρώο *meetro-o*
   register (n)
μηχανή *meekhanee* engine,
   machine
μηχανικός *meekhaneekos*
   engineer, mechanic
μιά φορά *meea fora* once
μίγμα *meeghma* mix
μίζα *meeza* starter (car)
μίζερος *meezeros* mean,
   nasty
μικρός *meekros* little, small
μικροσκοπικός *meekro-skopeekos* tiny
μίλι *meelee* mile
μιλώ *meelo* speak, talk
μισθοφόρος *meesthoforos*
   freelance
μισθώνω *meesthono*
   lease (vb)
μισός *meesos* half
μνημείο *mneemeeo*
   monument
μοίρα *meera* lot
μοιράζομαι *meerazome*
   share (vb)
μολονότι *molonoti*
   although
μόλυβδος *moleevdhos*
   lead (n, metal)
μολύβι *moleevee* pencil
μόλυνση *moleensee*
   infection
μολυσμένος *moleesmenos*
   polluted

μοναστήρι *monasteeree*
   abbey, monastery
μονή *monee* monastery
μόνο *mono* just, only
μονό εισιτήριο *mono eeseeteereeo* single
   ticket
μονό κρεββάτι *mono krevatee* single bed
μονόκλινο δωμάτιο *mono-kleeno dhomateeo*
   single room
μόνον *monon* only (adv)
μονοπάτι *monopatee* path,
   footpath
μόνος *monos* alone, odd
   (number), only (adj), single
μοντέρνος *mondernos*
   fashionable
μοσχάρι *moskharee* calf,
   veal
μοτοσικλέτα *motoseekleta*
   motorbike
μου αρέσει *aresee* like (vb)
μουντός *moondos* dull
μουσείο *mooseeo*
   museum
μουσικός *mooseekos*
   musician
Μουσουλμάνος *Moosool-manos* Muslim
μουστάκι *moostakee*
   moustache
μουστάρδα *moostardha*
   mustard
μοχθηρός *mokhteeros*
   nasty
μοχλός *mokhlos* lever
μοχλός ταχυτήτων
   moklos takheeteeton
   gear lever
μπαγιάτικος *baghee-ateekos* stale
μπαίνω *mbeno* come in,
   enter, shrink
μπαίνω σε ουρά *mbeno se oora* queue (vb)
μπακαλιάρος *bakaleearos*
   cod

μπαλκόνι **balkonee**
balcony

μπανιέρα **mbanee-_era_**
bathroom

μπάνιο **mbaneo** bath

μπαστούνι του γκολφ
bastoonee too golf
golf club (stick)

μπαχαρικό **mbakhareeko**
spice

μπέικον **mbe-eekon**
bacon

μπέρδεμα **mberdhema**
mix-up

μπερδεμένος **mberdhe-menos** confused

μπιζέλι **mbeezelee**
pea (dry)

μπισκότο **beeskoto** biscuit,
cookie

μπλούζα **blooza** blouse

μπογιά **bogheea** paint (n)

μπορώ **mboro** can (vb),
may

μπότα του σκι **mbota too skee** ski boot

μπότες **botes** boots

μπουζί **boozee** spark plug

μπουκάλι **bookalee** bottle

μπούτι **bootee** thigh

μπροστά **mbrosta** before,
front

μπύρα **beera** beer

μπύρα χύμα **beera kheema** draught beer

μύγα **meegha** fly (n)

μύδι **meedhee** mussel

μυθιστόρημα **meethee-storeema** novel

μυρίζομαι **meereezome**
smell

μυρμήγκι **meermeengee**
ant

μυς **mees** muscle

μυτερός **meeteros** sharp

μύτη **meetee** nose

μυωπικός **meeopeekos**
short-sighted

N

ναι **ne** yes

ναός **naos** temple

ναρκωτικό **narkoteeko**
drug (narcotic)

ναυτία **nafteea** nausea,
seasickness, travel sickness

ναυτικό **nafteeko** navy

νέα **nea** news

Νεα Ζηλανδία, Νεο-
ζηνανδός, Νεοζηλανδή
**Nea Zeelandheea,
Neozeelandhos, Neo-
zeelandhee** New Zealand,
New Zealander

νεκρός **nekros** dead

νεκροταφείο **nekrotafeeo**
cemetery

νέο **neo** new

Νέο Έτος **Neo Etos** New
Year

νέος **neos** young

νερό **nero** water

νεροχύτης **nerokheetees**
sink

νεφρό **nefro** kidney

νηπιαγωγείο **neepeeagho-gheeo** nursery school

νησί **neesee** island

νηφάλιος **neefaleeos**
sober

νιπτήρας **neepteeras**
washbasin

Νοέμβριος **Noemvrios**
November

νοικιάζω **neekeeazo** hire,
rent (vb)

νοικιασμένο αυτοκίνητο
**neekeeazomeno
aftokeeneeto** hire car

νόμισμα **nomeesma**
currency

νόμος **nomos** law

Νορβηγία **Norveegheea**
Norway

Νορβηγίδα **Norvee-gheedha** Norwegian (f)

Νορβηγός **Norveeghos**
Norwegian (m)

GREEK → ENGLISH

νοσοκόμα **nosokoma** nurse

νοσοκομείο **nosokomeeo** hospital

νοσταλγός **nostalghos** homesickness

νοστιμώτατος **nosteem-otatos** delicious

Νότια Αφρική **Noteea Afreekee** South Africa

Νοτιοαφρικάνα **Noteeoafreekana** South African (f)

Νοτιοαφρικάνος **Noteeoafreekanos** South African (m)

νότιος **noteeos** south

νουβέλα **noovela** novel

νους **noos** mind

νταντά **dada** nanny

ντεκαφεϊνέ **dekafe-eene** decaffeinated

ντεμοντέ **ndemode** old-fashioned

ντήζελ **ndeezel** diesel

ντομάτα **domata** tomato

ντόνατ **donat** doughnut

ντουζίνα **doozeena** dozen

ντουλάπα **ndoolapa** cupboard

ντούς **ndoos** shower

ντροπαλός **ndropalos** shy

ντροπή **ndropee** shame

νυσταλέος **neestaleos** sleepy

νύφη **neefee** bride, daughter-in-law, sister-in-law (brother's wife)

νύχι **neekhee** nail

νυχτικό **neekhteeko** nightdress

Ξ

ξανά **xana** again

ξανθή μπύρα **ksanthee beera** lager

ξανθός **kshanthos** fair, blonde

ξαπλώνω **ksaplono** lie (vb, recline)

ξαπλώνω κάτω **ksaplono kato** lie down

ξαπλώστρα **ksaplostra** deck chair

ξαφνικά **ksafneeka** suddenly

ξεβιδώνω **kseveedhono** unscrew

ξεκλειδώνω **ksekleedhono** unlock

ξένος **ksenos** foreign (person), foreigner, strange, stranger

ξενώνας **ksenonas** hostel

ξενώνας νεότητας **ksenonas neoteetas** youth hostel

ξεπακετάρω **ksepaketaro** unpack

ξέρω **ksero** know

ξεσκονόπανο **ksesko-nopano** duster

ξεφλουδίζω **ksefloo-dheezo** peel (vb)

ξεφούσκωτα λάστιχα **ksefooskota lasteekha** flat tyre

ξεχνάω **ksekhnao** forget

ξίδι **kseedhee** vinegar

ξινός **kseenos** sour

ξοδεύω **ksodhevo** spend (money)

ξύλο **kseelo** wood

ξυπνάω **kseepnao** wake up

ξυπνώ **kseepno** awake

ξυράφι **kseerafee** razor

ξυρίζομαι **kseereezome** shave

ξυριστική λεπίδα **kseereesteekee lepeedha** razor blade

Ο

ο εαυτός μου **o eaftos moo** myself

ο παπούς και η γιαγιά **o papoos ke ee gheea-gheea** grandparents

ο περισσότερος *o peree-*
soteros most

οδήγηση από τα δεξιά
**odheegheesee apo ta
dhekseea** right-hand
drive

οδήγηση στα αριστερά
**odheegheesee sta
areestera** left-hand
drive

οδηγός **odheeghos** driver,
guide, guide book

οδηγός ταξί **odheeghos
taksee** taxi driver

οδηγώ **odheegho** drive,
lead (vb)

οδικά έργα **odheeka ergha**
road works

οδικός χάρτης **odheekos
khartees** road map,
street map

οδοντίατρος **odhon-
deeatros** dentist

οδοντόβουρτσα **odhon-
dovoortsa** toothbrush

οδοντογλυφίδα **odhondo-
ghleefeedha** toothpick

οδοντοστοιχία **odhondo-
steekheea** dentures

οδυνηρός **odheeneeros**
painful

οικιακός **eekeeakos**
domestic

οικογένεια **eekogheneea**
family

οικοδομή **eekodhomee**
building

οικονομία **eekonomeea**
economy

οινοπνευματώδη ποτά
**eenopnevmatodhee
pota** spirits (drink)

Οκτώβριος **Oktovreeos**
October

όλα **ola** everything

όλα καλά **ola kala** OK

Ολλανδία **Olandheea**
Netherlands

Ολλανδός, Ολλανδή
Olandhos, Olandhee
Dutch, Dutchman,
Dutchwoman

ολοκηρώνω **olokleerono**
wrap up

ολόκληρος **olokleeros**
whole (entire)

ομάδα **omadha** group, team

ομελέτα **omeleta** omelette

ομίχλη **omeekhlee** fog, mist

όμοιο **omeeo** like (adj)

όμοιος **omeeos** similar

όμορφος **omorfos** beautiful,
handsome, lovely, pretty

ομός **omos** raw

ομοφυλόφιλος **omofeelo-
feelos** gay, homosexual

ομπρέλα **ombrela** umbrella

ομπρέλα ηλίου **ombrela
eeleeoo** sunshade

όνομα **onoma** name, first
name

όπερα **opera** opera

όπισθεν **opeesthen** reverse
gear

οποιοσδήποτε **opeeos-
dheepote** anybody

οπτικός **opteekos** optician

όραση **orasee** sight

οργανικά λαχανικά
**orghaneeka lakha-
neeka** organic vegetables

οργανωμένη εκδρομή **or-
ghanomenee ekdhro-
mee** package holiday

οργανωτής εκδρομών
**orghanotees ekdhro-
mon** tour operator

ορειβασία **oreevaseea**
mountaineering

ορθογραφώ **orthoghrafo**
spell

όριο ταχύτητας **oreeo
takheeteetas** speed limit

οριστικά **oreesteeka**
definitely

ορκίζομαι **orkeezome**
swear (an oath)

όροφος **orofos** floor, storey

ορχήστρα **orkheestra**
orchestra

οσφυαλγία **osfeealgheea**
backache

οτιδήποτε **oteedheepote**
anything

οτοστόπ **otostop** hitchhike

Ουαλή **Ooalee** Welsh,
Welshwoman

Ουαλία **Ooaleea** Wales

Ουαλός **Ooalos** Welsh,
Welshman

Ουγγαρέζα **Oongareza**
Hungarian (f)

Ουγγαρέζος **Oongarezos**
Hungarian (m)

Ουγγαρία **Oongareea**
Hungary

ουρά **oora** queue (n)

ουρανός **ooranos** sky

οφειλόμενος **ofeelomenos**
due

οφθαλμίατρος **ofthalmee-
atros** ophthalmologist

οχετός **okhetos** drain (n)

όχημα της ξηράς **okheema
tees kseeras** vehicle

όχι **okhee** no, not

όχι άνετος **okhee anetos**
uncomfortable

όχι καλά ψημένο **okhee
kala pseemeno**
underdone

όψη **opsee** view

Π

π.μ. (προ μεσημβρείας, **pro
meseemvreeas)** a.m.
(before noon)

παγετός **paghetos** frost

παγετώνας **paghetonas**
glacier

παγοδρόμιο **paghodhro-
meeo** skating rink

παγοπέδιλα **pagho-
pedheela** ice skates

παγοπέδιλο **pagho-
pedheelo** skate (gear)

πάγος **paghos** ice

παγούρι **paghooree** flask

παγωμένος **paghomenos**
frozen

παγωμένος καφές
paghomenos kafes
iced coffee

παγωτό **paghoto** ice cream

παιδί **pedhee** child

παιδική χαρά **pedheekee
khara** playground

παιδικό αμαξάκι **pedheeko
amaksakee** pushchair

παίζω **pezo** play (vb)

παίρνω **perno** take

παιχνίδι **pekhneedhee**
game, play (n), toy

πακέτο **paketo** package,
packet

παλαιό **paleo** old (object)

παλάτι **palatee** palace

πάλι **palee** again

παλίρροια **paleereea** tide

παλούκι σκηνής **palookee
skeenees** tent peg

παλτό **palto** coat, overcoat

πάνα **pana** diaper, nappy

πανδοχείο **pandhokheeo**
inn

πανεπιστήμιο **panepees-
teemeeo** university

πάνες μιάς χρήσης **panes
meeas khreesees**
disposable diapers/nappies

πανί **panee** cloth

πανί για πιάτα **panee
gheea peeata** dishtowel

πανσιόν **panseeon** guesthouse, boarding house

παντελόνι **pandelonee**
pants, trousers

παντεσπάνι **pandespanee**
sponge cake

παντζούρι **pantzooree**
shutter

πάντοτε **pandote** always

παντού **pandoo** everywhere

παντόφλες **pandofles**
slippers

παντρεμένος *pandre-menos* married

πάνω από *pano apo* over

πάνω πάτωμα *pano patoma* top floor

παξιμάδι *pakseemadhee* nut (for bolt)

παπαρούνα *paparoona* poppy

παπάς *papas* priest

πάπια *papeea* duck

παπιόν *papeeon* bow tie

πάπλωμα *paploma* duvet, quilt

παπούς *papoos* grandfather

παπούτσι *papootsee* shoe

πάρα πολύ *para polee* too much

παραβάν *paravan* screen

παραγγελεία *parangeleea* order (n)

παραγγέλνω *parangelno* order (vb)

παράδειγμα *paradheegh-ma* example

παραδίδω *paradheedho* deliver

παράδοση *paradhosee* delivery

παραζεσταμένο *parazesta-meno* overheat

παράθυρο *paratheero* window

παρακαλώ *parakalo* please

παράκαμψη *parakampsee* detour

παράκληση *parakleesee* request (n)

παρακολουθώ *parako-lootho* watch (vb)

παραλαμβάνω *para-lamvano* get

παραλία *paraleea* coast, seaside

παραλία γυμνιστών *para-leea gheemneeston* nudist beach

παραμάνα *paramana* nanny, safety pin

παραμονή *paramonee* stay

Παραμονή Πρωτοχρονιάς *Paramonee Protokhro-neeas* New Year's Eve

Παραμονή Χριστουγέννων *Paramonee Khreesto-ghenon* Christmas Eve

παράξενος *paraksenos* peculiar, strange, weird

παραπάνω *parapano* above

παραποιώ *parapeeo* fake (vb)

παραπονιέμαι *paraponee-eme* complain

παράπονο *parapono* complaint

παράρτημα *pararteema* branch (office)

Παρασκευή *Paraskevee* Friday

παραχώρηση *para-khoreesee* concession

παραψημένο *parapsee-meno* overdone

παρέα *parea* company

παρεκκλήσι *parekleesee* chapel

παρελθόν *parelthon* past

παρεξήγηση *parekseegheesee* misunderstanding

παρκάρω *parkaro* park (vb)

πάρκο *parko* park (n)

παρκόμετρο *parkometro* parking meter

παρμπρίζ *parbreez* windscreen

πάροδος *parodhos* bypass (road)

παρόν *paron* present (now)

παρουσιάζω *parooseeazo* present (vb)

πάρτυ *partee* party (celebration)

πάστα *pasta* pastry

παστίλιες για το λαιμό *pasteelee-es ghea to lemo* throat lozenges

Πάσχα **Paskha** Easter

Πασχαλιάτικο αυγό **Pas-khaleeateeko avgho** Easter egg

πατάτα **patata** potato

πατατάκια **patatakeea** chips, crisps

πατέρας **pateras** father

πατριός **patreeos** stepfather

πατσαβούρα **patsavoora** floorcloth

πάτωμα **patoma** floor (of room)

παυσίπονο **pafseepono** painkiller

παχύ **pakhee** greasy

παχύς **pakhees** fat

πεδιάδα **pedheeadha** plain (n)

πέδιλα **pedheela** flip flops, sandals

πεζοδρόμιο **pezodhro-meeo** pavement, sidewalk

πεζός **pezos** pedestrian

πεθαίνω **petheno** die (vb)

πεθερά **pethera** mother-in-law

πεθερικά **pethereeka** in-laws, parents-in-law

πεθερός **petheros** father-in-law

πεινασμένος **peenas-menos** hungry

πειράζει – δεν πειράζει **peerazee – dhen peerazee** matter – it doesn't matter

πελάτης **pelatees** client, customer

πέλμα **pelma** sole (shoe)

Πέμπτη **Pemptee** Thursday

πένα **pena** pen

πένσα **pensa** pliers

πεντάλ **pedal** pedal

πεπόνι **peponee** melon

πέρα από **pera apo** beyond

περιγραφή **perighrafee** description

περιγράφω **perighrafo** describe

περίεργος **peree-erghos** odd, strange

περιήγηση **peree-eegheesee** tour

περικυκλωμένος **peree-keeklomenos** surrounded

περιμένω **pereemeno** wait

περιοδικό **pereeodheeko** magazine

περίοδος **pereeodhos** period

περιοχή **pereeokhee** district, region

περίπου **pereepoo** about, approximately

περίπτερο **pereeptero** kiosk, stall

περίπτωση **pereeptosee** case

περισσότερο **pereesotero** mostly

περισσότερος **peree-sotero** more

περίστροφο **pereestrofo** gun

περιφραστικός **peree-frasteekos** roundabout

περίχωρα **pereekhora** outskirts

περμανάντ **permanand** perm

πέρνω τηλέφωνο **perno teelefono** call (vb, phone)

περούκα **perooka** wig

περπατώ **perpato** walk

πέστροφα **pestrofa** trout

πεταλούδα **petaloodha** butterfly

πετάω **petao** fly (vb)

πέτρα **petra** stone

πετσέτα **petseta** napkin, towel

πετώ **peto** throw

πέφτω **pefto** fall

πηγαίνω **peegheno** go
πηγαίνω με αυτοκίνητο **peegheno me afto-keeneeto** go (by car)
πηγαίνω με τα πόδια **peegheno me ta podheea** go (on foot)
πηγαίνω πίσω **peegheno peeso** go back
πηγούνι **peeghoonee** chin
πηδάλιο **peedhaleeo** pedal, rudder
πήδημα **peedheema** jump (n)
πηδώ **peedho** jump (vb)
πηρούνι **peeroonee** fork
πιάνο **peeano** piano
πιάνω **peeano** catch (vb)
πιατάκι **peeatakee** saucer
πιατικά **peeateeka** crockery
πιάτο **peeato** dish, plate
πίεση **pee-esee** pressure, blood pressure
πιθανόν **peethanon** perhaps, probably, possibly
πικάντικος **peekandeekos** savoury
πικνίκ **peekneek** picnic
πιλότος **peelotos** pilot
πίνακας **peenakas** painting
πίνακας ανακοινώσεων **peenakas anakeenoseon** noticeboard
πίνακας με ασφάλειες **peenakas me asfalees** fuse box
πινακίδα **peenakeedha** number plate, signpost
πίνω **peeno** drink (vb)
πίπα **peepa** pipe (smoking)
πιπέρι **peeperee** pepper (spice)
πιπεριά **peepereea** pepper (vegetable)
πιπίλα **peepeela** dummy, pacifier
πισίνα **peeseena** pool

πιστεύω **peestevo** believe
πιστοποιητικό **peestopee-eeteeko** certificate
πιστοποιητικό γεννήσεως **peestopee-eeteeko gheneeseos** birth certificate
πιστωτική κάρτα **peesto-teekee karta** charge card, credit card
πίσω **peeso** back, behind
πίτα **peeta** pie
πλαγιά για αρχάριους **plagheea gheea arkhareeos** nursery slope
πλαγιά για σκι **plagheea gheea skee** ski slope
πλαζ **plaz** beach
πλάι **plaee** beside
πλάκα **plaka** fun (to make ... of)
πλάκα σοκολάτας **plaka sokolatas** bar of chocolate
πλαστική σακούλα **plasteekee sakoola** plastic bag
πλαστικό **plasteeko** plastic
πλάτη **platee** back
πλατίνες **plateenes** points (car)
πλατύς **platees** wide
πλεκτά **plekta** knitwear
πλέκω **pleko** knit
πλένω **pleno** wash
πλεξούδα **pleksoodha** plait
πλευρά **plevra** side
πλευρό **plevro** rib
πλέω **pleo** sail
πληγή **pleeghee** ulcer
πληγή στο στόμα **pleeghee sto stoma** mouth ulcer
πλήθος **pleethos** crowd
πληθυσμός **pleetheesmos** population

GREEK → ENGLISH

GREEK → ENGLISH

πληκτικός *pleekteekos* boring

πλημμύρα *pleemeera* flood

πλημμυρίδα *pleemee-reedha* high tide

πληροφορίες *pleeroforee-es* information, enquiry desk

πληρωμένος *pleeromenos* paid

πληρωμή *pleeromee* payment

πληρώνω *pleerono* pay

πλήσιμο αυτοκινήτου *pleeseemo afto-keeneetoo* car wash

πλοίο *pleeo* boat, ship

πλούσιος *plooseeos* rich

πλυντήρια *pleendeereea* laundry

πλυντήρια ρούχων *pleen-deereea rookhon* launderette, Laundromat

πλυντήριο πιάτων *pleen-deereeo peeaton* dishwasher

πνεύμα *pnevma* spirit (soul)

πνεύμονας *pnevmonas* lung

ποδήλατο *podheelato* bicycle, cycle (vehicle)

πόδι *podhee* foot, leg

ποδιά *podheea* apron

πόδια *podheea* feet

ποδόσφαιρο *podhosfero* football

Ποιά; *Peea?* Which?

ποινή *peenee* sentence (law)

Ποιός; *Peeos?* Who?

ποιότητα *peeoteeta* quality

πόλεμος *polemos* war

πόλη *polee* city, town

πολίτης *poleetees* citizen

πολλά *pola* many, plenty

πολλοί *polee* several, many

πολύ *polee* much, very

πολυάσχολος *poleeas-kholos* busy

πολυθρόνα *poleethrona* armchair

πολυκατάστημα *poleekata-steema* department store

πολυκατοικία *poleekatee-keea* block of flats

πολυτελείς *poleetelees* luxury

πολύτιμος *poleeteemos* valuable

Πολωνία *Poloneea* Poland

Πολωνός *Polonos* Pole, Polish

πονάει *ponaee* sore, it's sore, hurts

πονάω *ponao* hurt (vb)

πονεμένος *ponemenos* sore

πονόδοντος *ponodhondos* toothache

πονοκέφαλος *ponokefalos* hangover, headache

πονόλαιμος *ponolemos* sore throat

πόνος *ponos* ache, pain

πόνος στο αυτί *ponos sto aftee* earache

ποντίκι *pondeekee* mouse

πόντος *pondos* centimetre

πορθμός *porthmos* channel

πορσελάνη *porselanee* china

πόρτα *porta* door

πορτατίφ *portateef* lamp

πορτ-μπαγκάζ *port-bagaz* trunk (of car)

πορτό *porto* port (wine)

Πορτογαλία *Portoghaleea* Portugal

Πορτογαλίδα *Porto-ghaleedha* Portuguese (f)

Πορτογάλος *Portoghalos* Portuguese (m)

πορτοκάλι *portokalee* orange

πορτοφολάς *portofolas* pickpocket

πορτοφόλι *portofolee* purse, wallet

πορτραίτο **portreto** portrait
πορφυρός **porfeeros** purple
Πόσα; **Posa?** How many?
ποσέ **pose** poached
πόσιμο νερό **poseemo nero** drinking water
ποσό **poso** amount
Πόσο κάνει; **Poso kanee** How much is it?
ποσοστό υπηρεσίας **pososto eepeereseeas** service charge
ποσότητα **posoteeta** quantity
πόστο **posto** post (n, mail)
ποταμός **potamos** river
ποτέ **pote** never
Πότε; **Pote?** When?
πότε-πότε **pote-pote** occasionally
ποτήρι **poteeree** glass, tumbler
ποτήρι του κρασιού **poteeree too kraseeoo** wine glass
ποτό **poto** drink (n)
Που; **Poo?** Where?
πούδρα **poodhra** talcum powder
πουκάμισο **pookameeso** shirt
πουλάω **poolao** sell
πουλί **poolee** bird
πούλμαν **poolman** coach
πουλόβερ **poolover** jumper, pullover
πουρές **poores** mashed potatoes
πούρο **pooro** cigar
πουτίγκα **pooteenga** pudding
πράγμα **praghma** thing
πραγματικά **praghmateeka** really
πρακτική **prakteekee** practice
πράξη **praksee** practice
πράσινος **praseenos** green
πράσο **praso** leek

πρέπει **prepee** must
πρέπει να **prepee na** have to
πρεσβεία **presveea** embassy
πρίζα **preeza** plug (elec), socket
πρίζομαι **preezome** swell
πριν **preen** before
πριν από μία εβδομάδα **preen apo meea evdhomadha** a week ago
πρίξιμο **preekseemo** swelling
πρισμένος **preesmenos** swollen
προάστειο **proasteeo** suburb
πρόβατο **provato** sheep
πρόβλημα **provleema** problem
προβολέας **provoleas** headlights
προβολείς **provolees** headlight
πρόγραμμα **proghrama** programme, program
προθάλαμος **prothalamos** lobby
προκαταβολή **prokatavolee** advance
προκαταβολικά **prokatavoleeka** in advance
προκυμαία **prokeemea** quay
προξενείο **prokseneeo** consulate
προορισμός **prooreesmos** destination
προς **pros** to
προσβλέπω **prosvlepo** look forward to
προσδένομαι με ζώνη ασφαλείας **prosdhenome me zonee asfaleeas** fasten seatbelt
προσδοκώ **prosdhoko** expect
προσεκτικός **prosekteekos** careful

προσεκτικός **prosekteekos**
safe (adj, sure)

προσεύχομαι **prosefkhome**
pray

πρόσθετος **prosthetos**
extra

πρόσκληση **proskleese**
invitation

πρόσοψη **prosopsee**
façade

προσπαθώ **prospatho** try

προσπερνώ **prosperno**
overtake, pass (vb)

προστατευμένος **pros-
tatevomenos** sheltered

πρόστιμο **prosteemo**
fine (n)

πρόσφατος **prosfatos**
recently

προσωπικός αριθμός
αναγνώρισης **proso-
peekos areethmos
anaghnoreesees**
pin number

πρόσωπο **prosopo** face

προσωρινός **prosoreenos**
temporary

πρόταση **protasee**
sentence (grammar)

προτείνω **proteeno**
recommend

προτιμώ **proteemo** prefer

προτιμώμενος **protee-
momenos** favourite

προφέρω **profero**
pronounce

προφορά **profora** accent

προφυλακτήρας **profeelakteeras** bumper, fender

προφυλακτικό **profeelak-
teeko** condom

πρωθυπουργός **prothee-
poorghos** prime minister

πρωί **proee** morning

πρωινό **proeeno** breakfast

πρώτα **prota** at first

πρώτες βοήθειες **protes
voeethee-es** first aid

πρωτεύουσα **protevoosa**
capital (city)

πρώτη τάξη **protee taksee**
first class

πρώτος **protos** first

πρώτος όροφος **protos
orofos** first floor

πτήση **pteesee** flight

πτήση ανταπόκρισης **pteesee andapokreesees**
connecting flight

πτήση τσάρτερ **pteesee
tsarter** charter flight

πτυχίο **pteekheeo** degree
(qualification)

πυξίδα **peekseedha**
compass

πύργος **peerghos** tower

πυρετός **peeretos** fever

πυροσβεστήρας
peerosvesteeras
fire extinguisher

πυροσβεστική **peeros-
vesteekee** fire brigade

πυτζάμες **peetzames**
pyjamas

πώληση **poleesee** sale

πωλητής **poleetees**
salesperson (m)

πωλήτρια **poleetreea**
salesperson (f)

Πως; **Pos?** How?

Πως είσαι; **Pos eese?**
How are you?

Ρ

ράβω **ravo** sew

ραδιόφωνο **radheeofono**
radio

ρακέτα **raketa** racket (sport)

ρακέτα του τένις **raketa
too tenees** tennis racket

ράμμα **rama** stitch

ραντεβού **randevoo**
appointment, date

ραπανάκι **rapanakee** radish

ράφι **rafee** shelf

ράφι αποσκευών **rafee
aposkevon** luggage rack

ράφτης *raftees* tailor

ρεζέρβα *rezerva* spare tyre

ρεσεψιόν *resepseeon* reception

ρεσεψιονίστας *resep-seeoneestas* receptionist

ρέστα *resta* change (money)

ρεύμα *revma* breeze, draught

ρευματισμός *revma-teesmos* rheumatism

ρηχός *reekhos* shallow

ριγέ *reeghe* striped

ρίχνω *reekhno* pour, drop (vb)

ρίχνω κάτω *reekno kato* knock over

ρόδα *rodha* wheel

ροδάκινο *rodhakeeno* peach

ροζ *roz* pink

ρολό *rolo* blind (n)

ρολόι *roloee* clock, watch

ρόμπα *romba* dressing gown

ρούμι *roomee* rum

ρούχα *rookha* clothes

ρουχισμός *rookheesmos* clothing

ροχαλίζω *rokhaleezo* snore

ρύζι *reezee* rice

ρυμούλκα *reemoolka* trailer (for goods)

ρυμουλκώ *reemoolko* tow

ρυτίδες *reeteedhes* wrinkles

ρώγα *rogha* teat (bottle)

Σ

Σάββατο *Savato* Saturday

σαββατοκύριακο *savato-keereeako* weekend

σαγόνι *saghonee* jaw

σαιζλόνγκ *sezlong* deck chair

σακάκι *sakakee* jacket

σακίδιο *sakeedheeo* backpack

σάλα *sala* hall

σαλάτα *salata* salad

σαλάχι *salakhee* skate (fish)

σαλόνι *salonee* lounge

σαλόνι αναχώρησης *salonee anakhoreese* departure lounge

σάλτσα *saltsa* dressing (salad), gravy, sauce

σαμπάνια *sampaneea* champagne

σανδάλια *sandhaleea* sandals

σανίδα κυματοδρομίας *saneedha keemato-dhromeeas* surfboard

σανίδα σιδερώματος *saneedha seedhero-matos* ironing board

σαντιγύ *sandeeghee* whipped cream

σάντουιτς *sadooeets* sandwich

σάπιος *sapeeos* rotten

σαπούνι *sapoonee* soap

σ'αυτόν *s'afton* to him

σαφής *safees* plain, clear (adj)

σβήνω *sveeno* switch off, turn off

σβηστός *sveestos* off

σβόλος *svolos* lump

σειρά *seera* row (n, line)

σεισμός *seesmos* earthquake

σέλα *sela* saddle

σελίδα *seleedha* page

σέλινο *seleeno* celery

σελοφάν *selofan* cling film

σελφ-σέρβις *self-servees* self-service

σεντόνι *sendonee* sheet

σεντόνια *sendoneea* linen

σεξ *seks* sex (intercourse)

Σεπτέμβριος *Septem-vreeos* September

σερβιέττες *servee-etes* sanitary pads

σερβιτόρος/σερβιτόρα **serveetoros/serveetora** waiter/waitress

σεσουάρ **sesooar** hairdryer

σεφ **sef** chef

σήμα **seema** dialling tone, signal

σήμα κυκλοφορίας **seema keekloforeeas** road sign

σήμα στοπ **seema stop** stop sign

σημαντικό **seemandeeko** important

σημείο **seemeeo** point (n)

σημείωμα **seemeeoma** note

σημειωματάριο **seemeeomatareeo** notebook

σήμερα **seemera** today

σήμερα το πρωί **seemera to proee** this morning

σηκώνομαι **seekonome** get up

Ση-Ντη Πλέγιερ **See-Dee Pleghee-er** CD player

σηπτικός **seepteekos** septic

σηπτικός βόθρος **seepteekos vothros** septic tank

σιγή **seeghee** silence

σίγουρος **seeghooros** sure

σίδερο **seedhero** iron (appliance)

σιδηροδρομικός σταθμός **seedheerodhromeekos stathmos** railway station

σιδηρόδρομος **seedheerodhromos** railway

σίδηρος **seedheeros** iron (metal)

σικ **seek** posh

σικάλινο ψωμί **sikaleeno psomee** rye bread

σινεμά **seenema** cinema

σιρόπι για βήχα **seeropee gheea veekha** cough mixture

σιωπή **seeopee** silence

σκάκι **skakee** chess

σκάλα **skala** ladder

σκαλί **skalee** step

σκαλιά **skaleea** stairs

σκαρφαλώνω **skarfalono** climb

σκάσιμο **skaseemo** puncture

σκάω **skao** burst

σκελετός **skeletos** frame

σκέπτομαι **skeptome** think

σκηνή **skeenee** tent

σκι **skee** ski, skiing

σκιά ματιού **skeea mateeoo** eye shadow

σκιάζω **skeeazo** shade

σκίζω **skeezo** tear (vb)

σκισμένος **skeesmenos** torn

σκληρά **skleera** rough

σκληρός **skleeros** hard, tough

σκληρός δίσκος **skleeros dheeskos** hard disk

σκοινί ρούχων **skeenee rookhon** clothes line

σκόνη **skonee** dust, powder

σκοπεύω **skopevo** intend

σκόπιμα **skopeema** deliberately

σκόρδο **skordho** garlic

σκοτάδι **skotadhee** darkness

σκοτεινός **skoteenos** dark, gloomy

σκοτούρα **skotoora** trouble

σκουλαρίκια **skoolareekeea** earrings

σκουλίκι **skooleekee** maggot

σκούπα **skoopa** broom

σκουπίδια **skoopeedheea** litter, rubbish, trash

σκουπιδοτενεκές **skoopeedhotenekes** dustbin

σκουριασμένος **skooreeasmenos** rusty

σκούρο μπλε **skooro ble** navy blue

σκούφος **skoofos** cap

σκύβω **skeevo** bend
σκύλος **skeelos** dog
σκωληκοειδίτιδα **skoleekoeedheeteedha** appendicitis
σκώρος **skoros** moth
Σκωτία **Skoteea** Scotland
Σκωτσέζος **Skotsezos** Scot, Scottish
Σλοβακινός **Slovakeenos** Slovak
σμέουρο **smeooro** raspberry
σοβαρός **sovaros** serious
σόδα **sodha** soda
σοκολάτα **sokolata** chocolate
σοκολατάκια **sokolatakeea** chocolates
σολομός **solomos** salmon
σορτς **sorts** shorts
Σουιδέζα **sooeedheza** Swedish, Swede (f)
Σουιδία **Sooeedheea** Sweden
Σουιδός **sooeedhos** Swedish, Swede (m)
σούπα **soopa** soup
σουτιέν **sootee-en** bra
σοφίτα **sofeeta** attic
σπάγγος **spangos** string
σπανάκι **spanakee** spinach
σπάνιος **spaneeos** rare
σπασμένο **spasmeno** broken
σπάω **spao** break
σπεύδω **spevdho** rush
σπηλιά **speeleea** cave
σπίρτα **speerta** matches (for lighting)
σπίτι **speetee** home, house
σπιτονοικοκυρά **speetoneekokeera** landlady
σπιτονοικοκύρης **speetoneekokeerees** landlord
σπονδυλική στήλη **spondheeleekee steelee** spine

σποραδικά **sporadheeka** occasionally
σπρώχνω **sprokhno** push
στάβλος **stavlos** barn
σταγόνες ματιού **staghones mateeoo** eye drops
σταδιακά **stadheeaka** gradually
στάδιο **stadheeo** stadium
σταθμός **stathmos** station
σταθμός ταξί **stathmos taksee** taxi rank
σταματάω **stamatao** stop
στάση **stasee** stopover
στάση λεωφορείου **stasee leoforeeoo** bus stop
σταυρόλεξο **stavrolekso** crossword puzzle
σταυρός **stavros** cross (n)
σταφίδα **stafeedha** raisin
σταφύλια **stafeeleea** grapes
στέγη **steghee** roof
στεγνοκαθαριστήριο **steghnokathareesteereeo** dry cleaner's
στεγνός **steghnos** dry
στεγνοτήριο **steghnoteereeo** spin-dryer
στεγνώνω μαλλιά **steghnono maleea** blow-dry
στεγνωτήριο **steghnoteereeo** dryer (for clothes)
στέλνω **stelno** send
στέμμα **stema** crown (royal)
στενό **steno** narrow
στενός **stenos** tight
στερεώνω **stereono** fasten
στήθος **steethos** breast, chest
Στην υγειά μας! **Steen eegheea mas!** Cheers!
στιγμή **steeghmee** moment
στιγμιαίος καφές **steeghmee-eos kafes** instant coffee

στιφάδο **steefadho** stew (with onions)

στοίχημα **steekheema** bet

στολή υποβρύχιου ψαρέματος **stolee eepovreekheeoo psarematos** wetsuit

στόμα **stoma** mouth

στοματικό διάλυμα **stoma-teeko dheealeema** mouthwash

στομάχι **stomakhee** stomach

στον/στην/στο **ston/steen/sto (m/f/n)** at

στου κοσμηματοπώλη **stoo kosmeematopolee** jeweller's

στου κομμωτή **stoo komotee** hairdresser's

στου μανάβη **stoo manavee** greengrocer's

στου σιδηροπώλη **stoo seedheeropolee** ironmonger's

στου χαρτοπώλη **stoo khartopolee** stationer's

στου ψαρά/ψαροπώλη **stoo psara/psaropolee** fishmonger's

στόφα υγραερίου **stofa eeghraereeoo** gas cooker

στραμπουλίζω **stram-booleezo** sprain (vb)

στριμωγμένος **streemogh-menos** jammed

στρίφωμα **streefoma** hem

στρσίδι **stroseedhee** bedspread

στροφή **strofee** turn

στρώμα **stroma** mattress

στυλός διαρκείας **steelos dheearkeeas** ballpoint pen

συγγνώμη **seenghnomee** apology

Συγγνώμη? **Seenghnomee** Pardon?

συγκομιδή **seengomee-dhee** harvest

Συγχαρητήρια! **Seengkhareeteereea!** Congratulations!

συγχωρώ **seengkhoro** excuse (vb)

συδεντήρας **seendhe-teeras** staple (n)

συκώτι **seekotee** liver

συλλαβίζω **seelaveezo** spell

συλλαμβάνω **seelamvano** arrest, catch

συμβαίνω **seemveno** happen

συμβόλαιο **seemvoleo** contract

συμβολή **seemvolee** junction

συμβουλή **seemvoolee** advice

συμπεριλαμβανόμενος **seembereelamva-nomenos** included

συμπλήρωμα **seemblee-roma** supplement

συμπληρωματικό φαγητό **seembleeromateeko fagheeto** side dish

συμπληρώνω **seem-bleerono** fill in

συμφωνία **seemfoneea** agreement, deal

συμφωνώ **seemfono** agree

συναγωγή **seenaghoghee** synagogue

συνάδελφος **seenadhelfos** colleague

συναισθανόμενος **seenes-thanomenos** conscious

συνάλλαγμα **seenalaghma** exchange (n), exchange rate

συνάντηση **seenandeesee** meeting

συναντώ **seenando** meet

συναρπαστικός **seenarpas-teekos** exciting

συναυλία **seenavl_ee_a**
concert

συνεδρίαση **seenedhr_ee_a-see** meeting

συνεργείο διάσωσης **seen-erg_hee_o dhee_a_sosees**
breakdown van

συνέταιρος **seeneteros**
partner (business)

σύνεφο **seenefo** cloud

συνεχίζω **seenekh_ee_zo**
continue

συνήθης **seen_ee_thees**
usual

συνηθισμένα **seeneethees-mena** usually

συνθέτης **seenth_e_tees**
composer

συνιστώ **seeneesto** advise,
introduce

συνολικά **seenol_ee_ka**
altogether

σύνολο **s_ee_nolo** total

σύνορα **s_ee_nora** border

συνταγή **seendagh_ee**
recipe

συνταγή γιατρού **seen-dagh_ee gheeatroo**
prescription

συνταξιούχος **seendaksee-_oo_khos** old-age
pensioner, retired, senior
citizen

σύντομα **s_ee_ndoma** soon

συντομότερος τρόπος
seendom_o_teros tropos
short-cut

συντριβάνι **seendree-vanee** fountain

σύντροφος **s_ee_ndrofos**
partner (companion)

σύρμα **s_ee_rma** wire

συρρικνούμαι **seeree-kn_oo_me** shrink

συρτάρι **seert_a_ree** drawer

συρτάρια **seert_a_reea** chest
of drawers

συσκευάζω **seeskev_a_zo**
pack (vb)

συστατικά **seestat_ee_ka**
ingredients

συστημένο γράμμα
seesteemeno ghr_a_ma
registered mail

συχνά **seekhna** often

συχνός **seekhn_o_s** frequent

σφήκα **sf_ee_ka** wasp

σφουγγάρι **sfoongaree**
sponge

σφράγισμα **sfragh_ee_sma**
filling (tooth)

σφυρί **sf_ee_ree** hammer

σχάρα **skhara** roof-rack

σχέδιο **skh_e_dheeo** pattern

σχεδόν **skhedh_o_n** nearly,
almost

σχεδόν ποτέ **skhedh_o_n
pote** hardly

σχέση **skh_e_see** relative,
relation

σχετικός **skheteek_o_s**
relative, relation

σχήμα **skh_ee_ma** form,
shape

σχοινί **skh_ee_nee** rope

σχολείο **skhol_ee_o** school

σώβρακο **s_o_vrako**
underpants

σώζω **s_o_zo** save (people)

σωλήνας **sol_ee_nas** pipe
(plumbing), tube

σώμα **s_o_ma** body

σωματοφύλακας **somato-f_ee_lakas** lifeguard

σώος **s_o_-os** whole (healthy)

σωσίβιο **sos_ee_veeo** life
belt

σωσίβιο-χιτώνας
sos_ee_veeo-kheet_o_nas
life jacket

σωστά **sost_a** properly

σωστός **sost_o_s** right,
correct (adj)

T

ταβάνι **tavanee** ceiling

ταΐζω **ta_ee_zo** feed

ταινία **ten_ee_a** tape

GREEK → ENGLISH

ταμειακή μηχανή **tameeakee meekhanee** cash register

ταμείο **tameeo** cash desk, counter, till

ταμίας **tameeas** cashier

ταμπέλα **tambela** sign (n), label

ταμπέλα αποσκευών **tambela aposkevon** luggage tag

ταμπόν **tampon** tampon

τάξη **taksee** class

ταξί **taksee** cab, taxi

ταξιδεύω **takseedhevo** travel

ταξίδι **takseedhee** journey

ταξίδι για δουλειά **takseedhee gheea dhooleea** business trip

ταξίδι με πλοίο **takseedhee me pleeo** boat trip

ταξιδιωτική επιταγή **takseedheeoteekee epeetaghee** traveller's cheque

ταξιδιωτικός πράκτορας **takseedheeoteekos praktoras** travel agent

τάπα **tapa** plug (bath)

τάση **tasee** voltage

ταυτότητα **taftoteeta** identity card

ταχυδρομείο **takheedhromeeo** mail (n), post office

ταχυδρομικά τέλη **takheedhromeeka telee** postage

ταχυδρομική επιταγή **takheedhromeekee epeetaghee** money order

ταχυδρομική θυρίδα **takheedhromeekee theereedha** post office box

ταχυδρομικό κουτί **takheedhromeeko kootee** postbox

ταχυδρομικός κώδικας/ τομέας **takheedhromeekos kodheekas/ tomeas** postal code

ταχυδρόμος **takheedhromos** postman/ postwoman

ταχυδρομώ **takheedhromo** mail, post (vb)

ταχύμετρο **takheemetro** speedometer

ταχύς **takhees** express (train)

ταχύτητα **takheeteeta** gear (car), speed

τέλειος **teleeos** excellent, perfect

τελειώνω **teleeono** finish (vb)

τελευταίος **telefteos** last

τελεφερίκ **telefereek** cable car, funicular

τελικά **teleeka** eventually

τέλος **telos** end

τελωνείο **teloneeo** customs

τεμπέλης **tembelees** lazy

τενεκές **tenekes** can (n), tin

τένις **tenees** tennis

τένοντας **tenondas** tendon

τέρμα **terma** terminal (bus, train)

Τετάρτη **Tetartee** Wednesday

τέταρτο **tetarto** quarter

τετράγωνος **tetraghonos** square

τέχνη **tekhnee** art, craft

τεχνητή ίνα **tekhneetee eena** man-made fibre

τζαμένια σκέπη **tzameneea skepee** sunroof

τζαμί **dzamee** mosque

τηγάνι **teeghanee** pan, frying pan

τηγανίζω **teeghan*eezo***
fry

τηγανίτα **teeghan*eeta***
pancake

τηγανιτές πατάτες
teeghan*eetes* pat*ates*
French fries

τηγανιτός **teeghan*eetos***
fried

τηλεόραση **teel*eorasee***
television

τηλεφώνημα **teelef*oneema***
telephone call

τηλεφώνημα για ξύπνημα
**teelef*oneema* gh*eea*
ks*eepneema*** wake-up
call

τηλεφώνημα μακράς
αποστάσεως **teelefon-
eema makr*as* apos-
t*aseos*** long-distance call

τηλεφώνημα με χρέωση του
καλούμενου **teelefonee-
ma me khr*eosee* too
kal*oomenoo*** collect call

τηλεφώνημα με χρέωση του
καλούμενου **teelefon-
eema me khr*eosee* too
kal*oomenoo*** reverse-
charge call

τηλεφωνητής **teelefonee-
tees** operator (phone)

τηλεφωνική σύνδεση **teelefon*eekee* s*eendhesee***
connection (phone)

τηλεφωνικός θάλαμος
**teelefon*eekos* th*ala-
mos*** phone booth

τηλεφωνικός κατάλογος
**teelefon*eekos* katalo-
ghos*** telephone directory

τηλέφωνο **teel*efono*** phone,
telephone

τηλέφωνο για το κοινό
**teel*efono* gh*eea* to
k*eeno*** payphone

τηλεφωνοκάρτα **teelefono-
k*arta*** phone card

την επόμενη εβδομάδα
**teen ep*omenee*
evdhom*adha*** next
week

την περασμένη εβδομάδα
**teen perasm*enee*
evdhom*adha*** last
week

της **tees** of

Τι; **Tee?** What?

Τι κάνεις; **Tee k*anees***
How do you do?

Τι συμβαίνει; **Tee seem-
v*enee?*** What is wrong?

Τι τρέχει; **Tee tr*ekhee?***
What's the matter?

Τι ώρα είναι; **Tee *ora*
*eene?*** What's the time?

τιμή **teem*ee*** price

τιμή εισόδου **teem*ee*
*eesodhoo*** entrance fee

τίμιος **t*eemeeos*** fair, just

τιμολόγιο **teemol*ogheeo***
invoice

τιμόνι **teem*onee*** steering
wheel

Τίνος; **T*eenos?*** Whose?

τίποτα **t*eepota*** nothing

τίποτε άλλο **t*eepote* *alo***
nothing else

τιρμπουσόν **teerb*ooson***
corkscrew

τμήμα **tm*eema*** compartment, department

το **to** it (indirect object), the

το γένος **to gh*enos*** maiden
name

τοίχος **t*eekhos*** wall

τόνος **t*onos*** tuna

τοπεία **top*eea*** scenery

τοπικός **top*eekos*** local

του **too** of

τουαλέτα **tooal*eta*** toilet,
cloakroom

τουαλέτες ανδρών
tooal*etes* andhr*on*
gents' toilet

τούβλο **t*oovlo*** brick

τούνελ **t*oonel*** tunnel

GREEK → ENGLISH

τουριστική θέση **tooreesteekee thesee** economy
class

τουριστικός συνοδός **too-
reesteekos seenodhos**
tour guide

Τουρκάλα **Toorkala** Turkish,
Turk (f)

Τουρκία **Toorkeea** Turkey

Τούρκος **Toorkos** Turkish,
Turk (m)

τουρκουάζ **toorkooaz**
turquoise

τούρτα **toorta** cake

τούτο **tooto** it (subject),
this

τραβώ **travo** pull

τραγουδάω **traghoodhao**
sing

τραγούδι **traghoodhee**
song

τραγουδιστής **traghoo-
dheestees** singer

τραίνο **treno** train

τράμ **tram** tram

τραπεζαρία **trapezareea**
dining room

τραπέζι **trapezee** table

τραπεζομάντηλο **trapezo-
mandeelo** tablecloth

τραύμα **travma** injury

τραυματισμένος **travma-
teesmos** injured

τραχιά **trakheea** roughly

τρελός **trelos** crazy, mad

τρέχω **trekho** run

τρέχων **trekhon** current (adj)

τριαντάφυλλο **treeanda-
feelo** rose (flower)

τριμμένο **treemeno** grated

τρομερός **tromeros**
dreadful

τροφική δηλητηρίαση **trofeekee dheeleetee-
reeasee** food poisoning

τροχάδι **trokhadhee** jog (n)

τροχαίο ατύχημα **trokheo
ateekheema** road
accident

τροχόσπιτο **trokhospeeto**
caravan, trailer, van, home-
on-wheels

τρύπα **treepa** hole

τρυπάνι **treepanee** drill (n)

τρύπημα σε λάστιχο
**treepeema se
lasteekho** puncture

τρυπητό **treepeeto** colander

τρώω **tro-o** eat

τσαγιερό **tsaghero** kettle,
teapot

τσάι **tsaee** tea

τσάι από βότανα **tsaee
apo votana** herbal tea

τσαμπί **tsambee** bunch

τσάντα **tsanta** bag, carrier
bag, handbag

τσεκάρισμα αποσκευών
και εισιτηρίου προ της
αναχώρησης **tsekarees-
ma aposkevon ke
eeseeteereeon pro
tees anakhoreesees**
check in (at airport)

τσέπη **tsepee** pocket

τσιγάρο **tseegharo**
cigarette

τσίμπημα εντόμου
tseembeema endomoo
insect bite

τσιμπιδάκι **tseembee-
dhakee** tweezers

τσιμπούκι **tseembookee**
pipe (smoking)

τσιπς **tseeps** chips

τσίχλα **tseekhla** chewing
gum

τσουγκράνα **tsoongrana**
rake

τσούκσιμο **tsookseemo**
sting

τσουλήθρα **tsooleethra**
slip

τσούχτρα **tsookhtra**
jellyfish

τύπος **teepos** type

τυρί **teeree** cheese

τυφλός **teeflos** blind (adj)

τύχη **teekhee** luck
τώρα **tora** now
τωρινός **toreenos** current

Υ

υγιείς **eeghee-ees** healthy
υγκαέριο **eeghraereeo** gas
υγρασία **eeghraseea** humid
υγρό για τα πιάτα **eeghro gheea ta peeata** washing-up liquid
υγρό συντήρησης φακών επαφής **eeghro seendeereesees fakon epafees** soaking solution
υγρό φρένων **eeghro frenon** brake fluid
υγρός **eeghros** damp, wet
υδατική κρέμα **eedhateekee krema** moisturizer
υδατοστεγής **eedhatosteghees** waterproof
υδραυλικός **eedhravleekos** plumber
υδρώνω **eedhrono** sweat (vb)
υδρώτας **eedhrotas** sweat (n)
ύλη **eelee** matter
υπαίθριο μαγαζί **eepethreeo maghazee** stall
ύπαιθρος **eepethros** countryside, outdoors
υπάλληλος **eepaleelos** shop assistant
υπέδαφος **eepedhafos** underground
υπέρβαρες αποσκευές **eepervares aposkeves** excess luggage
υπέρταση **eepertasee** high blood pressure
υπερχρεώνω **eeperkhreono** overcharge
υπηρεσία **eepeereseea** service
υπηρεσία κούριερ **eepeereseea kooree-er** courier service

υπηρέτρια **eepeeretreea** maid
υπνοσάκος **eepnosakos** sleeping bag
υπνωτικό χάπι **eepnoteeko khapee** sleeping pill
υποβρύχια κατάδυση **eepovreekheea katadheesee** scuba diving
υπόγειο **eepogheeo** basement
υπόγειος σιδηρόδρομος **eepogheeos seedheerodhromos** subway, underground
υπογραφή **eepoghrafee** signature
υπογραφή στο ξενοδοχείο κατά την άφιξη **eepoghrafee sto ksenodhokheeo kata teen afeeksee** check in (at hotel)
υπογράφω **eepoghrafo** sign (vb)
υποδερμική βελόνα **eepodhermeekee velona** hypodermic needle
υπολογιστής **eepologheestees** computer
υπόλοιπο **eepoleepo** rest, remainder
υπομονετικός **eepomoneteekos** patient (adj)
υπόσχεση **eeposkhesee** promise (n)
υπόσχομαι **eeposkhome** promise (vb)
υπότιτλος **eepoteetlos** subtitle
υπουργός **eepoorghos** minister
υποχρεωτικός **eepokhreoteekos** compulsory
ύστερα **eestera** after
ύφασμα **eefasma** cloth, fabric, material
υψηλός **eepseelos** high
ύψος **eepsos** height

Φ

φαγητό *fagheeto* food

φαγητό μωρού *fagheeto moroo* baby food

φαγητό σε πακέτο *fagheeto se paketo* take-away food

φαγούρα *faghoora* itch (n)

φάκελος *fakelos* envelope, file, folder

φακές *fakes* lentil

φακοί *fakee* lenses

φακοί επαφής *fakee epafees* contact lenses

φακός *fakos* lens

φανάρι φρένων *fanaree frenon* brake light

φανέλα *fanela* flannel, jersey

φαξ *faks* fax

φαράσι *farasee* dustpan

φαρδύς *fardhees* wide

φάρμα *farma* farm

φαρμακείο *farmakeeo* chemist, pharmacy

φαρμακείο πρώτων βοηθειών *farmakeeo proton voeetheeon* first-aid kit

φάρμακο *farmako* drug, medicine

φαρμακοποιός *farmakop-eeos* chemist, pharmacist

φασαρία *fasareea* noise, racket, row, trouble

φασόλι *fasolee* bean

Φεβρουάριος *Fevrooareeos* February

φεγγάρι *fengaree* moon

φελλός *felos* cork

φερμουάρ *fermooar* zipper, zip fastener

φέρνω *ferno* fetch

φερυμπώτ *fereembot* ferry

φερυμπώτ αυτοκηνίτων *fereembot aftokee-neeton* car ferry

φέρω *fero* bring

φεστιβάλ *festeeval* festival

φέτα *feta* slice

φεύγω *fevgho* go away, leave

φθάνω *fthano* arrive

φθινόπωρο *ftheenoporo* autumn

φίδι *feedhee* snake

φιλάω *feelao* kiss (vb)

φιλενάδα *feelenadha* girlfriend

φιλέτο *feeleto* fillet

φιλί *feelee* kiss (n)

φιλικός *feeleekos* friendly

φιλμ *feelm* film (n)

φιλοξενία *feeloksenea* hospitality

φίλος *feelos* boyfriend, friend

φίλος δι'αλληλογραφίας *feelos dhee'aleelo-ghrafeeas* penfriend

φίλτρο *feeltro* filter

φίνος *feenos* posh

φλάσκο *flasko* flask

φλέβα *fleva* vein

φλοιός *fleeos* bark (n, of tree)

φλούδι *floodhee* peel (n)

φλυτζάνι *fleetzanee* cup

φοβάμαι *fovame* afraid, be afraid of

φοβερός *foveros* dreadful

φοιτητής *feeteetees* student (tertiary)

φοιτητική έκπτωση *feetee-teekee ekptosee* student discount

φονεύω *fonevo* kill

φόρεμα *forema* dress

φορητή κουκέτα *foreetee kooketa* carry-cot

φόρμα *forma* form (document), tracksuit

φορολογική απόδειξη *foro-logheekee apodheek-see* receiver (tax)

φόρος *foros* tax

φόρος προστιθέμενης αξίας *foros prosteethemenees akseeas* VAT

φορτηγάκι *forteeghakee* van (for goods)

φορτηγό *forteegho* lorry, truck

φουλ πανσιόν *fool panseeon* full board

φουλάρι *foolaree* scarf

φουντούκι *foondookee* hazelnut

φούρνος *foornos* bakery, oven

φούρνος μικροκυμάτων *foornos meekrokeematon* microwave oven

φουσκάλα *fooskala* blister

φουσκώνω *fooskono* inflate, swell

φούστα *foosta* skirt

φραγμένο *fraghmeno* blocked

φράουλα *fraoola* strawberry

φράχτης *frakhtees* fence

φρένο *freno* brake (n)

φρέσκος *freskos* fresh

φρούριο *frooreeo* fortress

φρουρός *frooros* security guard

φρούτα *froota* fruit

φρουτοχυμός *frootokheemos* fruit juice

φταρνίζομαι *ftarneezome* sneeze

φτέρνα *fterna* heel

φτηνή τιμή *fteenee teemee* cheap rate

φτηνό *fteeno* cheap

φτηνότερος *fteenoteros* cheaper

φτιαγμένος *fteeaghmenos* made

φτιάχνω *fteeakhno* fix

φτυάρι *fteearee* spade

φτωχός *ftokhos* poor, impecunious

φύκι *feekee* seaweed

φύλακας *feelakas* guard, security guard

φυλακή *feelakee* prison

φυλάω *feelao* look after

φυλή *feelee* race (people)

φυλλάδιο *feeladheeo* brochure, leaflet

φύλλο *feelo* leaf

φύλο *feelo* sex (gender)

φύση *feesee* nature

φυσικός *feeseekos* natural

φυστίκι *feesteekee* peanut

φυτεύω *feetevo* plant (vb)

φυτό *feeto* plant (n)

φυτώριο *feetoreeo* nursery (plants)

φωλιά *foleea* nest

φωνάζω *fonazo* call, shout (vb)

φωνή *fonee* voice

φως *fos* light (n)

φωτεινός σηματοδότης *feteenos seematodhotees* traffic light

φωτιά *foteea* fire

φωτίζω *foteezo* light (vb)

φωτογραφία *fotoghrafeea* photograph, photo, picture

φωτογραφίζω *fotoghrafeezo* photograph (vb)

φωτοτυπία *fototeepeea* photocopy (n)

Χ

χαϊδεύω *khaeedhevo* stroke, caress

χαιρετισμός *khereteesmos* greeting

χαλάζι *khalazee* hail

χαλάκι *khalakee* rug

χαλαρός *khalaros* loose

χαλί *khalee* carpet

χαλώ *khalo* spoil

χαμηλός *khameelos* low

χαμηλών λιπαρών *khameelon leeparon* low fat

χαμμένος *khamenos* lost

GREEK → ENGLISH

χαμογελώ **khamoghelo**
smile (vb)

χάμπουργκερ **kham-boorger** hamburger

χάνω **khano** lose

χάπι **khapee** pill

χαρά **khara** joy

χάρακας **kharakas** ruler
(for measuring)

χαρακτηριστικός **kharak-teereesteekos** typical

Χάρηκα που σας γνώρισα!
Khareeka poo sas ghnoreesa Pleased to
meet you!

χαρούμενος **kharoomenos**
glad, happy

χάρτης **khartees** map

χαρτί **khartee** paper

χαρτί αλληλογραφίας
khartee aleeloghra-feeas writing paper

χαρτί σημειώματος **khartee seemeeomatos**
notepaper

χαρτί τυλίγματος **khartee teeleeghmatos** wrapping
paper

χαρτικά **kharteeka**
stationery

χαρτόκουτο **khartokooto**
carton

χαρτόνι **khartonee**
cardboard

χαρτοπετσέτα **kharto-petseta** serviette

χαρτοπετσέτες **kharto-petsetes** paper napkins

χαρτοφύλακας **kharto-feelakas** briefcase

χασάπης **khasapees**
butcher

χείμαρρος **kheemaros**
stream

χειμώνας **kheemonas**
winter

χειραποσκευές **kheerapos-keves** hand luggage

χειροποίητο **kheeropee-eeto** handmade

χειρότερος **kheeroteros**
worse

χειρουργική **keeroorghee-kee** surgery (procedure)

χειρόφρενο **kheerofreno**
handbrake

χέλι **khelee** eel

χέρι **kheree** hand

χερούλι **kheroolee** handle

χήνα **kheena** goose

χήρος, χήρα **kheeros, kheera** widower, widow

χθες **khthes** yesterday

χίλια **kheeleea** thousand

χιλιόγραμμο **kheeleeo-ghramo** kilogram

χιλιόμετρο **kheeleeometro**
kilometre

χιόνι, χιονίζει **kheeonee, kheeoneezee** snow,
it is snowing

χιονοστιβάδα **kheeonos-teevadha** avalanche

χιούμορ **kheeoomor**
humour

χλωμός **khlomos** pale

χοιρινό **kheereeno** pork

χοντρός **khondros** thick

χορεύω **khorevo** dance (vb)

χορωδία **khorodheea** choir

χώρος στάθμευσης για
τροχόσπιτα **khoros stathmefshees ghea trokhospeeta** caravan
site

χορταρικά **khortareeka**
vegetables

χορτοφάγος **khortofaghos**
vegetarian

χουρμάς **khoormas** date
(fruit)

χρέη **khre-ee** debts

χρειάζομαι **khreeazome**
need (vb), require

χρεώνω **khreono** charge

χρήματα **kreemata** money

χρήση **khreesee** wear

χρησιμοποιώ *khreesee-mopeeo* use
χρήσιμος *khreeseemos* useful
Χριστούγεννα *Khreestooghena* Christmas
χρόνος *khronos* year
χρυσός *khreesos* gold
Χρυσός Οδηγός *Khreesos Odheeghos* yellow pages
χρώμα *khroma* colour
χρωστάω *khrostao* owe
χτένα *khtena* comb (n)
χτενίζω *khteneezo* comb (vb)
χτίζω *khteezo* build
χτυπάω *khteepao* hit
χτυπάω την πόρτα *khteepao teen porta* knock
χτυπώ και ρίχνω κάτω *khteepo ke reekhno kato* knock down
χτυπώ κάτω (τα πόδια) *khteepo kato (ta podheea)* stamp
χύμα κρασί *kheema krasee* house wine
χυμός *kheemos* juice
χυμός ντομάτας *kheemos domatas* tomato juice
χυμός πορτοκαλιού *kheemos portokaleeo* orange juice
χύνω *kheeno* pour, spill
χώμα *khoma* ground
χώρα *khora* country
χωράφι *khorafee* field
χωρίζω *khoreezo* separate (vb)
χωριό *khoreeo* village
χωρίς *khorees* without
χωρίς ζάχαρη *khorees zakharee* sugar-free
χωρίς καφεΐνη *khorees kafe-eenee* decaffeinated
χωρισμένος *khoreesmenos* divorced
χωριστός *khoreestos* separate (adj)

Ψ
ψαλίδι *psaleedhee* scissors
ψαλλίδι νυχιών *psaleedhee neekheeon* nail scissors
ψάρι *psaree* fish
ψάχνω *psakhno* look for
ψεύδομαι *psevdhome* lie (vb, fib)
ψεύτικος *psefteekos* false
ψηλή καρέκλα *pseelee karekla* high chair
ψηλός *pseelos* tall
ψητός *pseetos* grilled
ψιλά *pseela* change (money)
ψυγείο *pseegheeo* fridge, radiator
ψυκτικός σάκος *pseekteekos sakos* cool bag
ψύλλος *pseelos* flea
ψωμάκι *psomakee* bun
ψωμί *psomee* bread
ψωμί με ακοσκίνιστο αλεύρι *psomee me akoskeeneesto alevree* wholemeal bread

Ω
ωκεανός *okeanos* ocean
ώμος *omos* shoulder
ώρα *ora* hour, time
ωραίος *oreos* nice
ώρες ανοίγματος *ores aneeghmatos* opening times
ώρες επισκέψεως *ores epeeskepseos* visiting hours
ωριαία *oree-ea* hourly
ώριμος *oreemos* ripe
ωρολόγιο πρόγραμμα *orologheeo proghrama* timetable
ωταλγία *otalgheea* earache

GREEK → ENGLISH

THE GREEK ALPHABET

The Greek alphabet may
look daunting at first, but it
only takes an hour or so to
memorize it. A knowledge of
the alphabet will enable you to
read road and other signs, and
the destinations of local buses.
The chart below shows upper
and lower case characters of
the alphabet, together with a
guide to the pronunciation of
their Greek names.

A	α	_ahl_fah
B	β	_vee_tah
Γ	γ	_ghah_mah
Δ	δ	_dhehl_tah
E	ε	_ehp_seelonn
Z	ζ	_zee_tah
H	η	_ee_tah
Θ	θ	_thee_tah
I	ι	_yee_otah
K	κ	_kah_pah
Λ	λ	_lahm_dhah
M	μ	mee
N	ν	nee
Ξ	ξ	ksee
O	o	_o_meekron
Π	π	pee
P	ρ	ro
Σ	σ	_seegh_mah
T	τ	tahf
Υ	υ	_eep_seelonn
Φ	φ	fee
X	χ	khee
Ψ	ψ	psee
Ω	ω	o_meh_ghah